W9-BLA-969

Washington on Foot

24 Walking Tours of Washington, D.C. Old Town Alexandria Historic Annapolis

Third Edition, Revised

Edited by John J. Protopappas and Lin Brown

National Capital Area Chapter
American Planning Association
and
Smithsonian Institution Press
Washington, D.C.

Library of Congress Cataloging in Publication Data
Main entry under title:

Washington on foot.

1. Washington (D.C.)—Description—1981—Tours.
2. Alexandria (Va.)—Description—Tours.   3. Annapolis
(Md.)—Description—Tours.   I. Protopappas, John J., (John
Joseph), 1946–.   II. Brown, Lin.   III. American Planning
Association. National Capital Area Chapter.
F192.3.W335 1984   917.53′044   83-12880
ISBN 0-87474-765-1 (Smithsonian)

First edition: 1976; revised 1977
Second edition: 1980
Third edition: revised 1984; second printing 1985;
third printing 1987; fourth printing 1989.

Printed in the United States of America

Typography: Polly Sexton

The paper in this book meets the guidelines for
permanence and durability of the Committee on
Production Guidelines for Book Longevity of the Council
on Library Resources.

Contents

Map of Tour Areas   4

About Washington on Foot   6

Washington, D.C.   7
Alexandria and Annapolis   11
How to Use This Guide   11
Taking the Right Bus   11
Using the Metro Subway   12
On Not Getting Lost on Washington Streets   13

Map of Metro Subway   14

L'Enfant's City

1/Capitol Hill***   16
2/Capitol Hill—East**   23
3/The Mall—East***   28
4/The Mall—West***   35
5/Independence Avenue, SW*, and L'Enfant Plaza**   41
6/Southwest**   49
7/Foggy Bottom**   59
8/White House***   69
9/Federal Triangle**   78
10/Downtown**   86
11/Midtown**   97
12/16th Street, NW, and Meridian Hill***   106
13/Dupont Circle***   120
14/Shaw School Urban Renewal Area* and Logan
    Circle**   131

The Other Washington

15/Kalorama***   136
16/Adams-Morgan**   149
17/Woodley Park** and National Zoo**   162
18/Cleveland Park** and Washington Cathedral***   166
19/Howard University*   178
20/LeDroit Park**   183
21/Old Anacostia**   190
22/Georgetown***   195

Nearby Historic Ports

23/Old Town Alexandria, Virginia***   206
24/Historic Annapolis, Maryland***   212

***Not to be missed   **Highly Recommended   *Recommended

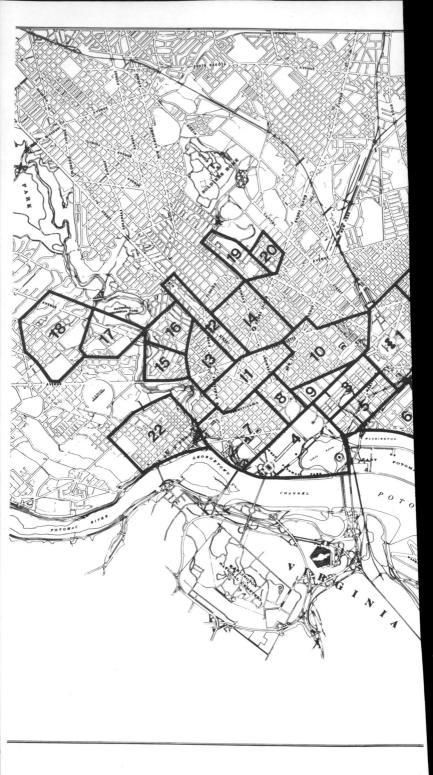

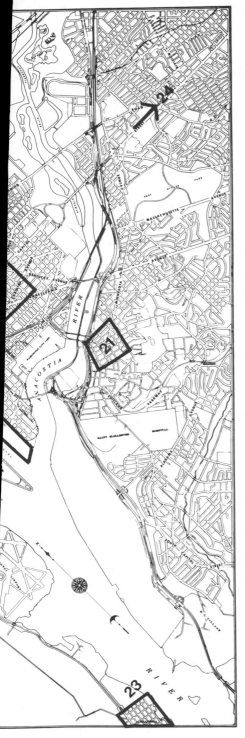

Tour Areas

1/Capitol Hill***

2/Capitol Hill—East**

3/The Mall—East***

4/The Mall—West***

5/Independence Avenue, SW*, and L'Enfant Plaza**

6/Southwest**

7/Foggy Bottom**

8/White House***

9/Federal Triangle**

10/Downtown**

11/Midtown**

12/16th Street, NW, and Meridian Hill***

13/Dupont Circle***

14/Shaw School Urban Renewal Area* and Logan Circle**

15/Kalorama***

16/Adams-Morgan**

17/Woodley Park** and National Zoo**

18/Cleveland Park** and Washington Cathedral***

19/Howard University*

20/LeDroit Park**

21/Old Anacostia**

22/Georgetown***

23/Old Town Alexandria, Virginia***

24/Historic Annapolis, Maryland***

About
Washington on Foot

There are many ways to see cities, but for anyone desiring a sense of the history and the character of an urban place, the city is best seen on foot. A mosaic on a garden wall, the framed view of a church dome from a narrow street, or the gleam of stained glass above a doorway—these are just a few of the visual rewards of a walking tour.

Washington on Foot is an informative guide to the neighborhoods and the monuments of the nation's capital. Twenty-two informative walking tours will steer you through the preserved colonial and federal quarters, the vital commercial districts, the long-standing residential neighborhoods, the revitalized urban-renewal areas, as well as the familiar memorials, public buildings, and museums of Washington. Two other tours will escort you through the 18th-century setting of Old Town Alexandria, Virginia, and to Annapolis, the colonial seaport and capital of the state of Maryland.

Originally published in 1976 for the National Planning Conference, *Washington on Foot* is now used by thousands of visitors and residents interested in a close-up look at the historical, cultural, and architectural aspects of these three cities. More than two dozen volunteers, including urban planners, architectural historians, and other urban professionals, have contributed to this volume. *Washington on Foot* is intended to serve the general public as a guide to many of the significant features of these three cities. The tours are designed for use by both pedestrians and by bicyclists.

The Editors

John Protopappas is currently the Deputy Long Range Planning Chief for the District of Columbia's Office of Planning. Over the past ten years he has practiced transportation- and land-use planning in the United States and in Europe. He has been a guest lecturer on Urban Planning at the Catholic University of America and the University of Maryland. He has written for professional journals, and was editor of the national award-winning APA newsletter, *Capital Comments*. He is also a decorated veteran of the Vietnam conflict.

Lin Brown has an M.A. in Regional and Community Planning and is the current editor of the APA's *Capital Comments*. She is active in civic association work and is an avid observer of the urban scene.

Wolcott Etienne, who prepared tour maps and addi-

tional sketches for this third edition of *Washington on Foot,*
is an urban designer who has worked with local architectural firms and the D.C. Office of Planning. He received
graduate degrees in both architecture and city planning
from the University of Pennsylvania, and has previously
worked in Atlanta and London.

About the NCAC-APA

The National Capital Area Chapter (NCAC) of the American
Planning Association (APA) is one of the oldest and largest
chapters of the 20,000-member national organization. The
chapter has more than 775 professional urban-planning
members in the District of Columbia and in Prince
George's and Montgomery counties, Maryland.

APA is the major organization in the country representing the interests of planning and planners. It was formed in
1978 by a merger of the American Institute of Planners and
the American Society of Planning Officials. Members include practicing planners, local officials, architects, engineers, students, educators, and other citizens interested in
developing and maintaining well-planned urban and rural
communities.

A subunit of APA, the American Institute of Certified
Planners (AICP) fosters the professional development of
APA members. It administers the certification exam for
planners. AICP also is concerned with planning education
and standards of planning practice.

Member interests are represented through 46 chapters
and 17 divisions concerned with areas of specialized
practice. The various disciplines range from transportation
and energy planning to law and environmental planning.
For more information, contact APA, 1776 Massachusetts Avenue, NW, Washington, D.C. 20036. Telephone: (202) 872-
0611.

Washington, D.C.

"Washington is a Capital City."—This tourist promotion theme
aptly describes the ambiance of the nation's capital. Long
regarded as a city of monuments, monumental buildings,
and government workers, but otherwise reminiscent of a
small town, Washington has emerged in recent years as a
more cosmopolitan, fast-paced, and vibrant city. This change
has been accomplished without transforming the city into a
monolithic and overwhelming metropolis. Overall, the human
scale has been retained.

Washington now rivals in entertainment and cultural of-
ferings cities whose reputations in this regard are well established. This change can be partly attributed to the opening
of the Kennedy Center for the Performing Arts in 1971. The

facilities of this imposing structure on the banks of the Potomac attract a variety of outstanding talent.

The Smithsonian Institution's contribution to Washington's culture is unsurpassed. It has one of the most impressive (and still expanding) arrays of museums in the world, a high-quality education program, and a unique performing-arts program, all available to the public. The most notable of the Smithsonian's newer museums are the National Air and Space Museum, the East Wing of the National Gallery, and the Hirshhorn Museum and Sculpture Garden.

In 1980, 638,000 persons lived in the city's diverse neighborhoods. The population has stabilized in the past few years, after a substantial decline of 116,000 persons from 1970 to 1980. The current population has a large component of single and small two-person households, many with relatively comfortable incomes that permit them to enjoy the city's cultural amenities and its restaurants and to purchase homes. These households have spurred much of the residential rehabilitation you will see as you visit the neighborhoods on your walking tours.

From August to May, Washington's resident population includes more than 90,000 students who attend the city's 20 universities and specialty schools.

Many minority groups are well represented in Washington. Blacks compose approximately 70 percent of the population. In recent years Hispanic and Asian populations have been growing rapidly.

Year-round, more than 17 million tourists and conventioneers visit the Smithsonian museums on the Mall, the White House, the Capitol, and the numerous memorials and monuments scattered throughout the monumental areas of the city.

More than 666,000 persons are employed in the city's many federal, District of Columbia, and private office buildings. Washington's image as a one-industry town is changing rapidly. While federal employment is still the single dominant factor in the city's employment base (about one-third of all workers in the city were federal workers in 1980), the vast majority are clearly in the private sector. This includes workers in finance, insurance, real estate, business, legal and health services, as well as restaurant and retail activities. More exclusive to Washington are the thousands of journalists, lobbyists, and employees of the large number of trade associations in the city. The combination of residents, tourists, conventioneers, and workers gives the city high levels of daytime activity and a very busy night life at theaters, movies, hotels, and restaurants.

The city is well endowed with parkland. Rock Creek Park, which includes the National Zoo, hiking and bicycling trails, the Carter Barron amphitheater, and many picnic and playground sites, extends from the city's northwest boundaries with Maryland into the central business area anchored at the Potomac River by the Kennedy Center. In the very heart of the federal area are parks providing tennis courts, open spaces, walking areas, skating ponds, and other attractions.

Washington has been subject to almost continuous planning since its inception. Untold numbers of planners, architects, developers, and other visionaries have influenced the cityscape. Three of the most prominent were the plans of L'Enfant, Andrew Downing, and the McMillan Commission.

The core of Washington is largely developed as envisioned by Pierre Charles L'Enfant in his 1791 plan for the city, as modified by the McMillan Commission. L'Enfant focused on the siting of the major federal buildings and other symbols of the national government. His plan established the formal pattern of streets, avenues, squares, and circles in the city today.

A second major plan, prepared in 1851 by Andrew Jackson Downing, was limited to the Mall area. It called for a natural landscape treatment of the Mall, which deviated from the formalism of L'Enfant. A third plan, which reinforced and extended L'Enfant's conception, was prepared by the McMillan Commission in 1901. This plan was a bold concept for development of the monumental core and formal federal areas of the city. A casual walk along the Mall allows you to observe remnants of all these earlier planning efforts. There is an excellent exhibit detailing the city's early planning history at the Smithsonian Building (the "Castle").

The original city planned by L'Enfant extended between the Potomac and Anacostia rivers, south of Florida Avenue. This area encompasses the Downtown area as well as some of the city's most desirable neighborhoods. Downtown contains Washington's three major department stores, hundreds of specialty shops and boutiques, and more than 48 million square feet of private and public office space. Most of the private office buildings are occupied by business services, associations, and the city's innumerable lawyers and consultants. Washington's low skyline, most noticeable in the Downtown area, resulted from the congressionally mandated 1910 Height of Buildings Act, which limits the maximum height of buildings from 90 to 130 feet, depending upon location and zone district. Only the north side of Pennsylvania Avenue, between 15th and 10th streets, NW, exceeds those legal limits to reach a height of 160 feet.

For over 150 years, Downtown Washington was the commercial center of the city and of the surrounding region. Although this role was challenged somewhat during the 1950s and 1960s, Downtown still offers the greatest variety of goods and services to be found anywhere in the Washington metropolitan area. During the past two decades, a number of plans and programs were initiated to revitalize Downtown. Some were very successful, while others languished. Much of the development in Downtown today resulted from ideas formed during the last decades. Metrorail, the newly opened Convention Center, and the refurbishing of Pennsylvania Avenue are notable examples.

The city has six major universities: George Washington, Georgetown, American, Catholic, Howard, and the rapidly growing University of the District of Columbia. Each campus has its own ambiance, ranging from the "Gothic" architecture of Georgetown University, the city campus flair of George Washington University, to the highly contemporary facade of the University of the District of Columbia.

Washington's two great cathedrals are the Washington National Cathedral in the Northwest section of the city, with the magnificent landscaping and city vistas, and the National Shrine of the Immaculate Conception on the campus of Catholic University in the upper Northeast. Their architecture and surroundings remain a very vibrant part of the whole region's life.

Outside the boundaries of the original city, there are more than 50 neighborhoods, largely developed during the 19th and 20th centuries. A few of the more notable ones are included in this publication. Others, not included, are significant because of their historic locations along streetcar routes or the prominent persons who resided in their boundaries. A visit to any one of these areas will leave you with indelible images of strong and vibrant neighborhoods. Many are undergoing physical as well as socio-economic change. Others remain unchanged. Most significant in all of these neighborhoods are the tree-lined streets, varied architectural styles, and diverse residents.

Washington has one of the country's most ambitious tree-planting programs, initiated in 1815, one year after construction started on the U.S. Capitol. Many of the streets in the neighborhoods you will visit have trees that are more than 150 years old. Spend some time observing the interesting tree canopies for which Washington neighborhoods are famous.

Two prominent organizations that have had a great influence on the scale and urban design of many of the city's neighborhoods are the Commission of Fine Arts and the Joint Committee on Landmarks. The Commission on Fine Arts was created in 1910 to carry forward the concepts of the McMillan Commission. The Joint Commission on Landmarks is a more contemporary preservation organization, charged with identifying and protecting historic resources in Washington and advising the city on preservation programs. Nearly 400 buildings, sites, streets, and places have been designated by the commission. In addition, several of the neighborhoods you will visit are within one of the 45 designated historic districts in the city. These include Capitol Hill, LeDroit Park, Old Anacostia, and Georgetown.

Before ending your tour of Washington, take time to attend one of the large number of free classical and pop concerts, or seek out the city's vigorous network of neighborhood art museums and galleries, or sample its spirited commercial and varied neighborhood theaters. Whatever you decide to do while visiting the city, enjoy yourself. The following pages, we hope, will help you in your discovery of Washington as a truly Capital City.

—ALVIN R. McNEAL

Alexandria and Annapolis

No visit to the nation's capital is complete without a trip to the nearby historic port cities of Old Town Alexandria, Virginia, and Historic Annapolis, Maryland. Both of these colonial port cities (along with Georgetown) are older than the District of Columbia. Today, both cities are bustling with active commercial life while retaining much of their 17th- and 18th-century residential atmosphere.

How to Use This Guide

Select any of the 24 tours listed here by the name of the area covered. For each, you'll find the walking distance and the time it takes to walk the route (not including visits to museums and historic houses). Public transit information to the starting point is provided (courtesy of the Washington Metropolitan Area Transit Authority). A map shows the route and locates the major sights by numbers keyed to the descriptive text. Sketches scattered throughout the book highlight the important sights. Finally, stars indicate a ranking for each tour and major sight, as follows:

***Not to be missed
 **Highly recommended
  *Recommended

Taking the Right Bus

The Washington Metropolitan Area Transit Authority (Metro) Information Service will tell you which Metrobus to take to any destination. Call (202) 637-2437.

When you board your bus, you will be expected to pay the exact fare in tickets, tokens, or cash. Metrobus operators do not carry change, nor do they sell tickets or tokens. Call (202) 637-1328 to find out where you can buy commuter tickets or tokens. The basic fare within the District of Columbia at this writing is 75 cents in nonrush hours, 80 cents in rush hours (defined as 6–9:30 a.m. and 3–6:30 p.m. weekday nonholidays based on the time of boarding). The fare increases as you cross the various zones into the suburbs.

If you need to change from one bus to another in order to reach your destination, you will be given a transfer at no additional cost. You must ask your bus operator for it when you pay your fare. Your transfer permits you to change to three more buses, if necessary. Transfers are valid for two hours and they cannot be used for a return trip or stopover, but only for on-going connections.

Route numbers and letters accompanying each tour in the guide refer to bus services available weekdays. These' routes pass the beginning point of each tour or near it. Note: special rush-hour and weekend routings are not listed.

Using the Metro Subway

Washington's subway system, called Metro, began operation in March 1976 and has revolutionized travel patterns in the city. It is a pleasant and quick way to travel to and from the tour areas in the guide, particularly those in central Washington.

Four Metrorail lines serve the Washington area. The Red Line currently provides service between Silver Spring and Shady Grove, Maryland. The Blue Line links National Airport and the Addison Road stations. The Yellow Line provides service from Gallery Place to Huntington Station in Alexandria, Virginia. The Orange Line's terminals are now at Ballston in Arlington, Virginia, and New Carrollton in Maryland. The Orange and Blue Lines share tracks between Rosslyn and Stadium-Armory. (See map of Metro subway on page 14.) Eventually, the subway will reach 101 miles, serving the far-out suburbs. Please check maps in each Metro station and car for new extensions.

Three of the lines intersect at the Metro Center station in downtown Washington, facilitating transfers between the Red Line (upper level) and the Blue and Orange Lines (lower level). The Yellow and Red Lines intersect at Gallery Place. The Yellow also intersects with the Blue and Orange Lines at L'Enfant Plaza, and with the Blue Line at the Pentagon.

The name of the Metro station, and the color of the line serving the beginning point of each walking tour, are indicated in this guide. The "M" symbol on each tour map locates station entrances.

Metro operates as follows:

Weekdays: 6:00 a.m.–12:00 midnight
Saturdays: 8:00 a.m.–12:00 midnight
Sundays: 10:00 a.m.–6:00 p.m.

There is a two-tier fare system based on time and distance traveled. As of April 1985, the fares during rush hours (6:00–9:30 a.m. and 3:00–6:30 p.m. on weekday nonholidays) range between 80 cents and $2.40. The fares during nonrush hours (all other times on weekday nonholidays as well as Saturdays, Sundays, and holidays) range from 80 cents to $1.10. Fares are paid with farecards which are for sale in machines in all stations: they can be bought in any value from 80 cents to $30, and are good until used. Exit gates automatically deduct the fare and print the remaining value, if any, on the farecard. Check the charts in each station for the exact fare between stations on your route.

Transfers from subway to bus, with a discount up to 100 percent, can be made only if the transfer ticket is acquired from any station other than the one at which the connection is to be made. Get your free transfer ticket from the dispensing machine within the paid area at the station where you enter the Metrorail system. Remember that free transfers obtained aboard a bus cannot be used on Metrorail.

Bon voyage!

On Not Getting Lost on Washington Streets

The quadrants (NW, SW, NE, SE) must be explained. The north/south axis through the Capitol, represented by South and North Capitol streets, divides the eastern and western sections of the city. The east/west axis through the Capitol, represented by East Capitol Street and the center line of the Mall, separates the northern and southern sections. All streets within each of the quadrants bear the quadrant designation, and the quadrant describes its direction on the compass from the Capitol.

Street names are generally in alphabetical or numerical order; names of states are used for the diagonal avenues. Measuring from the center line of the Mall in either direction, north or south, the parallel streets are designated by letters (A, B, C, etc.). Then, two-syllable names follow the letters from A to about W (such as Adams, Bryant, Channing, etc.) Three-syllable names continue the pattern from A to about W (Albemarle, Brandywine, Chesapeake, etc.). Beyond that point, along the longest north/south line approximating 16th Street, NW, the streets are named after trees and flowers, also in alphabetical order (Aspen, Butternut, Cedar, etc.). Running east and west from the line representing North and South Capitol streets, the streets are numbered 1st, 2d, 3d, 4th, to somewhere in the 50s.

Numbering of addresses is also orderly. Between 1st Street and 2d Street (on lettered and named streets), the house numbers are between 100 and 199; between 40th Street and 41st Street, the house numbers are between 4000 and 4099. An easy rule in locating an address on numbered streets is that 10 blocks from A Street would be K Street; hence, 1000 15th Street would be the intersection of K and 15th streets.

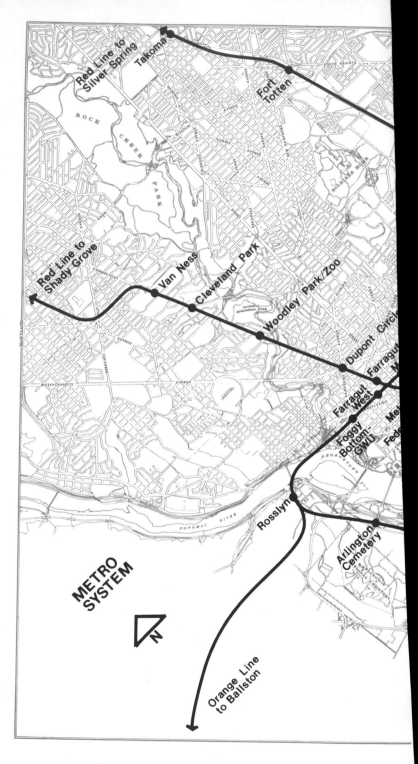

METRO
SYSTEM

N

Red Line to Silver Spring

Takoma

Fort Totten

Red Line to Shady Grove

Van Ness

Cleveland Park

Woodley Park/Zoo

Dupont Circle

Farragut

Farragut West

Foggy Bottom-GWU

Fed

Rosslyn

Arlington Cemetery

POTOMAC RIVER

Orange Line to Ballston

ROCK CREEK PARK

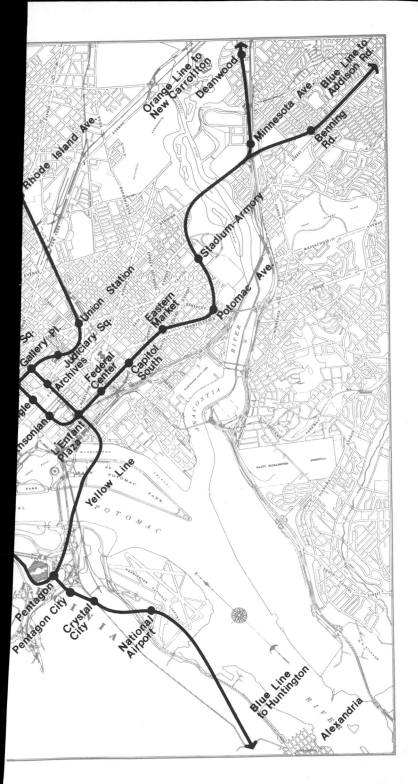

Orange Line to
New Carrollton

Deanwood

Blue Line to
Addison Rd.

Minnesota Ave.

Rhode Island Ave.

Benning
Rd.

Stadium-Armory

Potomac Ave.

Union Station

Eastern
Market

Sq.

Gallery Pl.

Judiciary Sq.

Archives

Federal
Center

Capitol
South

gle

smonian

L'Enfant
Plaza

Yellow Line

POTOMAC

Pentagon

Pentagon City

Crystal
City

National
Airport

Blue Line
to Huntington

Alexandria

L'Enfant's City

1/**Capitol Hill*****

(U.S. Capitol, Union Station-National Visitors Center, Library of Congress, Supreme Court, active residential restoration area)

by Clifford W. Moy

Distance: 2¾ miles
Time: 1¼ hours
Bus: 16, 38, 40, 42, 80, 96, 98, D2, D4, D8, X2, X4, X6, and X8
Metro: Union Station-Visitors Center (Red Line)

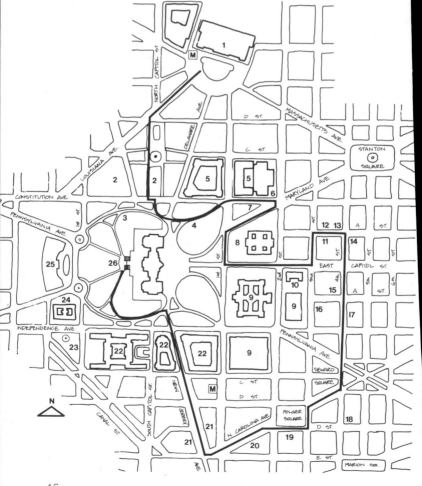

1 The tour begins at **Union Station***** and the
Plaza***, about 4 blocks north of the Capitol at Massachusetts and Delaware avenues, NE. Architect Daniel H.
Burnham designed Union Station in response to the
McMillan Commission's wish that all the train stations be
consolidated into one terminal. Since 1908, the station has
also served as a monumental gateway into Washington,
D.C. To further that end, the 40-million-dollar **National
Visitors Center*,** housed within the railroad terminal,
was dedicated on July 4, 1976. Unfortunately, its use has
not lived up to its promotion. However, the cosmetic treatment of Union Station Plaza was well received. The redesign of the Plaza stresses "people-orientation" (meaning
a rechannelization of traffic) and the placement of flag-
poles along the perimeter. An impressive structure in the
center of the Plaza is the **Columbus Memorial Foun-
tain*,** sculpted in 1912 by Lorado Taft.
　　In 1981 Congress passed the Union Station Redevelopment Act, providing for the development and restoration
of Union Station. This act envisions a "multi-modal transportation center" concept for the future development of
Union Station.

2 This Capitol Hill **park**** is one of the favorites of many
congressional aides, particularly the younger set, who
brown-bag their lunches. If you are here in the spring and
summer you can see why. The many red oak trees and a
sparkling water fountain are invitations one cannot refuse.
To the west juts a concrete **monolith honoring Sen.
Robert A. Taft*** of Ohio. Designed by Douglass W. Orr in
1959, this memorial houses 27 bells that chime every quar-
ter-hour.

3 The **Capitol Grotto**** (1879) is one of the best features of the Capitol grounds, which were designed by landscape architect Frederick Law Olmstead. Originally

Union Station

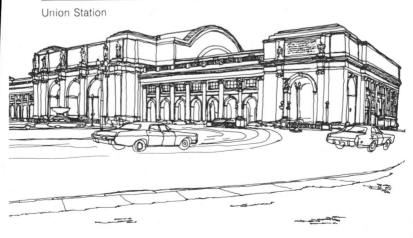

conceived to tap fresh spring water, the grotto now provides municipal water.

4 Also designed by Frederick Law Olmstead, the **Trolley Waiting Station*** (about 1876) was served by horse-drawn trolley cars. The other waiting station is located on the southeast corner of the U.S. Capitol.

U.S. Capitol

5 Asked by President George Washington to design a plan for the federal city, Major Pierre Charles L'Enfant, French engineer and architect, chose to position the **U.S. Capitol***** in one of two significant locations in the future city (the other was for the President's House). Jenkins Hill, in L'Enfant's estimate, was like '. . . a pedestal waiting for a monument. . . ." The cornerstone for the U.S. Capitol was laid in 1793 by President Washington. After being partly destroyed by British troops in 1814, the Capitol was restored with the addition of a wooden dome. In 1857 two wings were added (the Senate and the House of Representatives), and an iron dome replaced the wooden one in 1865. Atop the dome stands the Statue of Freedom. According to its sculptor, Thomas Crawford, the statue represents "Armed Liberty," her right hand grasping a sheathed sword while the other holds the wreath and shield. The **Capitol guided tour**** is recommended. If possible, take the Capitol subway to either the Richard B. Russell Senate Office Building (Senate Caucus Room; scene of the famous Watergate hearings) or the Everett M. Dirksen Senate Office Building. (The subway, which generally runs from 9:00 a.m. to 4:30 p.m. weekdays and 9:00 a.m. to 12:00 p.m. Saturdays, will stay open until the Senate recesses, when there is a night session.)

6 The **Sewall-Belmont House*,** at 144 Constitution Avenue, was saved from demolition in 1974 by a special act of Congress, and was subsequently entered into the National Register of Historic Places. Otherwise, the site would have been used to complete a Senate parking lot that now abuts the Sewall-Belmont House. Robert Sewall, from an illustrious Maryland family, in 1800 built this three-story townhouse, which was characteristic of the Federal period in style. His Capitol Hill home was leased to Albert Gallatin, Secretary of the Treasury (1801–13). In 1929 the National Women's Party purchased the house from Sen. Porter Dale. Some of the unusual furnishings include desks once owned by Henry Clay and Susan B. Anthony. (Visiting hours: 10:00 a.m.–2:00 p.m. weekdays; noon–4:00 p.m. weekends and holidays.)

7 The **Mountjoy Bayly House** (known also as the Chaplain's Memorial Building), at 122 Maryland Avenue, is also representative of the Federal period and is listed in the National Register of Historic Places. Mountjoy Bayly was a former sergeant-at-arms and doorkeeper of the Senate. Hiram Johnson, a progressive U.S. senator from 1917 until his death in 1945 and vice presidential candidate to Theodore Roosevelt on the Bull Moose ticket, purchased the property in 1929 and resided there from 1930 to 1945. Since 1947, the house has been owned by the Headquarters for the General Commission on Chaplain and Armed Forces Personnel.

8 Built entirely of marble, the **Supreme Court Building***** was completed in 1935. A spacious 100-foot-wide oval plaza precedes the main steps of the building. On the east front are a group of marble figures representing Confucius, Solon, and Moses (sculpted by Herman A. MacNeil).

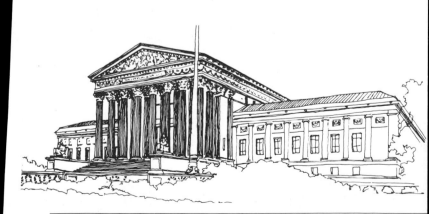

Supreme Court Building

9 Created by an act of Congress in 1800, the **Library of Congress***** housed its materials in the Capitol until 1896, when the Army Corps of Engineers built its main building. The Library serves not only the members of Congress. but also government agencies and the general public. Outstanding collections of rare Chinese, Russian, and Japanese books are among its many treasures. A visit to the main reading room is a must. Directly behind the main building is the Library Annex. The **James Madison Memorial Library,** another annex on Independence Avenue between 1st and 2d streets, was opened in 1980.

10 The **Folger Shakespeare Library**** (1932—Paul Cret), on 201 East Capitol Street, is certainly a must for Shakespeare followers; especially the reproduction of an **Elizabethan Theater**,** which is in active use all year.

11 The use of Folger's side entrance at 311 A Street, NE, is quite refreshing.

12 Frederick Douglass's first Washington residence was at 316 A Street, NE. According to a Capitol Hill Restoration Society plaque, Douglass was the "precursor to the Civil Rights Movement . . . [and] . . . resided in this building from 1871–1877."

13 Opening in a residential area in 1964, the **Museum of African Art*** (318 A Street, NE) was the first museum to house and thereby promote African heritage. (Hours: weekdays, 10:00 a.m.–5:00 p.m.; weekends and holidays 12:00–5:00 p.m.)

14 The townhouse on the corner of 4th and A streets, NE, is a converted store built around 1869. Compare this with the same style, but unrestored, townhouse at 1100 Independence Avenue, SE, located on the corner of Independence Avenue and 11th Street (at this juncture, the hearty walker can test his/her stamina by detouring onto East Capitol Street into Tour 2. This tour will lead you back into Tour 1 at Pennsylvania Avenue and 4th Street, SE).

15 The **Brumidi House,** 326 A Street, SE, was built about 1850. It was purportedly the home of Constantino Brumidi, an Italian artist, who at the age of 60, painted in 11 months the Apotheosis of Washington over 4,664 square feet of the Capitol dome. He was also responsible for the Rotunda frescoes and other Capitol decorations.

16 St. Marks Episcopal Church (1888), located on 3d and A streets, SE, is listed in the National Register of Historic Places. A frequent visitor was the late President Lyndon B. Johnson.

17 The townhouse at 120 4th Street, SE (built about 1876), is typical of the 1870s, with flat facade, elaborate cornices and lintels.

18 The **Ebenezer United Methodist Church,** on 4th and D streets, SE, originally known as the Little Ebenezer Church, was constructed in 1838 and rebuilt in 1897. From March 1864 to May 1865, the church served as the first schoolhouse for blacks in Washington. The church is also the oldest black church on Capitol Hill.

19 This vacant square is the site of the old Providence Hospital. It is now under the jurisdiction of the Architect of the Capitol as one of the "Capitol Grounds." It is currently committed as the site for a congressional page school and dormitory. How would one properly design the building to harmonize with the residential area?

20 This stretch of **North Carolina Avenue,** is a fine example of the L'Enfant plan for the Federal City: the superimposition of bold, diagonal avenues over a standard grid pattern. The side streets, particularly E Street, have been the scene of many touch football games.

21 This stretch of **New Jersey Avenue, SE**,** frames a magnificent sight. This transition between residential and federal buildings, along with the view of the Capitol dome, is startling. Consequently, New Jersey Avenue residents have acquired great pride in restoring their homes. The "Master Plan for Future Development of the Capitol Grounds and Related Areas" was completed in 1981 and is being introduced in Congress for adoption. According to the "transition zone" classification, New Jersey Avenue will be able to retain its historic, residential character in the face of congressional growth.

22 The **House Office Buildings** along Independence Avenue are, from west to east, the Sam Rayburn Building, the Nicholas Longworth Building, and the Joseph Cannon Building. You may want to stop by and visit your congressman. (The subway between the Rayburn Building and the U.S. Capitol generally runs from 9:00 a.m.–8:00 p.m. weekdays and 9:00 a.m.–5:00 p.m. Saturdays; it stays open until Congress recesses when there is an evening session.)

23 The **Bartholdi Fountain*** (between Canal and 1st streets on Independence Avenue, SW) was designed by Frederic Auguste Bartholdi in 1876.

24 The **Botanic Gardens*** (Independence Avenue, Maryland Avenue, and 1st Street, SW) was constructed in 1931–33 and is worth a visit. (For more details see Tour 3, The Mall—East, no. 9.)

25 The **Grant Memorial*** (1922) is the largest and most expensive statuary grouping in Washington. The **Capitol Reflecting Pool*** was designed by Skidmore Owings and Merrill. Completed in 1970, the pool is directly over Interstate Highway 395, which underlies the Mall.

26 The tour ends at the steps of the west side of the U.S. Capitol. The **view***** across the Mall to the Washington Monument is memorable. In the words of Pierre L'Enfant, the site of the U.S. Capitol is truly like "a pedestal waiting for a monument."

2/**Capitol Hill—East****

(active residential restoration area)

by Clifford W. Moy

Distance: 2¾ miles
Time: 1¼ hours
Bus: 40, 96, 98 on East Capitol Street; 92 and 94 on 8th
    Street, SE
Metro: Eastern Market (Blue and Orange Lines)

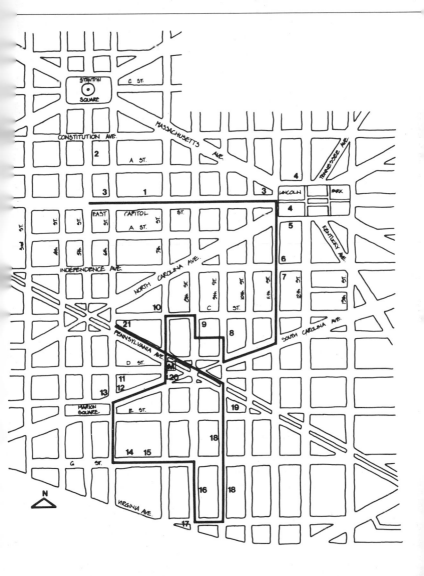

1 The tour begins at 5th and East Capitol streets. **East Capitol Street**** is considered the "Grand Street" of the Capitol Hill Community. The smaller scale of development of adjacent streets north and south of East Capitol provides a sharp contrast. In 1974 Michael Franch prepared a report for the Joint Committee on Landmarks for the National Capital in which he discovered that "the general area of elite residence (for the years 1888, 1889, 1909, and 1918) was a diamond-shaped district between the Capitol and Lincoln Park, Stanton Park and Seward Square." As was suspected, the heaviest concentration of elite residences was along East Capitol Street. The diversity of housing types and styles is tremendous, quite unlike the Georgetown Historic District. Everything from manor houses, federal townhouses, and brick row houses to the contemporary style of housing exists in the Capitol Hill Historic District. A community group, the Capitol Hill Restoration Society, has done much to encourage and to maintain the "Capitol Hill" image.

2 There is an interesting **view from East Capitol Street,** looking north along 5th Street, which includes a statue of Maj. Gen. Nathaniel Greene on horseback in Stanton Park.

3 The **townhouses at 512 and 514 East Capitol Street*** (1879) are representative of the 1870s, with flat facades and elaborate cornices and lintels. Some of the townhouses, for instance 1014 **East Capitol Street*** (1899), have balconies and/or roof decks on which to enjoy the hot summer evenings.

512 and 514 East Capitol Street

4 Lincoln Park* and the **Emancipation Statue** (completed and dedicated April 1876; President Ulysses S. Grant and Frederick Douglass were present at the ceremony) were constructed in memory of Abraham Lincoln. The other statue (dedicated July 1974) at the east end of the park is in honor of **Mary McLeod Bethune,** black educator. The entire seven-acre park was designed by Hilliard Robinson, landscape architect, in conjunction with the National Park Service. The homes surrounding Lincoln Park are predominantly from the 1890–95 period. Pay particular attention to the townhouse at 1125 **East Capitol Street*** (1892) near the northwest corner of Lincoln Park.

5 The **granite row houses** with balconies (1111 to 1119 East Capitol Street) were built in 1892.

6 Philadelphia Row* (124 to 154 11th Street, SE) was built by James W. Gessford, about 1866. He built 16 row houses in the style of Philadelphia to soothe his wife's homesickness for her native city.

Philadelphia Row

7 This **group of 15 row houses*** (200 to 228 11th Street, SE) was built by Charles Gessford in 1891, some 25 years after Philadelphia Row.

8 Constructed in 1967, the **Thomas Simmons House*** (314 to 316 9th Street, SE) is a fine example of the contemporary homes that are in keeping with the physical scale of the Capitol Hill Historic District. (Slip through the alley between houses 321 and 319 9th Street; more cautious individuals may continue on 9th Street before turning on C Street.)

9 This set of **contemporary row houses** (801–819 C Street, SE) was constructed in the mid-1960s.

10 A swing through an alley will lead directly to the **Eastern Market**** on 7th and C streets, SE. The open-market activity will mesmerize even the most tough-skinned of individuals. Designed by Adolph Cluss and constructed in 1873, this market is the heart of the Capitol Hill community. Be sure to sample the cannoli at the bakery. More boutiques and shops line 7th Street into Pennsylvania Avenue, SE.

Eastern Market

11 The **Maples House*,** now named the Friendship House Settlement, was built during the Federal period 1795–96 by architect-builder William Lovering. Francis Scott Key was one of the many distinguished owners. The front entrance of the Maples House originally opened onto South Carolina Avenue, but today it goes by the 619 D Street, SE, address.

12 This stretch of **South Carolina Avenue*** provides a spacious and charming residential atmosphere that is typical of the Capitol Hill community.

13 The **Carbery House,** 423 6th Street, SE, was built about 1813, and designated a historic site/structure by the Joint Committee on Landmarks. This stretch of 6th Street to G Street, SE, comprises some of the oldest houses on Capitol Hill, many built in the 1840s–50s.

14 Christ Church* (1806—Benjamin H. Latrobe). In the past, this church at 620 G Street, SE, served many individuals from the Navy Yard and Marine Barracks. It is believed to have been visited by Presidents James Madison, Thomas Jefferson, and James Monroe.

15 The house at 636 G Street, SE, the **birthplace of John Philip Sousa,** conductor, composer, and bandmaster of the U.S. Marine Corps, was built in 1844.

16 The **Marine Commandant's House**** and the **Marine Barracks**** occupy the entire square. Constructed in 1801–4 after George Hadfield's designs, the physical scale of the commandant's house sets it apart from the nearby homes. The Marine Barracks surrounds an interior courtyard and parade ground, extremely manicured in the traditional military style. The Marine Corps Band and the ceremonial units are housed at the barracks. Along 8th Street, from Pennsylvania Avenue to the SE Freeway (also known as Barracks Row), commercial rejuvenation is progressing.

17 One of the textbook results of a major freeway splicing through a community is the creation of vacant lots. In 1975, this site was a vacant lot. Today it is called a "missed opportunity." Ironically, the two affected advisory neighborhood commissions were involved in the planning process. The resulting decision was a compromise. Hence, half the site is paved for metered parking and the other half for recreational use.

18 Note the abrupt contrast of housing styles between the contemporary and the older housing in the 700 and 500 blocks of 9th Street.

19 Constructed in 1865–66, the **Old Naval Hospital** (Center for Youth Services) on Pennsylvania Avenue, between 9th and 10th streets, SE, still retains what may be the original cast-iron fence.

20 The square at Pennsylvania Avenue, between 7th and 8th streets, SE, is the site of the **Eastern Market Metro** subway station. The interplay of the design with the commercial strip along Pennsylvania Avenue could have been more interesting.

21 On the corner of Pennsylvania Avenue and 6th Street, SE, is the National Permanent Building (formerly named the Eastern Liberty Federal Building), which was occupied in 1976. Designed by the architectural firm of Mills Petticord (now merged with HOK), the metal mansard roof houses 90 solar collector panels designed for domestic hot water.

3/**The Mall—East*****
(major axis of monumental core, Smithsonian museums, art galleries)

by Wilcomb Washburn and Kathryn Cousins

Distance: 2 miles
Time: 1 hour
Bus: On or near Independence Avenue: 16B, 16C, 52, V4, or V6
Metro: Smithsonian (Blue and Orange Lines)

1 The tour begins at the **Smithsonian Building*****
(1855—James Renwick), Jefferson Drive between 9th and 11th streets, SW. The **Great Hall***** contains an excellent exhibit on the history of the planning of Washington, D.C. It introduces planning concepts to laymen, as well as orienting the public to the city. Note particularly the innovative "perspective" models of the four major plans—L'Enfant (1791), Downing (1851), McMillan Commission (1902), and National Capital Planning Commission/Pennsylvania Ave-

Smithsonian Institution Building (The Castle)

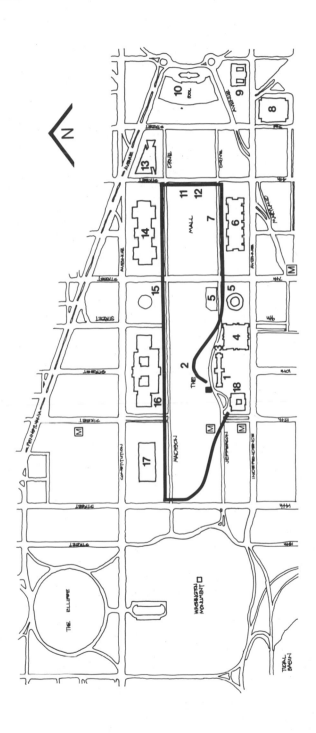

nue Development Corporation (1975). The original McMillan Commission models are also on display.

2 Walk outside to the center of the **Mall***.** You are midway on the major axis of the monumental core of this capital city as planned by L'Enfant. (The Mall was extended beyond the Washington Monument to the Lincoln Memorial in the 20th century after the tidal flats and marshes west of the monument were filled in.) The greensward was planned by L'Enfant as a broad avenue, 400 feet wide, lined with grand residences. The Mall now represents a sensitive compromise between the monumental plans of L'Enfant and the McMillan Commission (executed without the broad central avenue L'Enfant proposed), softened at the edges with humanistic touches suggestive of Downing (exemplified by the present-day ice rink, carousel, sports activities, Constitution Gardens, and the annual Festival of American Folklife).

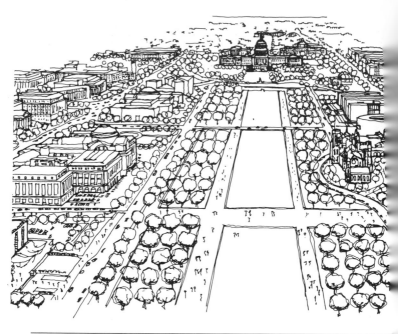

The Mall, looking east

3 Directly east of the Smithsonian Building is the **urn commemorating Andrew Jackson Downing.** His plan for the Mall created the first landscaped American public park. In the 1930s, many of the mature trees planted in conformity with his plan were removed from the center of the Mall as it was "restored" to L'Enfant's more formal concept by the McMillan Commission. Behind the Smithsonian Building, construction is underway for the Smithsonian Center for African, Near Eastern, and Asian Cultures. The center will be almost entirely underground.

4 The **Arts and Industries Building*** (1881—Cluss and Schulze, after plans by Montgomery Meigs), at Jefferson Drive and 9th Street, SW, features exhibits from the 1876 Centennial Exhibition held in Philadelphia.

5 Continue east along Jefferson Drive to 7th Street, SW, to the **Joseph H. Hirshhorn Museum and Sculpture Garden**** (1974—Gordon Bunschaft of Skidmore Owings and Merrill). Note the sunken outdoor sculpture garden, north of Jefferson Drive, as well as the cylindrical building that contains paintings and sculptures from the late 1800s to the present.

6 Continue on Jefferson Drive across 7th Street to the **National Air and Space Museum***** (1976   Gyo Obata of Helmuth, Obata and Kassabaum). Since its official opening on July 4, 1976, this has become the most popular Smithsonian museum—and the most heavily visited museum in the world.

National Air and Space Museum

7 The elms on the north side of Jefferson Drive are part of a continuous band of trees on both sides of the Mall that serve to emphasize the east-west axis. Unfortunately, the barrenness of these deciduous trees in winter leaves the Mall dull and lifeless. Downing's argument that the Mall should be attractive above all in the winter when Congress is in session has lost to questionable arguments that evergreens are not tolerant of urban conditions, are messy, or present security problems.

8 At the corner of 4th Street and Jefferson Drive, SW, one can view the **Hubert Humphrey Federal Office Building*,** designed by Marcel Breuer, who also designed the Housing and Urban Development Building (1968). The core of the building contains a 10-story exhaust shaft of the Interstate Highway 395 tunneled beneath the Mall.

9 The **Botanic Garden Conservatory*,** to the north of the Humphrey Building, is better known in Washington for supplying an amazing number of free plants for congressional offices, than for some of its well-conceived attempts to experiment with innovative plantings around the Mall. Open to the public, the conservatory contains special exhibits, lush tropical plants, ferns, cacti, and succulents.

10 Walk north on 4th Street. On your right is the **Grant Memorial*** and the **Reflecting Pool*** (see Tour 1, Capitol Hill, no. 25), at 1st Street between Maryland and Pennsylvania avenues, NW.

11 As one looks toward the Washington Monument, it is interesting to realize that this impressive, open, grassy mall was not completely implemented until 1975, when traffic and parking on the interior streets were replaced by the current pedestrian and bicycle paths. During the years between 1791 and 1972, the Mall had been the location of a cow pasture and slaughtering site, swamps, a Civil War hospital, a "murderers' row," a railroad station and numerous railroad tracks, a trash-filled and stagnant canal, and "temporary" government buildings that existed from World War I to 1972.

12 This is a good site from which to note how the position of the **old Smithsonian Building** offended the sense of order of the monumental-minded park planners of the 1900s. The McMillan Plan assumed the building would be removed, but the "defects" of Renwick's Norman "Castle," as seen by the formal eye of 1900, have become assets in the eyes of those forced to live in marble halls. The warm, rusty colors, which glow in the evening sun, serve as a standing rebuke to the colorless and lackluster white sepulchers around it. Its irregular dimensions and projections—vertically and horizontally—give us welcome relief from the symmetrical boxes constantly spawning in the Federal City. Even its failure to stand back of the line prescribed by the turn-of-the-century planners warms our hidden rebelliousness.

13 This striking building is the widely acclaimed **East Building of the National Gallery of Art**** (I. M. Pei), which opened in 1978. Pei's building is an unabashedly modern solution to an awkward site. Yet its pink Tennessee marble echoes the material, if not the form, of the adjacent main building of the National Gallery of Art to which it is connected by an underground passageway running under 4th Street. The East Building repeats its triangular theme throughout: in the ceiling designs and in the finely crafted walls whose sharp edges show wear from the admiring hands of many visitors. The museumgoer enters the building under a low ceiling and is then overwhelmed by a sunlit, four-story atrium around which the many galleries of the building are grouped.

14 Turn west on Madison to the **National Gallery of Art, Main Building**** (1941—John Russell Pope). It contains the richest **collection of fine arts***** in the city.

National Gallery of Art

15 Continue west to the **pool and ice-skating rink*** (1974—Skidmore Owings and Merrill), between 7th and 9th streets. This joint project of the National Park Service and the National Gallery of Art has been extremely successful in humanizing the edges of the Mall.

16 In front of the **National Museum of Natural History and National Museum of Man***** (1911—Hornblower and Marshall; 1965 wings, Mills, Petticord and Mills), between 9th and 12th streets, you will see a few evergreens planted in conformity with the 1851 Mall plan of Andrew Jackson Downing. The holly tree that you see in the midst of the elms, slightly to the southeast of the Natural History building's steps, was scheduled for removal during the leveling process. The tree was saved in the 1930s by Smithsonian Secretary Alexander Wetmore, an ornithologist, because it was the nesting place of his pet mockingbird. The museum is the home of the famous Hope Diamond.

17 The **National Museum of American History***** (1964—McKim, Mead and White), at Madison Drive between 12th and 14th streets, is characteristic of the museums of the 1960s. Note the contrast with the lighter, more "open" Smithsonian museums of the 1970s. Popular exhibits include the

Star Spangled Banner, Horatio Greenough's monumental sculptured figure of George Washington, and the First Ladies' gowns.

18 Walk across the Mall to the **Freer Gallery of Art**** (1923—Charles A. Platt), at 12th Street and Jefferson Drive. Built around a delightful interior court, the museum contains a small but choice collection of oriental art, and the world's largest collection of James Abbott McNeill Whistler's works (including the famous Peacock Room).

4/**The Mall—West*****
(national memorials)

by Wilcomb Washburn and Kathryn Cousins

Distance: 2¾ miles
Time: 2 hours
Bus: On Constitution Avenue: 16A, 16D; on 14th Street:
    50, 52, 9, 11A, 11E, and 11W
Metro: Federal Triangle or Smithsonian (Blue and Orange
Lines)

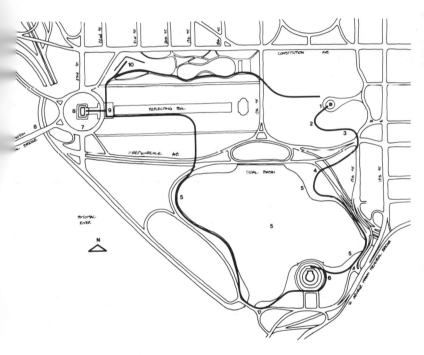

This tour includes the Washington, Jefferson, and Lincoln memorials. Because of the tour length and inadequate parking, you may wish to buy a ticket for the Tourmobile, which enables you to see each site at your own pace. You can get on and off the Tourmobile at 11 sites along the Mall for the entire day of purchase. Adult tickets can be purchased at major tourist spots on the Mall, including the three memorials on this tour. Call (202) 554-7950 for Tourmobile rates and information.

1 The tour begins at the **Washington Monument*****
(1884—Robert Mills), 15th Street and center of the Mall.
Pierre L'Enfant chose this site for the equestrian statue proposed by Congress. George Washington approved the site.
Because Congress failed to act decisively on the proposal,
a group of private citizens, organized in 1833 as the Washington National Monument Society, offered a prize for the
best design for a monument. Robert Mills's design for a
600-foot obelisk rising from a colonnaded base won; the
society accepted the design minus the colonnaded base.
Construction began in 1848, but funds ran out in 1854.
Construction began again in 1876 after Congress authorized the monument's completion at government expense.
It was finally completed in 1884 by the Army Corps of Engineers. If you look about one-fourth the way up you will
see a distinct break in the color of the stone indicating the
pause between construction phases.

L'Enfant's plan called for the monument to Washington
to be located at the crossing of the north-south axis south
from the White House at its crossing with the east-west axis
due west from the Capitol. The ground at that point, however, was low and marshy, and when the present monument
was started early in the 19th century, it was placed on more
solid ground 360 feet east and 120 feet south of the
planned position. Down the hill to the northwest you will
see the "Jefferson Pier," a stone monument placed there in
1810 to mark the true intersection of L'Enfant's proposed
north-south and east-west axes. It was later removed—but
was replaced in 1889. The Senate Park Commission planners sought to rectify the off-center Washington Monument
in its north-south axis by creating an elaborate sunken garden with a large circular pool to the west. It was never built
because engineers asserted that the monument's stability
would be threatened as a result. The planners sought to
rectify the off-center monument in its east-west axis by
slanting the Mall one degree south of its true east-west direction.

2 Walk to the west of the Washington Monument and look
west toward the Lincoln Memorial. All of the land toward
the Potomac River was reclaimed from marsh and tidal
land between the 1880s and the 1920s. Until then, the Potomac occasionally flooded right to the south lawn of the
White House. The McMillan Commission proposed extending the Mall from the Washington Monument to the proposed site for a Lincoln Memorial. The planners connected
the two monuments with a reflecting pool and aligned the
extension along the Park Commission's slanted new east-
west axis.

3 Go south toward the Jefferson Memorial. The **Sylvan
Theater,** at 15th Street and Independence Avenue, southeast of the Washington Monument, is the site of open-air
summer musical, dramatic, and dance productions.

Shakespearean plays are favorites.

4 Continue south across Independence Avenue and walk west to East Basin Drive, near 17th Street, to the **Tulip Library.** This outdoor garden is planted with flowering annuals, which are well identified. The tulips in the spring are spectacular.

5 The site of the **Tidal Basin***** (1897—W. T. Twining), Independence Avenue and East Basin Drive, was originally part of the Potomac River. In 1882 the tidal basin was created as part of a plan to improve navigation on the Potomac and to reclaim some land for parks. The basin serves to flush clean the Washington Channel, as gates between the basin and channel are opened at low tide to release the Potomac waters that have filled the basin at high tide. The **cherry trees***** surrounding the basin are among 3,000 given by Japan in 1912. The Cherry Blossom Festival—held each year in early April—celebrates their enchanting but short-blooming period.

6 Continue along the Tidal Basin to the **Jefferson Memorial***** (1943—John Russell Pope, architect; Rudulph Evans, sculptor). The McMillan Commission recommended a memorial in this location, but not specifically for Jefferson. There was considerable controversy on the design of the monument before approval. It was criticized as combining outmoded classical architectural styles, for being too similar to the Lincoln Memorial, and for blocking the view of the Potomac from the White House. Defenders of the design said it

Jefferson Memorial

was influenced by Jefferson's respect for classical styles, which he introduced to this country, and particularly by the Pantheon, which much of his own architecture resembled. The grounds are landscaped after designs of Frederick Law Olmsted, Jr. The site forms the south end of the major cross axis of the Mall with the White House at the north. This axis is difficult to perceive on the ground because the Tidal Basin presents a barrier to direct access to the memorial from the north. It is readily apparent, however, on a map or from the air.

Take the Tourmobile to the Lincoln Memorial or walk northwest across West Potomac Park to Independence Avenue.

Lincoln Memorial

7 The site of the **Lincoln Memorial***** (1922—Henry Bacon, architect; Daniel Chester French, scuptor) had been debated since 1867. Many early proposals stressed commemorating Abraham Lincoln as a war hero rather than as a humanitarian. Alternatives considered were a Lincoln Highway between Gettysburg and Washington and sites near Union Station and the Capitol. In 1911 the decision was made to locate the memorial here on the continuation of the axis of the Capitol and Washington Monument, as called for on the McMillan Plan, despite many objections that the land was swampy and inaccessible. Designed in a form derived from a Greek temple, the columns are tilted slightly inward to avoid the optical illusion of a bulging top. Many motifs representing Lincoln and America are incorporated in the monument, including the 36 columns that symbolize the 36 states of the Union while Lincoln was President. While some people questioned the design of a Greek temple to commemorate someone who was born in a log cabin and who proudly acknowledged that heritage, Daniel French said, "The Greeks alone were best able to express in their building . . . the highest attributes and the greatest beauty known to man." The memorial pays homage to "his simplicity, his grandeur and his power."

8 Walk around the Jefferson Memorial to the rear, or west, side for the **view***** across the Potomac. The **Arlington Memorial Bridge**** (McKim, Mead and White, architects;

Leo Freidlander, sculptor) is considered to be one of the finest bridges in the country. Designed with the concept of symbolically reuniting the North and South, it was recommended by the McMillan Commission and built in the 1920s. The bridge, which contains an operable (though rarely used) draw span, cleverly concealed in the center section, provides access to the **Arlington National Cemetery*.** About half way up the hill straight ahead of the bridge is the **grave of President John Kennedy*,** where the eternal flame can be seen at night. Farther up the hill is **Arlington House*** (Custis-Lee Mansion), home of Robert E. Lee. Looking back along the Potomac, the island to the right is a nature preserve and **memorial to President Theodore Roosevelt*.**

9 Walk around the Jefferson Memorial to the entrance and look toward the Capitol. The **view***** is one of the most photographed in Washington because it is truly spectacular. It is here that the current design policy maintaining a formal treatment of the center of the Mall and a more people-oriented treatment at the edges is most apparent. The **Reflecting Pool***** is designed to mirror, and to link in a formal and inspiring setting, both monuments. When an artificial ice-skating facility was proposed for the pool in the 1960s, it

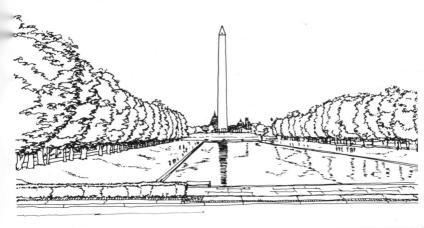

Washington Monument/Reflecting Pool

was turned down by the National Park Service as out of keeping with the dignity of the Mall. Such a facility has more recently been installed in the area between the National Gallery of Art and the National Museum of Natural History (see Tour 3, Mall—East, no. 15). To the north (formerly the site of "Main Navy"—temporary buildings from World War I that outlasted World War II) is the site of **Constitution Gardens*** (Skidmore Owings and Merrill). Originally planned as a vibrant, day- and nighttime attraction (modeled on the Tivoli Gardens in Copenhagen), the proposed concessionary activities were almost entirely eliminated in order to reduce initial costs. Since is opening in 1976, the gardens have failed to attract the crowds expected. An irregularly shaped lake forms the center of the park. Note the total absence of evergreens, which makes the landscape barren in winter.

10 The **Vietnam Memorial***,** dedicated in 1982, is one of Washington's most unusual monuments, both in its design and in the manner of its creation. Initiated by private citizens who had fought in Vietnam, it was built without public funds, and its winning design—by a young Chinese-American student at Yale, Maya Lin—was the product of an open architectural competition. The monument forms an open V-shaped slash in the ground, the ends of which point to the Washington Monument on the one side and the Lincoln Memorial on the other. On its polished black marble panels are inscribed chronologically, in order of their deaths, the names of the more than 50,000 Americans killed during the U.S. involvement in Vietnam. The monument has attracted great numbers of visitors who move reverently past the panels, leaving small tokens of remembrance—flowers, pictures, flags for those lost in the war. While the final judgment has yet to be written (and, indeed, the addition of a flagpole and a representational sculpture of these servicemen has been added to meet the criticisms of those who assert that the monument is too funerary and not sufficiently celebratory in character), it can be said that the monument is a moving work of art rising above the controversial character of the Vietnam War.

5/Independence Avenue, SW*, and L'Enfant Plaza**

(federal office buildings, large commercial urban redevelopment project)

by Charity Vanderbilt Davidson; 1983 update by Lin Brown

Distance: ¾ mile
Time: 1½ hours
Bus: 16B, 16C, 30, 32, 34, 36, 52, A2, A4, A6, and A8.
Metro: Federal Center, SW (Blue and Orange Lines)

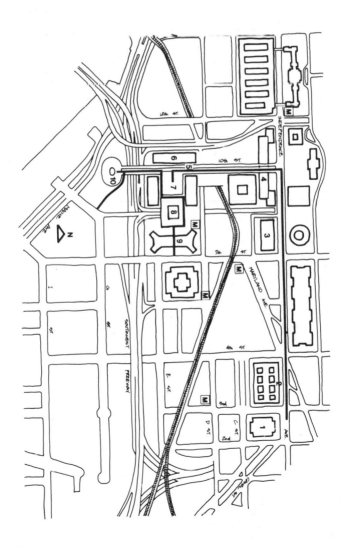

The Independence Avenue/L'Enfant Plaza area is the northern edge of Washington's Southwest quadrant. During the first half of the 19th century, it was a desirable residential area with a smattering of commercial uses (including the most famous of the city's slave pens). After the Baltimore and Potomac Railroad laid tracks along Maryland and Virginia avenues, SW, in 1873, the western end of the area between B Street, SW (Independence Avenue), and the waterfront became a vast railroad yard, and its desirability as a residential section diminished.

Prior to 1900 the only government agencies with a strong interest in the area were the Department of Agriculture, with buildings along B Street, and the Bureau of Printing and Engraving. Federal interest in the northern fringes of the Southwest increased during the first decades of the 20th century with the erection of more buildings for Agriculture and Printing and Engraving. The area retained much of its 19th-century appearance because the departments rented space in existing structures rather than erecting new buildings.

During World War I, the federal bureaucracy mushroomed, and it became all too apparent that the departments could no longer "make do" with a multitude of offices scattered all over the city. This area was included in the kite-shaped monumental core proposed by the Senate Park Commission in 1902, but its use was undefined and little action was taken. By the 1920s, a new building program had become a necessity. Most of the attention was focused on the Federal Triangle between Pennsylvania Avenue, NW, and the Mall. But by the 1930s, the newly created National Capital Park and Planning Commission (today the National Capital Planning Commission) was drawing up plans for similar developments in other parts of the city. One of the areas proposed was the Southwest Rectangle, bounded by B Street, SW (which was to be given the more pretentious name of Independence Avenue), 14th Street, the railroad tracks, and 2d Street, SW. Several large federal buildings (Health and Human Services), most of Agriculture, and Printing and Engraving were erected before the outbreak of World War II. In addition, Independence Avenue (B Street) was widened to form a south parallel to Constitution Avenue on the other side of the Mall.

Nothing further was done until the 1950s, when plans for the redevelopment of the entire Southwest were drawn up. Although an area roughly the same as the old Southwest Rectangle was set aside for development as government offices, no plan specified the location of any of the proposed buildings or their spatial relationship to one another. The awkward positioning of many of the offices in the redeveloped federal area is a result of this omission from the recent plans.

Hubert Humphrey Federal Office Building

1 The **Hubert Humphrey Federal Office Building*,** on Independence Avenue between 2d and 3d streets, SW, was completed in 1976 (Marcel Breuer and Herbert Beckhard). This six-story rectangular building presented a particular design challenge because it spans part of the adjacent freeway. Exhaust ducts from the freeway tunnel and a large mechanical equipment shaft had to be designed into the building. Interior offices are lighted by two interior light wells (one of which can be entered from the plaza). There are three levels of parking and mechanical equipment spaces, as well as the freeway under the plaza. The plaza itself, like the HUD building (see no. 9, this tour), is notable for its crisp or hard urban finish rather than the soft planting typical of Washington parks and plazas.

2 The **Department of Health and Human Services,** on Independence Avenue between 3d and 4th streets, SW, was completed in 1939–41 by the Office of the Supervising Architect of the Treasury. Originally intended for the Social Security Administration, this monolithic building was part of the Southwest Rectangle development. It is typical of federal architecture of the period, except that its openings (for ventilation) are screened, Egyptian style, for more overall massing (note later how this compares with the rear of the south building at the Department of Agriculture).

3 Federal Office Building No. 10, at 800 Independence Avenue, SW, was designed in 1963 by Holabird & Root. It is probably the most conspicuous of the "universal office buildings" constructed under the General Services Administration program of not assigning proposed buildings to any specific government agency or department. Occupied

by the Department of Transportation, this building is an example of the fallacy of the 1950s belief that two buildings
were harmonious if they had the same mass. It was hoped
that the similarity in mass, height, and setback between FOB
No. 10 and the National Archives building directly across the
Mall would emphasize the 8th-Street axis as it crossed the
Mall; unfortunately, there was no effort to relate such other
features as fenestration, columns, portico, etc. The result was
so visually unsatisfactory that few objected when the
Hirshhorn Museum interrupted the vista between two supposedly matching buildings. FOB No. 10's ground floor is
raised, giving it the appearance of an arcade; the result in
this building, with the loggia separated from the street by its
landscaping, is markedly different from that achieved by the
Forrestal Building, where it is part of the plaza.

4 The **James Forrestal Building (FOB No. 5),** at Independence Avenue and 10th Street, SW (1970—Curtis &
Davis), which is the only federal office building to have both
a name and a number, is probably the most special of the
"universal" buildings. It actually consists of three structures:
the 660-foot-long main building fronting on Independence
Avenue, a taller office annex behind, and a separate cafeteria building. The large horizontal building originally was
conceived as two of the General Services Administration's
"universal office buildings," one on each side of 10th Street.
The Department of Defense convinced Congress that the
specialized nature of the department's activities required that
the majority of its facilities on this site be contained in a single structure. Congress then approved the concept of a single building spanning 10th Street, SW. It finally was agreed
that the first floor of the horizontal building would be lifted 30
feet above the street level in order to avoid blocking the 10th
Street vista of the Smithsonian Castle tower. It was felt that
the sense of space created by the horizontal opening between the plaza and the first floor more than compensated
for the loss of the narrow view up 10th Street. The feeling of
unity between the Forrestal Building and the developing 10th
Street Mall/L'Enfant Plaza complex to the south was reinforced by the use of coordinated paving materials on all
three projects. The presence of the surface railroad on Maryland Avenue required that the two building complexes be on
different levels. A lower-level passage serves as a circulation
system for the three parts of the building and as a boarding
area for commuter buses.

5 The 10th Street Mall** and L'Enfant Plaza**
(1965—10th Street Mall, Wright & Gane, architects; 1965—
10th Street Overlook, Office of Dan Kiley, landscape architect; 1965—L'Enfant Plaza, North & South Buildings & Plaza,
I. M. Pei and Partners; 1970–73—L'Enfant Plaza Hotel,
Vlastimil Koubek). Original development plans for 10th
Street, SW, envisioned it as an esplanade lined with restricted commercial and residential uses. A slightly later

L'Enfant Plaza and 10th Street Mall

plan proposed that 10th Street be widened and serve as a throughway between downtown Washington and the Southwest Expressway.

Early in 1954, Webb & Knapp, the New York developers, proposed a renewal plan for the entire Southwest, including 10th Street and L'Enfant Plaza. As originally worked out by William Zeckendorf of Webb & Knapp and I. M. Pei, this proposal called for widening 10th Street and developing it as a 1,200-foot-long mall. This mall was to be flanked with public and semipublic office buildings. L'Enfant Plaza, originally farther east of 10th Street, was to be an enclosed square surrounded by private office buildings. It was also expected to develop as a cultural and entertainment/convention center with a hotel, performance hall, theater, and outdoor cafés. The mall itself was to terminate in a semicircular reflecting pool and waterfront park on the Washington Channel, balancing another large fountain treatment in the Smithsonian yard.

By the time construction began, significant changes had been made in the plan. In 1960 urban designer Willow von Molke proposed the development of the 10th Street axis to a waterfront overlook. I. M. Pei & Associates drew up a master plan for the mall and plaza that brought the plaza west to its present location; after public hearings, this master plan was incorporated into the official renewal plan approved by the National Capital Planning Commission (NCPC). Webb & Knapp had withdrawn and the project had been taken over by the L'Enfant Plaza Corporation.

6/7 Walk up the west side of the **10th Street Mall (6)** past the Postal Service building to the **Plaza** (7).** Note that the mall bridges the railroad tracks that cut through the site and that nothing has been done to develop the Maryland Avenue vista toward the Capitol. The Pei proposal had included a major focal sculpture for the plaza, but this too has been eliminated. The paving for both the mall and L'Enfant

Plaza is Hastings block inlaid with red granite. No effort has been made to differentiate visually between public and private property along the mall or in the plaza. The center strip down the mall was intended as a cascade of water flowing toward Independence Avenue, but leakage forced its draining.

8 The buildings to the north and south of the plaza are office towers; and one to the east is the **L'Enfant Plaza Hotel.** There is parking for 1,300 cars under the plaza, with direct ramps on and off the nearby expressway. There is also direct access to the Metro subway system.

Proceed across 10th Street and down the stairs on either side of the fountain. These lead to the 100,000-square-foot underground shopping mall. As with the plaza above, this retail facility gets intensive use by workers from the surrounding buildings. Once the shopping mall has been explored, continue east along the main corridor of the shopping arcade to the exit to the curvilinear HUD building.

L'Enfant Plaza Hotel

9 Department of Housing & Urban Development**
(1968—Marcel Breuer and Herbert Beckhard), 451 7th Street, SW. Walk through the HUD building to the 7th Street, SW, entrance and plaza. Commissioned in 1963, when HUD was still the Housing and Home Finance Agency, this was one of the first buildings constructed after President Kennedy issued his directive on "Guiding Principles for Federal Architecture." To raise the aesthetic standards of federal buildings, the General Services Administration provided that a percentage of the construction costs could be devoted to artistic embellishments (such as plazas and sculpture).

Breuer became involved with curvilinear structures while designing a building for UNESCO and a research lab for

IBM at LaGaude, France. The French favor such buildings because they permit a maximum amount of natural light in a maximum number of offices (thereby reducing the amount of electricity required), while keeping the distance between offices to a minimum. The architect selected a curvilinear shape for the HUD building partly because it would yield the best window-distance ratio in a large structure on a restricted site, and partly because its lines would be sympathetic to the curves of the Southwest Freeway adjacent to it. The building is a double-Y, with each wing touching the property lines only at the corners. It provides office space for more than 6,000 employees and has three levels of parking under the plaza. The plaza itself is also an effort to relate the 7th Street connection to the Mall.

The rectangular white building (Edward Durell Stone, architect) directly across 7th Street was privately built, but is occupied by the Department of Transportation. Return to the underground arcade and follow the overhead signs to the L'Enfant Plaza Hotel lobby. Exit from the lobby via the south doors in order to walk around the hotel's terrace. The section of terrace just south of the hotel is provided with umbrella-shaded tables, available to anyone wishing to use them; additional seating is provided elsewhere around the terrace.

Walk along the terrace in a counterclockwise direction. Note the small, walled, grassy space that separates the hotel from the HUD building; small as it is, this open space also is used intensively. This juxtaposition of buildings results from the fact that there was never a single design plan for the section of the redevelopment area designated for office use; each building was developed without direct coordination with its neighbors.

Continuing along the terrace, the railroad track barrier is once again very evident. The north side of the terrace provides an excellent **view**** of the Arts and Industries Building and the downtown skyline beyond the Mall.

10 Now walk back to the front of the hotel, across the plaza, and back to the 10th Street Mall. Continue south along the mall to the **Benjamin Banneker Fountain**,** where it terminates. This overlook provides a **panoramic view**** of the Washington Channel and the redeveloped Southwest. Moving around the overlook in a counterclockwise direction, one can see:

Department of Agriculture—South Building. This structure covers three city blocks. A portion was completed as part of the 1930s Southwest Rectangle project.

Bureau of Printing and Engraving. This building at the intersection of 14th and C streets is where millions of dollars, as well as stamps and other official documents, are printed every day. It is open to the public from 8:00 a.m. to 2:00 p.m. daily except Saturdays, Sundays, and holidays.

East Potomac Park, created by the Army Corps of Engineers during dredging operations along the Potomac in the 1880s, includes facilities for active and passive recreation. Initial redevelopment plans for the waterfront included provision for wharves and slips on the park side of the channel; eventually, it was decided to emphasize the shape and the landscaping of the park instead.

Crystal City, visible beyond East Potomac Park, is a privately developed complex of offices, apartments, and shops. Most of its tenants are government agencies.

The **Waterfront.** The major problem in its redevelopment was determining the intensity to which it should be rebuilt. At the time of renewal, most of the waterfront was taken up by commercial activities, dilapidated warehouses, the railroad yards, and a hodgepodge of rotting piers. The Washington architectural firm of Satterlee and Smith prepared a tentative redevelopment plan, but it was rejected by the National Capital Planning Commission as too intense. NCPC then drew up a list of plan objectives for the waterfront. Some of these objectives have been realized—buildings in the commercial waterfront area have been kept low so that the interior buildings also have a view of the channel, street ends have been kept open with parklets, and decking for underground parking and development was included as a public amenity. Unfortunately, most of the objectives have not yet been realized, and the northern section of the waterfront leaves a great deal to be desired (see Tour 6, Southwest).

The **vista down the Washington Channel** to its juncture with the Potomac River.

Fort Leslie J. McNair and the **National War College** (see Tour 6, Southwest, nos. 13 and 15).

The **Southwest Expressway,** which isolates the residential Southwest from the rest of the city.

6/**Southwest****
(Waterfront urban renewal area)

by Charity Vanderbilt Davidson; 1983 update by Lin Brown

Distance: 2 miles
Time: 1½ hours
Bus: To 7th and I (Eye) Streets, SW: 70, M8, V4, and V6.
Metro: L'Enfant Plaza (Blue and Orange Lines), exiting at
7th Street, SW.

When the Federal City was laid out in 1791–92, it was expected that the Southwest would develop as a mixed residential/commercial center. During the last decade of the 18th century, a number of wealthy citizens built homes in the area and a real estate syndicate built several rows of substantial brick dwellings for speculative purposes. Unfortunately, the Southwest's commercial dreams were never realized. It was hoped that the City Canal would enable the area to attract some of Georgetown's trade, but the mismanaged, decaying canal proved to be a barrier, which isolated the Southwest from the rest of the developing city, rather than a commercial link. During the 19th century, the central portion of the Southwest became a working-class residential area ringed by commercial uses such as the transporting and storing of goods and produce. The sections along B Street, SW (today Independence Avenue), continued to be occupied by more prominent citizens.

The area's isolation was reinforced and further emphasized in 1873 when the Baltimore and Potomac Railroad laid tracks along Maryland and Virginia Avenues, SW. By the early 20th century, the services provided by the Southwest's commercial waterfront had lost much of their importance, but the area where the Department of Agriculture is now located gained in importance when a railway depot was established nearby. However, the development of the depot led to the departure of the wealthier residents. The area further declined and acquired a reputation for having a high crime rate and innumerable squalid inhabited alleys. The Army Corps of Engineers redeveloped part of the waterfront in the 1930s, but even this did not halt the area's downward spiral. Also during the 1930s, the federal government began to redevelop the northern fringes as the Southwest Rectangle, a complex of government buildings similar to the Federal Triangle development. The buildings for the Department of Health and Human Services, the Department of Agriculture, and the complex of buildings for the Bureau of Printing and Engraving, were the only ones completed before construction was halted. By the late

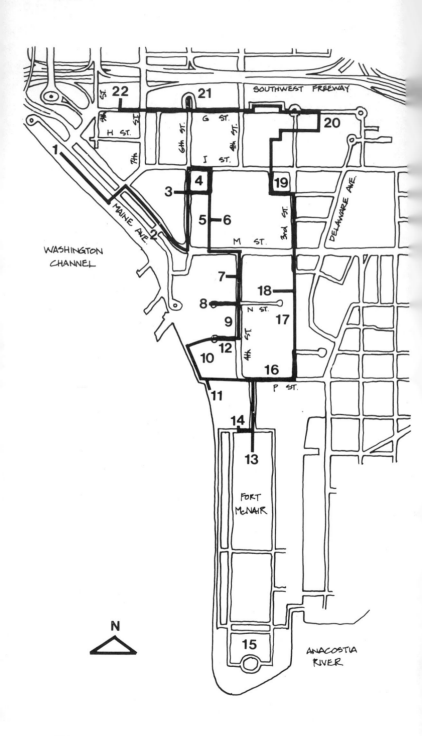

1940s, the Southwest was considered a vast slum, with three quarters of its buildings regarded as substandard.

Early in 1952, two plans were offered for the redevelopment of 427 acres in the Southwest. The first plan, prepared by Elbert Peets for the National Capital Planning Commission (NCPC), called for the rehabilitation of many of the residential structures, but it was rejected as socially and financially impossible. The second plan, commissioned by the District of Columbia Redevelopment Land Agency (RLA—today part of the D.C. Department of Housing and Community Development) was prepared by the St. Louis planning firm of Harland Bartholomew and Associates and by two Washington architects, Louis Justement and Chloethiel Woodard Smith. The Smith-Justement plan called for the demolition of nearly all existing structures and the erection of approximately 5,000 new dwelling units. NCPC then prepared a third plan, stressing redevelopment rather than rehabilitation. RLA began to accept bids for Area B, the section east of Canal Street and Delaware Avenue, reserved for public housing.

In 1953 President Eisenhower succeeded in persuading the New York development firm of Webb and Knapp to prepare a plan for 440 acres, which had been set aside for private development. Prepared by Webb & Knapp's architectural and planning staff, headed by I. M. Pei, and Chicago architect Harry Weese, the plan was unveiled early in 1954. The area south of the freeway was to be residential, with high-rise apartment towers interspersed among clusters of townhouses; this proposal for the mixing of building types was innovative, since developers had previously segregated high-rise and low-rise structures. The plans prepared by Peets and Smith-Justement had called for the rebuilding of retail commercial streets. However, the new plan called for a Town Center, or shopping mall, designed to serve the entire Southwest. The waterfront was to be completely redeveloped. In exchange for formulating the plan, Webb & Knapp was given a choice of areas to develop; the firm chose the area of the Town Center—what is today L'Enfant Plaza (see Tour 5) and the residential section north of M Street. The basic concepts of the Webb & Knapp plan (sometimes also referred to as the Zeckendorf-Pei plan) were finally adopted by NCPC in 1956, but many of the details were altered. Webb & Knapp began work on its portion of the project, but was forced to withdraw later for financial reasons.

The Peets plan of 1951 had tried to work with the original street plan, but subsequent development plans called for substantial changes, such as the creation of "super blocks" by closing many of the streets. One of the recurring themes in the redevelopment area is the various ways in which different developers have used the old street spaces.

In an effort to insure variety in the redevelopment area, RLA divided the portions not already assigned to the government or to Webb & Knapp into development parcels, some of which were awarded on the basis of design/development competitions. One of the plan requirements was that there be no ground-floor residences in any of the high-rise buildings; it is interesting to note the various efforts to utilize this under-building space; e.g., from parking (Capitol Park), to activity rooms and large lobbies (River Park), or arcades (Town Center).

1 The **small urban park*** between the Flagship and Hogate's restaurants was designed by Sasaki, Dawson and Demay. This section of the bulkhead along the water's edge is deserted even in nice weather. Both its landscaping and the amount of use it gets contrast markedly with the situation farther down the channel.

2 Arena Stage** and the **Kreeger Theater,** 6th and M Streets, SW (Arena, 1961; Kreeger, 1970—Harry Weese & Associates). Arena Stage's company was one of the pioneers of theater-in-the-round in America and is today one of the best resident theater companies in the country. The polygonal theater building, which seats 750, is separate from but connected to the elongated administration building that houses the supporting facilities.

The three-story Kreeger Theater wraps around one corner of this administration wing. It seats 500 and allows the company to expand its program of experimental plays, children's theater, and teaching. Unlike Arena Stage, which is truly theater-in-the-round, the Kreeger's stage is fan-shaped.

The exterior materials of both buildings are identical in order to make the two buildings "an aesthetic, functional whole," according to architect Weese.

Arena Stage

3 Waterside Towers*, 905-947 6th Street, SW (1970—
Chloethiel Woodard Smith & Associated Architects). This
complex of townhouses and high-rise apartments can be entered by walking down the driveway entrance. The townhouses serve as a wall around a large, landscaped interior
courtyard that covers the underground parking. The uninter-
rupted openness of this courtyard contrasts with the courtyard treatments in a number of other developments in the
area.

4 The **park**** with the pond was designed by Ian McHarg,
landscape architect.

5 Town Center Plaza*, 1100 block of 6th Street, SW
(1961–62—I. M. Pei Associates). Built in two phases, these
apartments were winners of an FHA Honor Award and are
significant because they demonstrate that good residential
architecture can be produced within the financial restraints
set by developers and still meet the requirements for FHA Title I funds. They are the only apartments in the redevelopment area that do not have balconies and are not
accompanied by townhouses. Their courtyards have been
created from the old street space and trees of L Street, SW.

6 Waterside Mall, 400 M Street, SW (1972—Chloethiel
Woodard Smith & Associated Architects). The large office
tower (housing the Environmental Protection Agency) is part
of the office and retail development known as Waterside
Mall. This still-to-be-completed commercial center expands
the original Town Center Plaza development. Originally designed along the lines of a suburban shopping center, the
mall was redesigned when it was determined that a more intensive facility was needed. It appears that this extension
was unwarranted by the Center's market area, for many of the
original stores have closed and the developers are reluctant
to complete the structure. The planned residential compo-
nents of the Center have been changed to offices.

7 Tiber Island**, bounded by M, N and 4th streets, SW,
and the waterfront (1965—Keyes, Lethbridge and Condon),
was the winner of the first RLA design competition and of a
1961 AIA Honor Award. It consists of four 8-story apartment
towers (368 units) and 85 two/three-story townhouses. It is
especially interesting because of the spatial relationship between its high-rise and low-rise elements, and the way in
which the District of Columbia zoning code was interpreted
in order to permit the design's implementation.

   The architects were particularly concerned with the organization and scale of the exterior spaces between and
around the buildings. The principal exterior space, a large
pedestrian court, is defined by the four apartment towers; the
fringes of this space are subdivided into smaller courts surrounded by the townhouses. The central plaza and the
courts are linked together by walkways, but variations in architectural detail and landscaping have given each court an

Tiber Island

individual character. The central pedestrian plaza covers a 280-car underground garage.

Local zoning regulations required that a row house have its own lot, off-street parking, individual utilities, and that it front on a street. The D.C. Government was willing to view the Tiber Island townhouses as apartments. This meant that the 64 houses on the perimeter could be sold under condominium agreements and the 21 houses entirely within the complex could be rented.

8 The **Thomas Law House*,** also known as the Honeymoon House, is located at 1252 6th Street, SW, in the southeast corner of Tiber Island. Law was a major promoter of south Washington development. His federal-style house, built between 1794 and 1796, is among Washington's earliest extant structures and is listed on the National Register of Historic Places. It was rehabilitated in 1965 to serve as a community center for residents of Tiber Island and Carrollsburg Square (no. 18, this tour).

9 Harbour Square**, bounded by 4th, N, and O streets, SW, and the waterfront (1966—Chloethiel Woodard Smith & Associated Architects). This complex includes not only new high-rise apartments and townhouses, but also has incorporated three of the late-18th/early-19th-century structures that survived the extensive demolition carried out in the renewal area:

The **Edward Simon Lewis House*,** at 456 N Street, was built about 1817, and is typical of the early-19th-century brick houses in Washington. Originally built as a single-family house, the structure was converted to apartments in the 1920s; during the 1930s, its tenants included journalists Lewis J. Heath and Ernie Pyle. After rehabilitation in 1964–66, the house was included in Harbour Square as a single-family townhouse.

The **Duncanson Cranch House*,** 468–470 N Street, SW, like Wheat Row, was built about 1794 by the Greenleaf syndicate. It now serves as two townhouses in Harbour Square.

Wheat Row**, at 1315–1321 4th Street, is an important example of the conservative, vernacular domestic architecture constructed during the Federal period. Built in 1794, it is believed to be the first speculative housing built in Washington City by the real estate syndicate of James Greenleaf (a former American consul in Amsterdam), Robert Morris (the Philadelphia financier), and John Nicholson (also of Philadelphia). It was rehabilitated in 1964–66 and included in Harbour Square as four townhouses.

Wheat Row in Harbour Square

10 The **Water Garden**** in the center of the Harbour Square complex is the dominant element in the development's pedestrian square. It includes sculptured forms, platforms, walks, and seating. Planting includes flowering water plants and willow trees. It is inoperative during the colder months of the year.

11 Waterside Park** (1967–68—Sasaki, Dawson and Demay). Walk around this park near a grove of willow trees and southwest along the seawall to the Titanic Memorial. This area is much more pleasant than the section of waterfront discussed earlier (no. 1) and receives much more use (partly because people are drawn to the nearby tourist boats to Mount Vernon and partly because of the nearby residential structures).

12 Riverside, Edgewater, and **1401–1415 4th Street** (formerly J. Finley House and Chalk House), bounded by 4th, O, and P streets and the waterfront (1966—Morris

Lapidus Associates). These apartments and townhouses were originally a single development. The Riverside and Edgewater have been converted to condominiums; 1401–1415 4th Street are now fee simple townhouses. This complex was the winner of the third RLA design competition. The O Street side is cold, but the interior area has a parklike quality. Note the use of old street space for a greenway along O Street.

13 Fort Leslie J. McNair* (1903—McKim, Mead and White) was established in 1794 as the Washington Arsenal. A feature of the L'Enfant plan, Fort McNair has been known by a variety of names (Washington Arsenal, U.S. Arsenal at Greenleaf Point, the Washington Barracks). The first fortifications were erected in 1794 and the first arsenal buildings in 1803–4. It was one of the earliest employers in Washington. All of the original buildings were destroyed by an explosion during the British occupation of Washington in August 1814. The arsenal buildings were rebuilt and served as a distribution center for arms.

14 The first **U.S. Penitentiary,** opened on the northern end of the arsenal grounds in 1826, is best known as the site of the trial and execution of four of the Lincoln conspirators and of the commandant of the Confederate prison at Andersonville, Georgia. Most of the penitentiary buildings were razed in 1869, but a portion remains in the center of the greensward. The arsenal grounds were used for storage by the Quartermaster Corps after 1881. Between 1898 and 1909, the general hospital on the grounds was the site of many of Major Walter Reed's experiments with yellow fever and diphtheria.

15 In 1903 the New York architectural firm of McKim, Mead and White was retained to design a building for the new **National War College** and to develop a master plan for the entire installation. Most of the firm's plan (which called for a long mall, flanked by white-columned officers' houses, with the War College at the end as the focal point) was implemented. An unconfirmed story relates that the designer was so angry when he learned that the War Department had refused to tear down the few remaining arsenal and penitentiary buildings in the middle of the proposed mall (thereby blocking the vista to the War College), that he refused to set foot on the site again. To this day the vista is still blocked, and in order to view the War College it is necessary to walk half the length of the mall, beyond the old penitentiary and arsenal buildings.

16 Channel Square, 325 P Street, SW (1968—Harry Weese & Associates), consists of tan-colored townhouses and an apartment tower, designed as middle-income housing under Section 221 D3 of the Housing Act of 1949. This section of the act subsidized the developer's interest rate, and in turn, rents have been kept well below existing market rates. The whole feeling of Channel Square is very different from that of other developments.

17 River Park Cooperative**, bounded by 4th, O, and N streets and Delaware Avenue, SW (1962—Charles M. Goodman Associates), was the first owner-occupied development in the new Southwest. It includes 134 townhouses and 384 adjacent apartments. The apartment building was designed to serve as a barrier between the development's barrel-vaulted townhouses and the public housing across Delaware Avenue.

This wall-like quality can best be experienced by walking north between the apartment building and the townhouses. The former street spaces in the complex have been landscaped and terminate in cul-de-sacs.

18 Carrollsburg Square*, bounded by M, N and 4th streets and Delaware Avenue, SW (1965—Keyes, Lethbridge and Condon, architects; Eric Paepcke, landscape architect), was the winner of the second RLA design competition. Like Tiber Island, Carrollsburg Square has a central pedestrian area over an underground garage, but here the plaza has been divided into a larger number of small residential courts. Here again, each court has been given its own character by means of variations in landscaping and architectural detail. Carrollsburg Square was intended as a transition between Tiber Island and the public housing immediately to the east.

19 Note the **park*** by landscape designer Ian McHarg that occupies the northern half of the square along the north side of the Town Center. Walk west through the **elongated park*** (also by McHarg) to the central plaza. These were intended as low-maintenance parks, but a great deal of work is still required. A variety of community facilities (library, churches, public transportation) are concentrated in this area. The large-scale dislocation of people, caused by the renewal, raised particular problems for local churches. The National Council of Churches worked with the Southwest's congregations in determining which would remain in the area, which would combine facilities if not congregations, and which would leave. Two of the remaining churches flank the park.

20 Capitol Park apartments & townhouses**, bounded by 4th and I streets, Delaware Avenue, and the SW Expressway (1959—Satterlee and Smith; 1963—Smith and Associates). Built on the site of Dixon's Court, one of Washington's largest and most infamous inhabited alleys, Capitol Park was the first of the new projects erected in the Southwest. It was given an AIA Merit Award in 1960. The apartment tower at 800 4th Street was the first building (402 units) of what was ultimately intended to be 1,600 units. Although built in stages, the complex was designed as a unified whole. The accompanying townhouses are FHA Honor Award winners. The development is best known for its parklike atmosphere. The feeling of openness that pervades Capitol Park with its use of glass, contrasts sharply with the feeling of containment present in other, later Southwest developments.

21   After exploring Capitol Park, cross 4th Street and walk west along G Street past the townhouses (1966–69—Walter Pater) to the **park** at the end of 6th Street. Walk north across the park to the retaining wall on the far side of the parking lot. This offers one of the most spectacular **views**** of just how major a barrier the Southwest Freeway is and how it cuts off the residential part of Southwest from the office-development areas. The townhouses are interesting because they are grouped around **common greens,** which are maintained and owned by the homeowners.

22   At the corner of G and 7th streets, SW, there is a bus stop. Nearby the tract (Parcel 76) now being used as a parking lot is the proposed site of a subsidized housing project—a selection the adjacent homeowners are successfully contesting in court. It is uncertain what this parcel will eventually be used for.

7/**Foggy Bottom****

*(Watergate, Kennedy Center, George Washington
University, State Department, Constitution Avenue)*

by Antoinette J. Lee;
original 1976 version by Zachary Domike

Distance: 2¾ miles
Time: 2 hours
Bus: Along Pennsylvania Ave.: 30, 32, 34, 36.
Metro: Foggy Bottom/GWU and Farragut West (Blue and
Orange Lines)

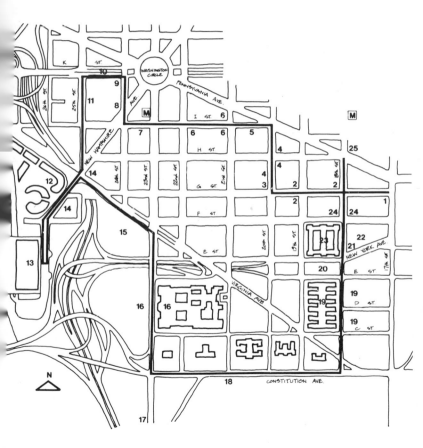

Foggy Bottom presents one of the most complex tapes-
tries of urban growth and change to be found in Washington, D.C. Its topography has been a decisive factor in
the patterns of its development. The ability of planners, en-

gineers, architects, and other designers to tame, exploit, and shape the area's topography accelerated the forces of change, as did the technological means available to them. Because of topographic and historical forces, the area served for more than a century as the site for a significant industrial settlement, thriving wharves, and a small, fashionable residential section. As the 20th century wore on, these historical settlements faded into memory and the area became the location for monumental buildings and parks and was overrun with expanding institutional structures and high-density development.

The origins of Foggy Bottom can be traced back to the mid-17th century, when it was part of the land grant known as Widdowe's Mite. In 1763 Jacob Funk purchased a tract of 130 acres, located generally between what is now 19th and 24th streets, H Street, and the Potomac River, and laid out the town of Hamburg. Also known as Funkstown, the area was one of a series of port towns situated along the Potomac in the mid-18th century, of which Georgetown and Alexandria were the most successful. Throughout the remainder of the century, little development occurred in Hamburg, and the area did not pose an obstacle to Pierre L'Enfant's street plan, which covered the Maryland side of the Potomac River as far north as Boundary Street (now Florida Avenue).

L'Enfant's plan set forth Washington Circle as the focus for growth in the Foggy Bottom area. The grid of numbered and lettered streets was cut through by radial avenues that tied the area to other focal points throughout the city. Market structures reinforced the growth plan, as did the residential and commercial development that clustered close to the President's House and along Pennsylvania Avenue.

In the 19th century, a thriving waterside settlement developed along the Potomac River and Rock Creek. On the high ground of Foggy Bottom, north of E Street and east of 23d Street, substantial residences were built to house the fashionable scientific and military communities and the diplomatic corps. On the low ground, south of E Street and west of 23d Street, modest dwellings were built to accommodate workers who toiled in the nearby glassworks, breweries, cement company, and gas works. The ill-built and much-polluted City Canal (along what is now Constitution Avenue), and the marshy lands merging into the Potomac, underscored the undesirable nature of the lowlands. In fact, the desolate character of this section is said to have given rise to Foggy Bottom's name, and the "incessant croaking of frogs at night furnished materials for ghost stories."

The filling-in of the City Canal and the reclamation of the "Potomac Flats" in the late 19th century transformed the lowland area and created a large swath of land available for development. This canvas stood ready for the grand plans of the McMillan Commission of 1901–2 as it recommended sites for public buildings and parks. The removal of the affluent residents to more fashionable neighborhoods elsewhere in the District, and a new appreciation of the proximity of the area to the White House and Downtown, changed the residential character of Foggy Bottom. Apartment buildings were wedged in between townhouses. Remaining townhouses were adapted to institutional use, as exemplified by the removal of George Washington University from 15th and I streets to 2023 G Street, NW, in 1912.

Throughout much of the 20th century, the area has served as the battleground between proponents of high-density development and defenders of the surviving townhouses, and between residents who prize Foggy Bottom's neighborly qualities and institutions that wish to expand their operations into office structures occupied only from nine-to-five. Foggy Bottom has also served as the stage for post-World War II urban renewal and highway plans, some of which were carried out and others aborted. More recently, the area has been further transformed by the arrival of the wealthy in the Watergate complex and other luxury residential high-rises.

1 Begin the tour at 17th and G streets. Heading west, you see on the left the new offices of the **Federal Home Loan Bank Board*.** Completed in 1978 after the designs of Max Urbahn, this lively office complex presents a small-scale version of New York City's Rockefeller Center, complete with skating rink, restaurants, and shops.

2 Starting at 18th and G streets and continuing up to 20th and G streets are the buildings occupied by the **World Bank** (International Bank for Reconstruction and Development) and the **International Monetary Fund*.** The addition to the complex on the north side of the block between 19th and 20th streets has a spectacular enclosed interior courtyard. On the south side of the block, the most recent building stands on the site of the early 19th-century **Lenthall Houses,** which were moved by George Washington University to 21st Street, between F and G streets, as part of a preservation compromise with the community. The block also retains the **F Street Club** (about 1853) and a portion of its garden at the northeast corner of 20th and F streets. On the same block, at the southeast corner of 20th and G streets, stands the **United Church-Church of Christ,** a combined German Lutheran and Methodist congregation. Originally built as the Concordia Lutheran Evangelical Church, it is a reminder of the former German settlement in Foggy Bottom. German language services are still offered.

3 The cross streets of 20th and G form one of the major entrances to **George Washington University.** Founded in 1821, the university was first located on College Hill in the area now known as Columbia Heights. In the early 1880s, the university moved to 15th and H streets, and later spread into other locations throughout the Downtown area. In 1912 it secured its first foothold in Foggy Bottom by purchasing the townhouse at 2023 G Street. Over the next 70 years, the university increased its land holdings many times over, until it, along with the federal government, constitutes the largest institutional presence in Foggy Bottom.

In the early years of its growth and expansion in Foggy Bottom, George Washington University constructed a quadrangle of Georgian-style buildings on the block bounded by 20th, G, 21st, and H streets. During the Great Depression, the university buildings became more spartan in design. In the post-World War II period, several limestone-faced buildings were constructed. More recently, the university has built a variety of academic buildings, some of which, like the Law Library, attempt to fit in with their surroundings. Others, like the Marvin Center, appear to replicate the office structures found elsewhere in the K Street canyon of office blocks.

The university has also taken on the role of a leading developer in the area by constructing large office buildings and then leasing them to other organizations, e.g., the World Bank, PEPCO, and the National Academy of Sciences. The expansionary role of the university has brought it into frequent conflict with the surrounding community. As the community groups have become more sophisticated, the university has been backed into a number of compromises that have preserved buildings in their entirety or portions thereof. The preservation and reuse of Quigley's Drugstore at the southeast corner of 21st and G streets is one of the more enlightened examples.

The zealous removal of paint from older campus buildings appears less well advised, since the buildings either needed the paint because of soft-brick construction or had their "chill-skins" removed by sandblasting. The removal of townhouses continues unabated, however, and one can expect that only a handful will survive to remind the observer of the once substantial residential neighborhood that graced Foggy Bottom.

4 Moving north along 20th Street, you can see the university's **Law School Complex** on the left and the **World Bank Complex** on the right. At the crossroads of 20th and H streets, the PEPCO-leased building sits on the right.

5 After you turn left at 20th and I streets, the **2000 Pennsylvania Avenue Complex*** comes into view. One of the most controversial preservation compromises struck between the university and the community, this assemblage attempts to preserve the front sections of a strip of 19th-century buildings referred to as the Red Lion Row, named after a popular eatery that formerly occupied one of the buildings. Behind the line of older buildings, a high-rise office structure looms, much in the same way that the New Executive Office Building stands as a backdrop to the residential-scale buildings along Jackson Place, facing Lafayette Square. Critics have decried this preservation solution as only "facade deep" and one that does little to improve the quality of design of the larger office structure. The architectural firm associated with the Lafayette Square project, John Carl Warneke, was also involved in the design of the 2000 Pennsylvania Avenue project, along with the firm of Hellmuth Obata and Kassabaum.

6 Continuing along I Street, you will pass the side of the **Marvin Center** (the university's student center) on the left and the **National Academy of Sciences**-leased building on the right. At the southeast corner of 22d and I streets, the **Academic Cluster** represents a new architectural style for the university. Sheathed in glass, this building suggests a lighter touch to large buildings and, one might hope, a more creative era for the university's construction program.

7 At 23d and I streets is another entrance to the university. The Foggy Bottom/GWU Metro stop is located here, at the conjunction of the George Washington University Hospital and the university's School of Medicine and Health Services. The closing of I Street between 23d and 24th streets provides for a pleasant plaza area at this juncture. Twenty-third Street also represents the boundary between the highlands to the east and the lowlands to the west.

During the first half of the 20th century, the lowlands area was largely occupied by a poor black population that inhabited the modest row houses and interior alley dwellings. **St. Mary's Church*,** located at 23d Street, was de-

St. Mary's Church

signed by James Renwick for a black congregation. Renwick was also the architect of the Renwick Gallery at 17th Street and Pennsylvania Avenue and the original Smithsonian "Castle" building. St. Mary's church has played a continuing role in the community, most recently with the construction of St. Mary's Court, a housing project for the elderly, behind the church on 24th Street. The next mile or so of this tour will be concerned with development on the lowlands.

8 At **24th Street,** the viewer can see streets of modest townhouses that formerly housed workers associated with Foggy Bottom's industrial past. These townhouses are fully rehabilitated for affluent occupants and are choice real estate. Unhappily, high-density zoning has permitted the intrusion of large apartment buildings into this area, further escalating the value of the land. At 900 24th Street is a recent development of pint-sized townhouses that attest to the floor space people are willing to forego in order to live in Foggy Bottom.

800 block of New Hampshire Avenue

9 At the corner of 24th and K streets is the **Immaculate Conception Academy,** a Catholic girls' school, which once served the nearby immigrant and ethnic community. The school now attracts students throughout the District of Columbia.

10 K Street, between 24th and 25th Streets, represents what post-World War II planners foresaw for Foggy Bottom—tall apartment buildings astride major thoroughfares. The construction of the K Street underpass was intended to facilitate commuter traffic to and from the Virginia suburbs. However, the traffic density and speed also effectively cut off the area south of K Street from its natural commercial strip along Pennsylvania Avenue. The high-rises along K Street represent an interesting mix of styles: art deco, modern, and postmodern. Several of the modern buildings have been converted into apartment-hotels, a major land-use problem in the neighborhood.

11 Turning south on **25th Street,** you can see one of the most intact residential streets in Foggy Bottom. Small alley dwellings, once notorious for their substandard level of housing but now rehabilitated and considered desirable, can be glimpsed along this street.

12 The juncture of **25th Street and Virginia Avenue** displays the new, superaffluent Foggy Bottom. Here, one sees the **Watergate*** complex developed by the Societa Generale Immobilaire of Rome and designed by Luigi Moretti. An example of "packaged living," with residential units, offices, a hotel, restaurants, and shops, the Watergate is one of Washington's premier addresses. The Watergate scandal in no way diminished the luster of the complex's reputation among the social elite. As you continue along New Hampshire Avenue toward the Kennedy Center, a major office section of Watergate complex comes into view, as do the entrances to **Les Champs,** home of Paris designer boutiques, Gucci shops, and other haute couture establishments.

13 The **Kennedy Center**** now comes into view. Completed in 1971 after the designs of Edward Durrell Stone, it represents the culmination of nearly two decades of plans to locate a major auditorium in Washington. The Center houses five auditoriums: the Concert Hall, Opera House, Eisenhower Theater, a film theater, and the Terrace Theater. The view of Rosslyn, Georgetown, and the Potomac River from the main-floor and roof-top terraces should not be missed.

14 On the way back to Virginia Avenue, you will pass the **Peoples Life Insurance Company,** a privately owned building of the late 1950s that appears to have aspirations to conform to public architecture of the time. This building, together with **Potomac Plaza** (completed in 1955 on the site of the Washington Gas Light Company) across Virginia Avenue, were early high-rise entrants into the lowlands of Foggy Bottom.

15 Columbia Plaza (Keyes, Lethbridge and Condon) comes next into view at 23d Street and Virginia Avenue. Another "package living" complex of apartments, offices, and shopping, Columbia Plaza represents the only residual product of two much larger urban renewal projects envisioned for Foggy Bottom in the post-World War II era. By the time ground was broken on the site in the mid-1960s, few could justify the project as a means to rid the area of substandard slum housing. The apartments have always been much in demand, although the ground-level shopping arcade has

Columbia Plaza

16 Continuing south along 23d Street, you come upon the entrance to the **Naval Medical Center** on the right, on the hill formerly occupied by the Naval Observatory. The **State Department** on the left was located in Foggy Bottom in the 1940s and its presence, together with the World Health Organization, the Organization of American States, and the World Bank, provides a distinctly international flavor to the area.

17 At the crossroads of 23d Street and Constitution Avenue, the **Lincoln Memorial***** is in view. The memorial, with its sculpture of a seated Lincoln by Daniel Chester French and the nearby Reflecting Pool, was a favorite among the followers of the City Beautiful movement. The **Memorial Bridge*,** just beyond, carries traffic into the Arlington Cemetery area. (See Tour 4, The Mall—West.)

18 Turning left on **Constitution Avenue,** you now face the ceremonial street, the picture-postcard qualities of which have captured the imaginations of countless tourists and would-be tourists. This is the area, bedecked by monumental buildings, that was carved out of the reclaimed lowlands and filled-in City Canal in the first half of the 20th century. On the left, the pedestrian will see a series of institutional and federal buildings designed by nationally famous architects.

At the northeast corner of 23d Street and Constitution Avenue is the first of this series, the **American Pharmaceutical Association** (1933—John Russell Pope). The next building is the **National Academy of Sciences** (1924—Bertram Grosvenor Goodhue). Don't miss the academy's **sculpture of Albert Einstein**** just to the left of its building. Dedicated in 1979 on the centennial of Einstein's birthday, this statue was based on a bust that Robert Berks sculpted from life in 1953. Einstein posed for Berks in his study, dressed in casual attire, a pose that is translated into this sculpture and contrasts with the highly formal environment of Constitution Avenue. As you continue east, the following buildings will come into view: the **Federal Reserve Board** (1937—Paul Cret); the **Department of Interior, South** (1931—J. H. DeSibour); the **Organization of American States Annex** (1948—Harbeson, Hough, Livingston and Larson); and the **Organization of American States** (1910—Albert Kelsey and Paul Cret). On the right are the parklands of the Mall, now including the site of the **Vietnam Memorial** and **Constitution Gardens.** (See Tour 4, The Mall—West, nos. 9 and 10.)

19 As you walk north along 18th Street, the large **Interior Department Building** (1937—Waddy B. Wood) comes into view on the left. On the right are the rears of **Constitution Hall** and the **American Red Cross.** (See Tour 8, White House, nos. 26 and 27.)

20 On the left at E Street is Rawlins Park, a pocket of tranquility that reaches its zenith in the early spring when its magnolia trees are in full bloom.

21 At the northeast corner of 19th Street and New York Avenue is the **Octagon House**** (1800—William Thornton).

Octagon House/AIA Headquarters

The Octagon, originally the home of Gen. John Tayloe, served as the site of a temporary President's House during the burning of the capital city by the British in 1814 and as the place where the Treaty of Ghent was signed, ending the War of 1812. The Octagon is now operated by the American Institute of Architects as a historic house museum and exhibition gallery.

22 Behind the Octagon is the headquarters building of the **American Institute of Architects,** completed in 1973 after the designs of the Architects Collaborative. Although criticized by some as a less than distinguished product of a major design profession, the AIA building does not try to compete with its historic frontispiece. The lobby area contains an exhibition gallery and its conference facilities are used by many design-related organizations in the city.

23 The **General Services Administration** building stands on the left, the symbolic, if not actual, center of the federal government's public building design operations. The GSA building was originally built for the Interior Department in 1917 after designs produced by the Office of the Supervising Architect of the Treasury, but was vacated by that department when its new building to the south on C Street was completed.

24 The crossroads of 18th and F streets contains two architectural oddities. To the west is the historic **Ringgold-Carroll House*** (also called the John Marshall House), which has survived the best attempts of developers to reduce it to dust. The house and its garden are protected from development by a preservation easement held by the National Trust for Historic Preservation. The last owner, Mrs. Robert Lowe Bacon, endowed the Bacon Foundation, the house's present occupant, as a center to promote international peace and understanding. To the east stand the remnants of **Michler Row,** cemented onto a modern office facade. Michler Row, constructed in the 1870s and named for Gen. Nathaniel Michler of the Department of Public Buildings and Grounds, was only recently home to a cleaners, a liquor store, an Asian restaurant, and several other neighborhood establishments. The firm of Skidmore Owings and Merrill provided for a virtual reconstruction of part of the Michler Row facade, while allowing for an otherwise mundane office structure to rise behind it. This project figures heavily in the debate about the desirability of facade preservation as a compromise solution.

25 The tour ends at 18th Street and Pennsylvania Avenue. At the northeast corner stands the **National Permanent Building,** completed in 1976 after designs by the firm of Hartman-Cox. With exposed utility ducts and cascading columns, this is one of Downtown's more innovative speculative office structures.

8/**White House*****

(White House, Renwick Gallery, Lafayette Square, Corcoran Gallery)

by Fred Greenberg; 1983 update by Julia Pastor

Distance: 2 miles
Time: 1½ hours
Bus: 30, 34, 36, 38, 42, 80, X2, X4, and X8
Metro: Farragut West and McPherson Square (Blue and Orange Lines)

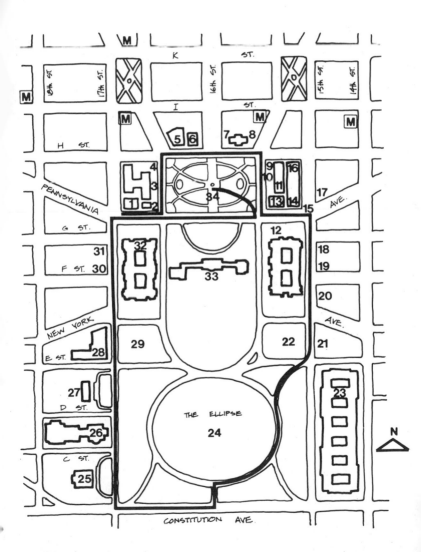

The White House precinct, the actual and symbolic center of the executive branch of government, is one of the most important and interesting areas in the city. Its core includes the White House grounds and the flanking Treasury and Executive Office Buildings, Lafayette Square and its bordering blocks, and the Ellipse. This area is almost entirely in federal ownership, deriving from the original "Reservation 1" purchased in 1791 as part of the original platting of the city. The blocks surrounding this core contain a variety of activities that support the federal presence, such as banks and national and international associations.

Beginning as a predominantly residential area around the White House, this precinct has evolved over time to an area that is now predominantly devoted to federal and private office buildings with related shops and services.

As a result of the initiatives of the Kennedy Administration in the 1960s, a plan to build massive federal office buildings flanking Lafayette Square was discarded. Instead, a plan to restore and enhance the area was adopted. This included restoration of the townhouses facing the square and placement of the higher federal office buildings behind them. In 1965 the Old Corcoran Gallery Building, threatened with demolition, was transferred to the Smithsonian Institution to be restored as a museum. Its opening in 1972, as the Renwick Gallery, represented an important step in bringing increased activity to the area.

The most recent additions in the area include the opening of the Federal Home Loan Bank Board complex with offices, shops, restaurants, and open plaza space; Pershing Park, with a café and an ice-skating rink in winter; and Metropolitan Square, with offices and shops (facing a dramatic interior atrium) contained behind the restored facade of the old Keith-Albee Theater Building.

1 Renwick Gallery*** (Old Corcoran Gallery and U.S. Court of Claims), 17th and Pennsylvania Avenue, NW (1859—James Renwick; 1972 restoration—John Carl Warnecke and Hugh Newell Jacobsen). Hours: 10:00 a.m. to 5:30 p.m. daily. Originally designed as an art gallery for W. W. Corcoran, this building was used by the government during the Civil War. When he was able to occupy his own building, Corcoran found that it was too small for his collection, so he built a larger gallery at 17th Street and New York Avenue. The U.S. Court of Claims took possession of the building in 1899 and used it for the next 65 years. The meticulous exterior and interior restoration was undertaken by the Smithsonian, beginning in 1965, and in 1972 the building was returned to its original function as an art gallery. The Renwick exhibits various aspects of U.S. design and craftsmanship. Two galleries are devoted to exhibitions of art from other countries.

Renwick Gallery

2 Blair-Lee Houses*, 1651 Pennsylvania Avenue, NW (1824; 1931 restoration—W. Faulkner). These fine houses are used by the government for entertaining distinguished visitors from foreign countries.

3 Lafayette Square Restoration**. Architect John Carl Warnecke was engaged by the Kennedy Administration to study the problem of development for Lafayette Square. The result was the integration of taller elements with the restored and infilling row houses. The "bookends" not only saved but enhanced the scale, fabric, and marvelous sense of space of Lafayette Square. The townhouses are used as offices for the various commissions created during presidential terms of office. The two office buildings referred to as the "bookends" flank the square on the west and east and contain secluded courtyards with fountains. They are: West—**New Executive Office Building*,** at 17th and H Streets, NW (Hours: 9:00 a.m. to 5:00 p.m. Monday through Friday); East—**United States Court of Claims*** (see no. 11, this tour).

4 Decatur House**, 748 Jackson Place (1818—Benjamin Latrobe). Hours: 10:00 a.m. to 2:00 p.m. weekdays, 12:00 to 4:00 p.m. weekends, closed Mondays. Admission charge. The house of Commodore Stephen Decatur, the suppressor of the Barbary pirates, was the first private house to be built on Lafayette Square. The upper two floors now serve as offices for the National Trust for Historic Preservation and the rest of the house displays period furnishings. Be sure to visit the preservation book store around the corner on H Street. (The National Trust Regional Offices and Conference Center are also located on H Street.)

5 U.S. Chamber of Commerce, 1615 H Street, NW (1925—Cass Gilbert). The Chamber of Commerce and Treasury Annex (see no. 13, this tour) buildings are the only completed portions of a plan to unify the architecture of Lafayette Square in the neoclassic style of the older Treasury Building.

6 Hay-Adams Hotel*, northwest corner of 16th and H streets, NW (1927—H. H. Richardson). This elegant hotel was built on the site of H. H. Richardson's houses for Henry Adams and John Hay.

7 St. John's Church*, 16th and H streets, NW (1816—Benjamin Latrobe; 1883—James Renwick). St. John's is among the oldest Episcopal churches in the city. It is commonly referred to as the "Church of the Presidents" because a pew has been set aside for the President and his family. Since its first services in 1816 every President has worshipped here, some quite regularly.

8 St. John's Parish Building (Old British Embassy), 1525 H Street, NW (1822–24—St. Clair Clarke). This house was designed by its owner, St. Clair Clarke, and in the 1840s served as the British prime minister's residence. St. John's Church acquired the building in 1954 for use as a parish house. (On Wednesdays, 12:30–1:30, a French lunch is served.)

9 Cutts Madison House (Dolley Madison House), at the corner of H Street and Madison Place, NW, was built in 1820. This house was originally owned by James Madison and upon his death his widow, Dolley Madison, took up residence here. The house was restored as part of the Federal Judicial Center in 1968.

10 The **Benjamin Ogle Tayloe House,** at 21 Madison Place, was built in 1828. It served as a social center during the Tayloe Period and was later referred to by President McKinley as the "Little White House."

11 The United States Court of Claims*, 717 Madison Place, NW (Hours: 9:00 a.m. to 5:00 p.m. Monday through Friday). An arcaded passageway leads pedestrians from H Street through a pleasant courtyard to Madison Place and Lafayette Square. The entrance to a "colonial style" cafeteria faces the courtyard.

12 Treasury Building**, 1500 Pennsylvania Avenue, NW (1836–69—Robert Mills, Thomas U. Walter). Exhibit hall hours: 9:30 a.m. to 3:30 p.m. Monday through Friday; entrance on East Executive Avenue. The Treasury is the third oldest federal building in Washington. The site, selected by Andrew Jackson, destroyed L'Enfant's vista between the Capitol and the White House. The view down Pennsylvania Ave-

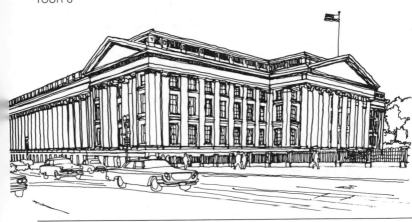

Treasury Building

nue as you walk past the Treasury on 15th Street is very dramatic. Take the time to visit the exhibit hall where currency, coins, stamps, and medals are on display.

The following five buildings (nos. 13–17) anchor the old financial district of the city, clustering in front of the Treasury building and along 15th Street. The unified facade treatment of buildings 13–16, and their massive columns, give the district a stately appearance.

13 Treasury Annex, Pennsylvania Avenue and Madison Place, NW (1919—Cass Gilbert).

14 Riggs National Bank, 1503 Pennsylvania Avenue, NW (1898—York and Sawyer).

15 American Security and Trust Company, northwest corner of 15th Street and Pennsylvania Avenue, NW (1899—York and Sawyer).

16 Union Trust Bank Building, southwest corner of 15th and H streets, NW (1906—Wood, Donnard and Deming).

17 National Savings and Trust Company*, northeast corner of 15th Street and Pennsylvania Avenue, NW (1880—James Windrim). The red brick Victorian-style structure provides a delightful relief from its more classic neighbors in the old financial district.

18 Metropolitan Square (Keith's Theater and Albee Building)*, southeast corner of 15th and G streets, NW (1911–12—Jules Henri de Sibour; 1982—facade retained and restored with new development behind—Koubek and Skidmore Owings and Merrill). A dramatic interior atrium and the historic facade restoration highlight this new private office and retail complex.

19 Rhodes Tavern, northeast corner of 15th and F streets, NW (1800). This is the oldest commercial structure left standing in Downtown. When the White House was being burned during the British invasion of 1814, the enemy officers ate dinner here. It was a home of one of the first banks in the city and the first home of the bank that became the Riggs National Bank.

20 Hotel Washington,** at the corner of 15th Street as it becomes Pennsylvania Avenue again (1917–18—Carrere and Hastings). The corner location of this fine hotel affords it one of the best views of the city. During spring, summer, and fall an outdoor rooftop terrace is open for food and drink.

21 Pershing Park,** between 15th and 14th streets on Pennsylvania Avenue, NW (1981—Lindsey and Friedberg). The park is a memorial to Gen. John J. Pershing that is an intimate retreat from the bustling city surrounding it. The large pool, fed by a waterfall, at the center of the park converts to a public ice-skating rink in winter. There is also a kiosk offering a café menu for outdoor dining.

22 Sherman Monument, 15th Street and Hamilton Place, NW. In addition to the statue of Gen. William T. Sherman, this monument includes the names of all of his battles and a chronology of his military assignments. The statues at the four corners represent branches of the army: infantry, artillery, cavalry, and engineers.

23 U.S. Department of Commerce (see Tour 9, Federal Triangle, no. 1).

24 The Ellipse*. Like Lafayette Square, the Ellipse (between 15th and 17th streets and Constitution Avenue) was the southern portion of the presidential grounds included in the L'Enfant plan. Note the visual relationship between the White House and the Jefferson Memorial and the strong axial relationship along 16th Street, through the White House to the Jefferson Memorial, enhanced by the granite fountains. L'Enfant intended the monument to George Washington to be located along this north-south axis, but soil conditions prevented its construction there. (See Tour 4, The Mall—West.) Note the imposing variety of styles of the buildings while progressing north along 17th Street to Pennsylvania Avenue.

25 Pan American Union* (Organization of American States), 17th Street and Constitution Avenue, NW (1910—Albert Kelsey and Paul Cret). Hours: Main Building—9:00 a.m. to 5:00 p.m. weekdays; Museum—9:00 a.m. to 4:00 p.m. Tuesday through Saturday. This building is the headquarters for the General Secretariat of the Organization of American States (there are 27 member states represented). The architectural styles of North and South America are blended into the building. The interior court, filled with many tropical plants, creates a wonderful space.

26 Daughters of the American Revolution (Constitution Hall), 1778 D Street, NW (about 1930—John

Russell Pope). Revolutionary period museum with tour: 9:00 a.m. to 4:00 p.m., Monday through Friday; Sundays 1:00–5:00 p.m. The DAR complex consists of Memorial Continental Hall, a library, a museum, an administration building, and Constitution Hall, which was the home of the National Symphony Orchestra prior to the opening of the Kennedy Center. The hall's program now consists of various concerts and lectures.

27 American Red Cross, 17th, D, and E streets, NW (1917—Trowbridge and Livingston). Hours: 9:00 a.m. to 4:00 p.m. Monday through Friday. The building is a monument to the women of the Civil War and serves as national headquarters for the National Red Cross.

28 Corcoran Gallery of Art***, 17th Street and New York Avenue, NW (1897—Ernest Flagg). Hours: 10:00 a.m. to 4:30 p.m. Tuesday through Sunday, Thursdays until 9:00 p.m. Closed Christmas and New Years Day. Admission free. This is one of Washington's finest art galleries, specializing in American art, fine art photography, modern art, and the education of artists. (The latter is accomplished through the Corcoran School of Art, located on the premises.) A fine example of beaux-arts style, the Corcoran has a magnificent interior atrium gallery.

Corcoran Gallery of Art

29 The **First Infantry Division Memorial** is the U.S. Army's testimonial to those of the 1st Infantry Division who died in World Wars I and II and Vietnam. A bed of flowers in the shape of a "one " is at the base of the memorial.

30 Winder Building, 604 17th Street, NW (1847–48). Although the building pioneered the use of central heating and steel beams and was a veritable high-rise in its time, its significance is more historical than architectural. It was the first, among many more to come, of the inexpensive, speculative office buildings designed for use by the federal government—its use today.

31 Headquarters building, **Federal Home Loan Bank Board,** 17th and G streets, NW (1977—Max Urbahn and Associates). An innovative and attractive design, the headquarters blends well with the renovated Winder building, harmonizing new with old. The project is significant in that it represents an effort by GSA to upgrade the quality of federal architecture and to incorporate lively commercial uses that bring much-needed nighttime activity into the area. The building features a lively urban park with an ice-skating rink in winter that converts into a fountain in summer, an outdoor restaurant, and retail uses at the street level.

32 Executive Office Building** (Old State, War and Navy) Pennsylvania Avenue and 17th Street, NW (1871–88—A. N. Mullett). Behind the 900 Doric columns was the world's largest office building at the time it was built. With its wealth of detail, it is probably the most eloquent government building in Washington. In an effort to beautify the nation's capital, President Kennedy saved the Old Executive Office Building from demolition. The Office of Management and Budget moved into the building in 1945. Sadly, it has been closed to the public since that time.

White House

33 The **White House***,** 1600 Pennsylvania Avenue, NW (begun 1792—James Hoban, Benjamin Latrobe, and others).

Hours: 10:00 a.m. to 12:00 p.m., Tuesday through Saturday, except holidays. Tour entrance is on East Executive Avenue. The simple, yet dignified, home of our President has more than 132 rooms, including the 54 rooms and 16 baths in the living quarters. The John Adamses were the first presidential family to occupy the White House, and soon after, in 1814, it was burned by the British. It is speculated that the building was first painted white at that time to cover the charring from the fire.

34 Lafayette Square*** was included in the President's Park in the L'Enfant plan of 1791. Jefferson authorized its separation into a park for public use. In 1824 the park was named in honor of the Marquis de Lafayette, a hero of the American Revolution. The central statue of Andrew Jackson, cast from the cannons captured by Jackson during the War of 1812, was the first equestrian statue in Washington, the second in the United States. The four other statues are of other American Revolutionary heroes. General Lafayette (southeast corner, 1890); Comte de Rochambeau (southwest corner, 1902); Gen. Thaddeus Kosciusko (northeast corner, 1910); and Baron Von Steuben (northwest corner, 1910). Lafayette Square is probably one of the nicest urban spaces in any American city and is actively used most of the year.

9/**Federal Triangle****

(government office buildings, Old Post Office)

by Pierre Childs;
original 1976 version by Sally Kress Tompkins

Distance: 1¼ miles
Time: ¾ hour
Bus: On 14th Street: 50, 52, 9, 11A, 11E, 11W; on
    Pennsylvania Avenue: 30, 32, 34, 36, 38, and 54
Metro: Federal Triangle (Blue and Orange Lines);
    Archives (Yellow Line)

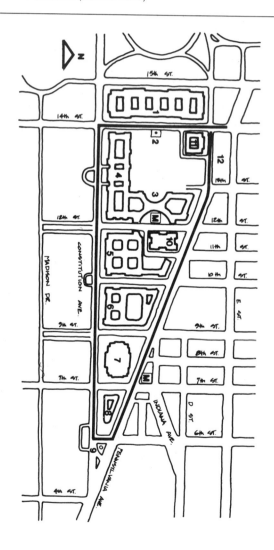

The Federal Triangle is formed by the intersection of Constitution Avenue, NW, with the diagonal Pennsylvania Avenue, and is bounded on the west by 15th Street and on the east by 6th Street. When Pierre L'Enfant imposed his grand design on the tobacco fields, farms, and wilderness that were to become the nation's capital, the Triangle was a swamp, subject to frequent flooding from the nearby Tiber Creek. Nevertheless, its exceptional location, south of Pennsylvania Avenue and north of the Mall between the White House and the Capitol, made it of obvious importance. L'Enfant marked it as the future site of municipal buildings.

After construction of the Tiber Canal in 1816 alleviated the flooding, the Triangle area developed rapidly, but as a commercial rather than as a governmental center. The Center Market, between 7th and 9th streets, NW, and dating from 1801, was replaced in 1870 by a large modern brick market whose stalls spread out as far as 11th Street, NW. Hotels, taverns, rooming houses, and printing and newspaper offices filled the area.

After the Civil War, the Triangle began to deteriorate. In 1899 the Old Post Office was erected at 12th Street and Pennsylvania Avenue, NW, and it was hoped that this would be the beginning of a renaissance for the area. The McMillan Commission plan of 1901 pictured the Triangle as a park dotted with various government buildings of a municipal nature; and, in 1908, the District Building was erected at 14th and E streets, NW, but no further action was taken. Conditions became increasingly scandalous: tattoo parlors, gas stations, cheap hotels, and chop suey signs were prevalent, and Ohio Avenue (eliminated by Triangle construction) was lined with brothels. At the same time, the government's need for more office space was growing acute. The Public Buildings bill, allocating 50 million dollars for buildings in the District of Columbia, was finally passed by Congress and signed by President Calvin Coolidge on May 5, 1926. Two years later, Congress appropriated the money to buy the entire Triangle.

Secretary of the Treasury Andrew Mellon was responsible for the construction and design of the buildings, and in 1927, he appointed a Board of Architectural Consultants to draw up a plan for the entire Triangle area.

The architects and the members of the National Commission of Fine Arts, who took an active role in formulating a plan, accepted the prevailing premise that the neoclassic style was the proper one for public buildings. They saw in the Triangle development a rare opportunity to plan a group of related monumental buildings designed to constitute a single great composition. Public enthusiasm was high for the project, and the capital was caught up in a quest for grandeur. Everyone looked forward to Washington becoming the "Paris of America" and talked of a capital "worthy of a great nation."

In 1929 a model of the composition designed by the Board of Architectural Consultants went on display. The Triangle had been given a treatment somewhat similar to that of the Louvre, with buildings reflecting a revival classical style. There were a series of courtyards around a central circular court. Vistas from this court extended into the other plazas, one of which—the Great Plaza—was to be as large as Lafayette Square. The main entrances of the buildings were planned to open onto these courts, so that a sense of quiet would pervade the scheme. The buildings had a uniform cornice line drawn from the Natural History Museum and following the diagonal of Pennsylvania Avenue. Pylons at the entrances and specially designed sidewalks served to unify the composition.

Unfortunately, the Triangle would never achieve the perfection for which its designers strove. The Great Depression—and the automobile—would sadly alter the final composition. The Great Plaza became a parking lot. The sweeping drives turned into major traffic arteries, and the pylons that were to flank them were declared a traffic hazard and were never constructed. The circular court was never completed because the Old Post Office, anathema to the Triangle's designers, was never demolished. Depression economies put the future of the final structure, with the Federal Trade Commission building at the apex, in doubt. When finally constructed in 1937, it was a simplified version of the original design. By that time the neoclassic style was out of favor and there was little interest in the buildings or in completing the design. The Triangle's imperial facade was deemed inappropriate for a democratic country.

Today the finished facade along Constitution Avenue is somewhat forbidding, and the Pennsylvania Avenue street line breaks up at 13th Street, exposing to view the huge unfinished parking lot that was to have been the Great Plaza. GSA has recently completed a master plan that proposes a redevelopment of this area and the renovation of the existing buildings, to invite the public into and through the Triangle, creating a link between the Mall and Downtown, and preserving the handsome architecture for the public enjoyment.

Start your walking tour at the 14th Street entrance to the Commerce Department building.

1 The **Commerce Department Building*** (14th Street between E and Constitution Avenue, NW) was designed by Louis Ayres of the firm of York and Sawyer and was intended to house all the bureaus of the department under one roof, which it did, except for the Bureau of Standards. At the time of its construction in 1932 it was the largest government office building in the world—1,050 feet long, exceeding the Capitol by 300 feet. Arched gateways two stories high give direct access through the building at what used to be C and

D streets. The central section of the 14th Street facade is patterned after the Perrault facade at the Louvre. The relief panels represent the various agencies of the department and were designed by James Earl Fraser. The building encloses six courtyards providing light and ventilation, which was necessary before air conditioning. Enter the lobby to view the coffered ceiling with gilded accents and richly colored marble floors and columns. Look out the windows into the landscaped courtyards and you will begin to sense the feeling the planners and architects had in mind when the building was laid out.

Located in the basement of the Commerce Department Building is the **Aquarium.** Enter from the 14th Street side. Hours: 9:00 a.m. to 5:00 p.m.

2 The **Oscar Straus Memorial Fountain** was designed by John Russell Pope, but a simplified version of his design was actually built. The figures were sculpted by Adolph A. Weinman. The large parking lot behind it is the Great Plaza. Picture the space as the designers envisioned it, landscaped as a huge formal garden. Then picture it as a building embracing the fountain and having a high glass galleria filled with exhibits and with a view of the hemicycle at the far end.

3 At the eastern end of the parking lot is the **hemicycle of the Federal Building.** It was designed by the firm of Delano and Aldrich and was meant to form a fitting terminus to the Great Plaza. The sculpted pediment is the work of Adolph A. Weinman. The bricks visible at the Pennsylvania Avenue side of the building mark the place where a final wing was to be added to enclose the Great Plaza.

Walk south on 14th Street and cross Constitution Avenue. The elaborate neoclassic facade of the Triangle buildings along Constitution Avenue can here be viewed from a distance. It is particularly impressive at night when the facades are illuminated. When GSA's master plan proposals are implemented, the projecting portico of the Departmental Auditorium will be flanked by major pedestrian paths through the monumental archways now restricted to parking cars. This will encourage public appreciation of the handsome architecture of the Triangle's interior.

4 Arthur Brown, Jr., of San Francisco, designer of the City Hall and War Memorial Opera House in that city, was the architect of the complex (between 12th and 14th streets on Constitution Avenue) made up of the **U.S. Customs Service** (originally built for the Labor Department), the **Departmental Auditorium,** and the **Interstate Commerce Commission Building.** Of particular interest is the second story relief panel of the Departmental Auditorium, which diverges from the neoclassic allegorical sculpture typical of the buildings' exteriors. Designed by Edmond Romulus Amateis, it depicts Gen. George Washington with Major Generals Nathanael Greene and John Sullivan. Greene's face is that of architect Brown and Sullivan's is that of sculptor Edgar Waiter. The doors to the auditorium are often open, and this beautifully restored monumental space is worth seeing, as are the rotunda and hearing rooms of the ICC and the landscaped courtyard of Customs.

Continue walking east along Constitution Avenue. As you cross 12th Street, note the new construction in the distance along Pennsylvania Avenue as well as glimpses of the recently cleaned Old Post Office Building. This is to become a major gateway to the city, and a connector between the Mall and Downtown under the master plan proposals to reduce vehicular traffic and enhance the landscaped treatments of the area.

5 After crossing 12th Street, you will be looking across Constitution Avenue at the **Internal Revenue Service Building** and the comforting words of Oliver Wendell Holmes inscribed on it: "Taxes are what we pay for a civilized society." The building was designed by the Office of the Supervising Architect of the Treasury Department under the direction of Louis Simon. It was completed in 1930, the first of the group to be finished. It is constructed of Indiana limestone and granite with columns of Tennessee marble. The building has four handsomely landscaped inner courtyards like the Commerce Department Building. The final wing, which was to form the eastern side of the circular court, was never completed.

6 When you have crossed 10th Street you are opposite the **Justice Department Building.** Its architecture is notably simplified, reflecting the influence of the art deco or modern styles of the period. This is reflected in the extensive use of aluminum in decorative lighting fixtures and monumental doors as well as in the polychrome details at the cornice and the soffits at the entries. It was designed by the Philadelphia firm of Zantzinger, Borie, and Medary, and completed in 1934.

Justice Department

7 As you proceed across 9th Street you should stop to admire John Russell Pope's **Archives Building***.** This was to be the most important and tallest building in the complex, designed as a shrine for the nation's most treasured documents. The structure is purely classical with completely plain walls, except for windows to accommodate the offices on the Pennsylvania Avenue side. It is adorned by 72 Corinthian pillars, 52 feet high, grouped in collonnades about the building. The great pediment on the Constitution Avenue facade displays a figure representing the Recorder of the Archives and two eagles standing guard at the sides. The sculptor was James Earle Fraser, who also designed the large seated figures that flank the monumental steps that lead into a public hall housing the **Declaration of Independence***,** the **Constitution***,** and the **Bill of Rights*****. All three are on display along with a changing special exhibit. (Enter from Constitution Avenue. Hours: 10:00 a.m. to 5:30 p.m. daily except Christmas.) The Archives' less notable records are housed in a central steel shaft.

National Archives

8 Proceed along Constitution Avenue to the last of the Triangle group, the **Federal Trade Commission.** This building, designed by Bennett, Parsons, and Frost, was considerably altered from the original model to be acceptable to a nation in the throes of a depression. It is still a very satisfying building, however, and its eastern end, a **rounded colonnade*** of Doric columns reminiscent of a blunted ship's bow, makes an excellent terminus to the Triangle composition. The art deco style that became increasingly popular in the 1930s is much in evidence in the relief panels, the decorative medallions, the aluminum doors, and most dramatically in Michael Lantz's horses, which flank the eastern colonnade.

9 The **Andrew Mellon Memorial Fountain*,** across

6th Street from the Federal Trade Commission building, is an exclamation point to the Triangle. The fountain, completed in 1952, could not be in a more appropriate position, filling the last sliver of the great Triangle that Mellon's influence brought to fruition and situated directly across from the National Gallery of Art, which he gave to the nation. The fountain was designed by Otto R. Eggers in bronze and granite; the signs of the zodiac, visible under the sheet of water formed by the overflow from the basins, are the work of Sidney Waugh. There are also benches to rest on before beginning the walk back along Pennsylvania Avenue.

The Pennsylvania Avenue side of the Triangle reveals all its weaknesses as well as its great potential. It is noticeable here that John Russell Pope did not follow the diagonal of the avenue as did the other architects. The resulting triangular slice of land is a small park, a memorial to Franklin Delano Roosevelt, located there according to his wishes. The flanking statues at the Archives' entrance are the work of Robert Aiken.

The Justice Department building returns to the concept of filling the entire block. Walk to the vehicular entrance in the center of its 9th Street facade for a glimpse of the largest and most elaborate of the Triangle's interior courtyards. Note the polychrome decorations of the soffits above the driveways. At 11th Street, the short, truncated facade of the IRS Building testifies that the design here was never completed, awaiting the planned demolition of the Old Post Office. It is here that some of the most dramatic proposals of GSA's master plan should be noted.

The Federal Triangle master plan creates a festive courtyard between the Old Post Office and the IRS Building, completing the blunt ends of IRS with facades replicating the original style and lining the courtyard with restaurants and exhibit space.

10 The **Old Post Office**** was designed by Willoughby Edbrooke in the Richardsonian Romanesque style popular at the time of its construction in 1899. It was considered an "object of permanent regret" by the neoclassicists, and the Triangle designers drew up a plan that demanded its demolition. Its bulk cuts across the space that would have been the pivotal circular court designed after the "gay fashion of Paris." It is worth walking down 12th Street to see the great eastern facade of the Post Office Department building that was to form half of that court. A small segment of the opposite side of the circular court is visible on the IRS building behind the Old Post Office.

Twelfth Street is to be renovated to respect the original concept of the Circular Plaza, with new paving and fountains. It is to serve as a major focal point in the Triangle and as an anteroom to the city. The Federal Triangle Metro Station is immediately below the center of the street. The Old Post Office, saved from the bulldozer, has been remodeled for government offices and commercial activities—producing a

Old Post Office Building

multiuse character seldom offered in government buildings.

Continuing down Pennsylvania Avenue past the unfinished wing of the Post Office Department one has another view of the Great Plaza—what the President's Temporary Commission on Pennsylvania Avenue called "potentially one of the finest urban land spaces in the country," now filled with cars. This site, under the master plan, will be developed with federal office buildings enclosing a number of large and small courtyards serving the public in various ways. The buildings will include publicly oriented housing, restaurants, shops, exhibit space, and visitor facilities. The great gap in the Pennsylvania Avenue south street line will be completed with a landscaped courtyard complementing the District Building and the new Western Plaza.

11 The **District Building*** (Pennsylvania Avenue and 14th Street) was designed by Cope and Stewardson in 1908 in a style described as "beaux-arts classicism." The original 1929 model of the Triangle did not include it, instead proposing its demolition, like that of the Old Post Office, in order to create a monolithic design.

12 In front of the District Building is the **Western Plaza,** designed by Robert Venturi for the Pennsylvania Avenue Development Corporation. The unique design incorporates a partial plan of the city in the paving of its raised platform. (See Tour 10, Downtown, for information on the area north of the Federal Triangle.)

10/**Downtown****

(central retail area, department stores, pedestrian malls, Washington Convention Center, Ford's Theater, FBI Building, Old Post Office, Pennsylvania Avenue)

by John Fondersmith;
original 1976 version by Robert Gray

Distance: 3 miles
Time: 2½ hours
Bus: Major routes are 40, 42, 60, S-2, S-4.
Metro: Metro Center (Red, Blue, and Orange Lines); Gallery Place (Red and Yellow Lines); Archives (Yellow Line); Judiciary Square (Red Line); Union Station (Red Line).

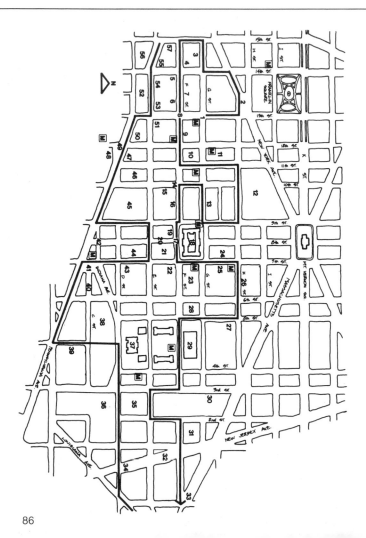

Since the 1950s, Washington's original Downtown area north of the Mall has undergone the problems that have afflicted other large American cities. The gradual reversal of this trend has been stimulated by the arrival of the still-expanding Metrorail system and a recognition by developers, the District of Columbia government, business leaders, and citizens of the area's vast economic potential. With future guidance by the Downtown Plan Policies, the extensive redevelopment and revitalization now underway are intended to achieve what Washington's Mayor Marion Barry calls a "Living Downtown." On this tour the numerous construction sites and recently completed developments mingled among some of Washington's oldest and finest buildings demonstrate the dynamic potential of this area.

1 Metro Center**, at the center of the Metro system, is expected to be the most heavily used of the 86 Metro stations in the 100-mile regional rapid-rail transit system. Subway service on a limited 4½-mile segment through Downtown started in 1976. The system now comprises 60.46 miles and 60 stations. Above the station, at 12, 13th, and G streets, NW, are publicly acquired urban renewal sites totaling 4.13 acres, which have a reuse potential of more than 1.7 million gross square feet of floor area for mixed-use development, including a new Hecht's department store, other retail space, a 400-room hotel, and office development.

2 New York Avenue between the White House and Mount Vernon Square is rapidly becoming a prestige business address. The **1300 block of New York Avenue** is the focus of recent office development, with six major new buildings and four renovations underway, and other developments planned. The largest and one of the most interesting of the new buildings, with a modern classical facade and a large interior atrium, is at **1300 New York Avenue;** by Skidmore Owings and Merrill.

3 Metropolitan Square is a large new office complex with a ground-floor retail mall. The beaux-arts facade of the Keith Albee Building on 15th Street has been retained and incorporated into the first phase of the project. The landmark interior of the **Old Ebbitt Grill,** formerly on F Street, has been relocated into the 15th Street frontage of the building. The second phase of the project will extend south to F Street, incorporating the landmark facade of the Metropolitan Bank Building.

4 Garfinckel's, Downtown's most fashionable department store, is the western anchor of the retail core. It has a direct connection to the Metropolitan Square shopping mall.

5 The **National Press Club Building,** at 14th and F streets, has housed a concentration of media offices since it opened in 1924. The top floor is often the scene of speeches by national and foreign leaders. The building recently underwent a major renovation, including a new facade, and includes a central atrium and two-level shopping mall, which will connect it with the adjacent National Place complex.

6 National Place is a retail/office/hotel project extending from F Street to E Street, developed by the Quadrangle Development Corporation and the Marriott Corporation. The three-level retail mall is managed by the Rouse Company.

7 The **north side of the 1300 block of F Street** includes a number of interesting small-scale retail buildings and several larger buildings, which have recently been renovated. The most interesting is the Romanesque Sun Building at 1315–17 F Street.

8 The **F Street Plaza,** between 12th and 14th streets, is bordered by roadways. It was intended to provide a sense of place for pedestrians. Though partly successful, the press of traffic on both sides of the narrow plaza hinders its use and attractiveness.

9 The **Ticketplace** pavillion, in the center of the F Street Plaza between 12th and 13th streets, opened in late 1981. It is operated by the Cultural Alliance of Greater Washington and provides half-price (day of performance) and full-price tickets (advance sales) for cultural events in the city and metropolitan region.

10 The **Woodward and Lothrop** department store forms the eastern anchor of the retail core. There is a direct underground connection to the Metro Center Station.

11 The block north of Woodward and Lothrop is the site of the future **Washington Center,** a major retail/office/hotel complex.

12 The **Washington Convention Center,** which opened in January 1983, is one of the country's largest and most modern convention centers, with 350,000 square feet of exhibit space and 40 meeting rooms. The Center, designed by Welton Becket and Associates, Gray and West, and H.D. Nottingham, stretches for two blocks along the north side of H Street. Hotels and other new developments are proposed for the 10 blocks surrounding the Center.

13 The **900 block of G Street, NW,** is now a pedestrian mall. The fountains have malfunctioned and are to be replaced with new and simpler landscaping. The **Martin Luther King Jr. Memorial Library,** at 9th and G streets, is the city's central library and the only work of the architect Mies van der Rohe in Washington. Other important buildings along this block include the new YWCA, St. Patrick's Catholic Church and Academy, and the First Congregational Church.

14 Tenth Street provides a vista between the new Washington Convention Center to the north and the National Museum of Natural History to the south on Constitution Avenue. The brick-paved portion of 10th Street between F and E streets is known as **"Lincoln Place."**

15 Ford's Theater***, where President Lincoln was assassinated, was restored by the National Park Service and reopened as a museum and theater in 1965. Across 10th Street, NW, the **Petersen House*** has also been restored to its appearance on April 14, 1865, when the dying President was carried there for treatment.

16 The **900 block of F Street,** a transition between the retail core and the Gallery Place areas, has a number of landmark buildings, including the **Atlantic Building** (930 F Street) and the **National Union Building** (918 F Street).

At the corner of 9th and F streets, NW, are several noteworthy commercial and architectural landmarks; the Richardsonian-style **Riggs National Bank*** (1891) and the **Lansburgh's Furniture Store** (1870).

Riggs National Bank

17 At **Gallery Place,** between 7th and 9th on F Street, NW, there is a pedestrian system that provides space for sitting, watching an occasional performance by street musicians or others, enjoying a casual lunch, and relaxing. This plaza is proposed to become a focus for street vendors. The Gallery Place Metro station underlies G Street—one block north.

18 The **National Portrait Gallery/National Museum of American Art***** building (F, G, 7th and 9th streets, NW) was formerly the U.S. Patent Office, a patent museum, then a repository for the Declaration of Independence, and a Civil War hospital before its renovation and reuse by the Smithsonian Institution in 1968 as a public art gallery. An excellent example of Greek revival architecture, the building now contains two excellent art collections plus a popular cafeteria, with seating in its interior and landscaped courtyard.

19 The buildings on the south side of the **800 block of F Street, NW,** including the **LeDroit Building,** are all landmarks. These facades complement that of the National Portrait Gallery. The LeDroit Building, an early nonelevated Victorian office building, now contains a number of artist studios.

20 The **8th Street vista** between the porticoes of the National Portrait Gallery and the National Archives on Pennsylvania Avenue is one of the special design relationships in the city.

21 The Greek revival-style **Tariff Commission Building** (1839—Robert Mills), at 701 E Street, NW, has provided space for a variety of government departments. The International Trade Commission currently occupies the building, and a Post Office is located on its main floor. Congress passed legislation in 1984 to transfer this building to the Smithsonian Institution for museum use.

22 **The Hecht Company,** at 7th and F Streets, is one of Washington's major department stores and occupies most of this block. When Hecht's moves to its new building at Metro Center, much of this block is expected to be rebuilt as a major mixed-use complex.

23 **Gallery Place** is a proposed development on a 2.77-acre renewal site, the block north of the Hecht Company. Plans call for a major retail/office/hotel/residential complex with a direct connection to the Gallery Place Metro Station.

24 The buildings along the west side of the **700 block of 7th Street,** between G and H streets, NW, were erected in the 1880s. These three- and four-story Victorian commercial structures have remained substantially unchanged except for the street floor windows.

25 **Gallery Place North** is another development site on land partly owned by the Washington Metropolitan Area Transit Authority. A WMATA development prospectus calls for a mixed-use complex with a Chinese design theme, in keeping with the character of the adjacent Chinatown.

26 The **600 block of H Street,** NW, forms the heart of **Chinatown,** with restaurants and shops. The Chinese New Year parade, which attracts large crowds, runs along H

Street each year. The **Wah Luck House** at the northwest corner of 6th and H streets provides 153 apartments, a Chinatown community room, and a Chinese meditation garden. This modern building with its Chinese design features was designed by Alfred Liu and developed by the Chinatown Development Corporation and the National Housing Partnerships.

27 St. Mary's Catholic Church, at 5th and H streets, was formed in the mid-19th century to serve German Catholic immigrants. The present church building (1891) was influenced by German Gothic architecture. The large but not very inspiring **General Accounting Office** wraps around the St. Mary's Church complex on two sides.

28 The Washington Metropolitan Transit Authority (WMATA)—builder of Metro and operators of Metrobus—moved into its new building in 1974 (Keyes, Lethbridge and Condon). It accommodates Metro's 1,100-person headquarters staff and houses the fare collection and central computer facilities for the entire rapid-rail transit system.

29 The **Old Pension Building**** (1882), 5th and G streets, NW, a Category I landmark in **Judiciary Square*,** was designed by Montgomery C. Meigs, engineer of the Capitol dome and the Cabin John Bridge. Its huge central hall, an innovation in lighting and ventilation at the time, was used for presidential inaugural balls in the 1800s. The building has been designated to house the National Building Museum, a center for display and study of American building arts, including city planning, architecture, landscape architecture, and construction.

Old Pension Building

30 The **Adas Israel Synagogue*,** 701 3d Street, NW, dedicated in 1876, was the first building constructed as a synagogue in the District of Columbia. It was moved to its present site in 1969, and its restoration was completed in 1974. A small museum inside is open Sundays 10 to 4 and weekdays by appointment. Phone: (202) 789-0800.

31 Designed by Edward Durrell Stone (architect also of the John F. Kennedy Center for the Performing Arts), the **Georgetown University Law Center*** (600 New Jersey Avenue) opened in 1969 with facilities for 1,700 students.

32 New Jersey Avenue is the spine of the Downtown East area. The **Capitol Place** complex, including a 265-room Sheraton Grand Hotel and office space, was recently completed at New Jersey Avenue and F Street. At F and North Capitol streets, the **Phoenix Park Hotel** is emerging from the major renovation of a previous hotel. The Dubliner is a popular Irish pub on the ground floor.

33 The monumental **Union Station,** designed by Daniel Burnham (1908), provides an impressive entrance into the city for rail travelers. A program to convert the station to a Visitors Center for the Bicentennial was less than successful, and in fact hindered its rail terminal function. Repairs and modifications are now underway and programmed to restore the building to a role as a modern transportation terminal. (Also see Tour 1, no. 1.)

34 The walk back through **Downtown East,** along North Capitol Street, New Jersey Avenue, E and F streets, NW, reveals a number of new buildings constructed during the past 10 years, including the office buildings Capitol Mall North and 400 North Capitol Plaza, the Hyatt Regency Hotel (400 New Jersey Avenue, NW) and the new headquarters of the National Association of Counties, located at 440 1st Street.

35 Designed by Victor Lundy, the new U.S. **Tax Court,** (east of 3d Street between D and E streets, NW) utilizes innovative structural concepts of post-tensioning to support a cantilevered courtroom on six columns. A landscaped pedestrian plaza spans the adjacent eight-lane Center-Leg Freeway. Since the dramatic front of this building faces the freeway, it is not fully seen by most visitors.

36 The **Department of Labor Building,** between 2d and 3d streets south of D Street, NW, accommodates approximately 4,000 employees. Below this large federal building is the Center-Leg Freeway, which crosses the Mall entirely in tunnel. The Department of Labor Building incorporates ventilation shafts for the freeway tunnel.

37 The **Old City Hall** (begun in 1820 and successively added to until completed in 1916), a Category I landmark in Judiciary Square, was the first public building constructed to house the District of Columbia Government. It has been put to various other uses, including a "jail lot" and a Civil War Hospital. The D.C. courts occupy the building, at present. A newer Municipal Center Building is located to the southeast across D Street.

38 The new home for the **District of Columbia Court of Appeals and Superior Court,** at Indiana Avenue, John Marshall Place, 6th and D streets, NW, opened in 1977. It has one appellate and 44 trial courtrooms plus ancillary space and totals 375,000 net square feet.

Walk south down the broad flight of steps and across the plaza and C Street into **John Marshall Park.** You have now entered the area where the Pennsylvania Avenue Development Corporation (PADC), a federal corporation, is undertaking a major program to improve and revitalize the north side of Pennsylvania Avenue between the Capitol and the White House.

39 John Marshall Park was completed in 1983 from the designs of Carol R. Johnson & Associates. On the east side of the park is the Federal Courthouse, scene of the Watergate trials. The now vacant lot on the west side of the park is the future site of the Canadian Chancery.

The **Market Square** area includes the Pennsylvania Avenue area east of the FBI Building, and is to be developed as a major housing area, with other retail, office, and hotel development. The PADC plan calls for retention and reuse of a number of landmark buildings.

40 The triangular area between Pennsylvania Avenue, Indiana Avenue, 6th and 7th streets, is the site of a mixed-use complex with a hotel, residential units, and retail and office space. Construction of the first phase began in 1983.

41 The area around the space at Indiana Avenue and 7th Street contains a concentration of small Victorian and earlier buildings. The Richardsonian-style **National Bank of Washington** (1886) has recently been renovated. Notice the **Temperance Monument** in front of the adjacent **Apex Building.** The three buildings on the north side of Indiana Avenue, housing Litwins, a restaurant, and the Artifactory, are some of the oldest commercial buildings in Washington, dating back to the 1820s.

42 The frontage north of Pennsylvania Avenue, across from the National Archives, is to be converted into **Navy Memorial Park,** a major new open space with an adjacent retail, office, and residential complex. The **Archives Metro Station** is located in the square.

43 The **Gallery Row** project at 7th and D streets is part of a program to create a 7th Street arts spine. The complex, which will include the replacement of landmark facades and new construction, will have space for 10 art galleries and retail and office space.

44 The building at 400 7th Street has been partially renovated to house the Washington Project for the Arts (WPA). Next door, **406 Seventh Street** has been renovated to house six art galleries. A few doors north at 420 7th Street is the **Lansburgh Cultural Center,** a landmark building that has been recycled to serve as a local arts center. The building also houses some District of Columbia government agencies, including the Office of Planning.

45 The **J. Edgar Hoover FBI Building** (between 9th and 10th streets and Pennsylvania Avenue and E Street), completed in 1975, provides space for more than 8,000 employees, 850 parking spaces, and has an interior courtyard. The **FBI Tour*** is a popular visitor attraction (enter from E Street).

46 1001 Pennsylvania Avenue is an office/retail complex on Pennsylvania Avenue between 10th and 11th streets. Architects of the Washington firm of Hartman-Cox have provided an interesting design incorporating portions of a number of older buildings on the site. Construction of the first phase began in 1984.

47 The **Old Evening Star Building** (1898—Marsh and Peter), on Pennsylvania Avenue at 11th Street, has a beautiful neoclassical facade. Renovation of this landmark building, once described as a "marble poem in the sky," and the addition of adjacent office space, is proposed.

48 The **Old Post Office** (1899) was a focus of preservation controversy for many years, but it has now been recycled for dramatic new uses, following the design of Arthur Cotton Moore and Associates (see Tour 9, Federal Triangle, no. 10, for more information).

49 The **Pennsylvania Avenue streetscapes** between the Capitol and 15th Street are being improved with special paving, lighting, and street furniture. Pennsylvania Avenue has also been rebuilt.

50 1201 Pennsylvania Avenue (Skidmore Owings and Merrill) opened in 1981. It has an unusual atrium, office and retail space, and two restaurants.

51 The **Warner Theater,** at 13th and E streets, NW, has a long history as an entertainment center in downtown Washington. An ornate movie palace in earlier decades, the Warner is now a live stage for various theatrical and musical productions.

52 Western Plaza (Venturi and Rauch) is a new open space formed by bending Pennsylvania Avenue into the line of E Street at 13th Street. The resulting rectangular plaza occupies a critical position between the Downtown area and the monumental Federal Triangle to the south, and offers a good view of the Capitol at the east end of Pennsylvania Avenue, about a mile away (see Tour 9, Federal Triangle, for more information.)

53 The **American City Building,** at 1301 Pennsylvania Avenue was completed in 1980, the first new private office building on Pennsylvania Avenue in over a decade.

54 The Pennsylvania Avenue frontage of the **National Place** complex (a joint venture of Mitchell-Giurgola and Frank Slessinger Associates) includes offices, the 774-room **J. W. Marriott Hotel,** and the entrance to the retail mall (see this tour, No. 6). As part of the project, the adjacent **National Theater** was renovated in 1983.

55 The **Willard Hotel*,** at 14th Street and Pennsylvania Avenue, NW, a Category III landmark, opened in 1901 and was one of Washington's top hotels for many years. In an earlier Willard Hotel on this site, Julia Ward Howe composed the "Battle Hymn of the Republic." The present hotel closed in 1968, and at one time there were plans to tear it down. However, the plans were changed in 1974 when the Pennsylvania Avenue Plan was revised to place more emphasis on historic preservation. Renovation of this historic hotel is now underway.

Willard Hotel

56 Pershing Park is a delightful new open space at the west end of Pennsylvania Avenue (designed as a joint venture of Jerome Lindsey/M. Paul Friedberg Associates). The central space is a pool in summer and a skating rink in winter.

57 The renovated **Washington Hotel** (1917) anchors the west end of Pennsylvania Avenue. If you take this tour in late spring or summer, you would do well to end the walk with a visit to the rooftop café overlooking 15th Street (open May––September), which provides a splendid view over the White House grounds and other parts of monumental Washington. The hotel also has a convenient ground-floor restaurant, overlooking Pershing Park, and the Two Continents restaurant.

11/**Midtown****
(office, hotel, high-quality restaurant and retail area)

by Allan A. Hodges, 1983 update by Joan Towles

Distance: 2¾ miles
Time: 1½ hours
Bus: 37, 46, D2, D4, D6, D8, G2, G4, G6, H1, L2, L4, N2,
N4, N5, and N6
Metro: Farragut North, Dupont Circle (Red Line); Farragut
West, McPherson Square (Blue and Orange
Lines)

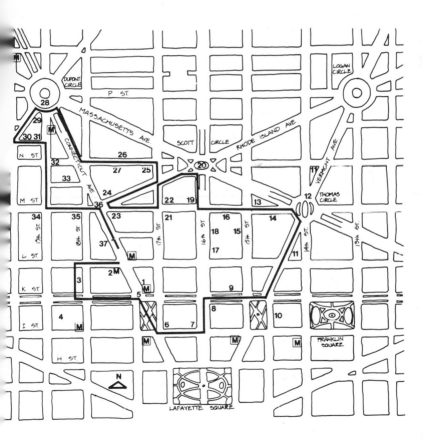

The Midtown tour begins at the Farragut North Metro
station at Connecticut Avenue and L Street, NW.

1 The increased accessibility that Metro has brought Washington has channeled new development near certain well-located stations. At this key Midtown corner, the developer leased the air rights above the Farragut North Metro Station, integrating its design to the economic potential of the attractive red brick office-retail building (Skidmore Owings and Merrill). Because the **"Connecticut Connection"** (the name of its four floors of retail space) has a direct underground connection to the rail station, no automobile parking spaces were required by the city—an innovative development incentive.

2 The protruding hexagonal tower diagonally across the street is part of the block-long, 130 foot-high **Washington Square** office building. The 600,000-square-foot building's exterior is sheathed in glass and panels of pink Tennessee marble from the same quarry that supplied the stone for the National Gallery of Art. This site, which also has a direct connection to the Farragut North Metro Station, has set the pace on recent rents for prime District office space at more than $30 per square foot.

The intersection of Connecticut Avenue and L Street is referred to by many as "Chloethiel's corner," in reference to Washington architect Chloethiel Woodard Smith. Her unreformed modernist designs can be seen in 1100 Connecticut Avenue, on the intersection's northwest corner, and in the Blake Building, on the southeast corner, both designs of the 1960s, as well as in the new Washington Square addition.

3 The corner of K and 18th streets, NW, is a good position from which to view the visual effect of the 130-foot height limit for buildings in the city. Restricted by Congress's Height of Buildings Act of 1910, Washington has developed a flat, low skyline unique for large U.S. cities. Some critics have complained that the height limit has restricted good architecture and contributed to a monotonous office-corridor effect, but many developers and architects have proven otherwise in recent years. In order to develop a site fully, with these height constraints putting building setbacks at a premium, enclosed center-block retail malls, such as the one at 1801 K Street, NW, have become increasingly popular.

4 **International Square,** covering almost the entire block from 18th to 19th streets south of K Street, NW, is a huge office-retail complex, graced by an attractive 10,000-square-foot, 12-story interior atrium. The project is another example of joint development between the transit authority, which has perpetual easements to the property for its Farragut West Metro Station, and the Carr Company developers, which had the foresight to combine construction efforts for over a decade so that the Square's innovative design might channel pedestrian traffic from the station through its two-level retail mall.

5 The corner of **Connecticut and K Streets, NW*,** is the center of Washington's booming private office district. This area, referred to by some as Midtown, accounts for nearly one-third of the total employment in the central city. In addition, Washington's major hotels, better restaurants, quality shops, and much of its growing night life are located here. Midtown is also a good place to experience the main features of L'Enfant's plan for Washington: diagonal radial avenues super-imposed over a grid street system, with circles and squares at their intersections.

6 "Damn the torpedoes! Full Speed Ahead!" said David G. Farragut during a Civil War battle in 1864 in Mobile Bay. A statue to the admiral is the centerpiece of lovely Farragut Square—and a roosting place for scores of pigeons. With good reason. **Farragut Square**** is one of the most heavily used urban parks in Washington. At noon, the "lunch bunch" congregates to eat brown bag lunches and be entertained by events ranging from concerts by the National Symphony to karate exhibitions. A Metro tunnel underlies the park.

Farragut Square

7 The striking hexagonal **Third Church of the Christ Scientist*** and the **Christian Science Monitor Building*** (NW corner of 16th and I streets, NW) were designed by I.M. Pei and Partners in 1972. The plaza between them is rarely used by pedestrians because it lacks benches to sit on and the exit is not clearly marked. However, the whole setting is visually satisfying.

8 The **Sheraton Carlton Hotel** (1926—Mihran Mesrobian) is as elegant on the main floor as is its facade. Have a look at the ceiling details in the lobby and the classical wine bar and magnolia-lined patio. Across the street is the busy Capital Hilton Hotel, which caters to convention, business, and local political groups. The hotel was recently restored to its original art deco style.

9 Busy **K Street** is the major east-west axis of the Midtown business district. The street channels commuter traffic westward to Virginia and Maryland and eastward to the redeveloping "Old Downtown" and the new D.C. Convention Center. (See Tour 10, Downtown.) Many airline offices, business services, and increasingly, professional offices are located here.

10 McPherson Square, the eastern counterpart of Farragut Square, is one of the many public reservations provided in the L'Enfant plan. A statue to Brig. Gen. James B. McPherson, who commanded the Tennessee Army in the Civil War, was erected in 1876. During the summer months, many local workers and tourists relax in the park while eating lunches and listening to free outdoor concerts.

11 Vermont Avenue, NW, is fast approaching its diagonal twin, Connecticut Avenue, as an important, albeit smaller, commercial corridor. The 1980s have seen the development of a dozen new office buildings on adjacent blocks, adding new life to this corner of Midtown. Vermont Avenue also provides a good **view** of the steeples of the colonial-style National City Christian Church (1930—John Russell Pope) and the NeoGothic Luther Place Memorial Church (1870—Judson York), located around Thomas Circle. The avenue's character changes from commercial to residential as it proceeds northeast to historic Logan Circle (see Tour 14, Shaw School Urban Renewal Area/Logan Circle).

12 Thomas Circle** is one of 15 major circles in the original L'Enfant Plan. It was intended as a quiet park, but now forms the junction of four of the city's busiest arteries. To relieve congestion, an underpass was built in 1940. In the late 19th and early 20th centuries, two- and three-story private dwellings surrounded the area. The low-density residential area has been replaced by apartment, hotel, and office complexes. An equestrian statue of Maj. Gen. George H. Thomas, a Union hero of the Civil War, commands the circle.

13 The **National Housing Center*** (1975—Vincent Kling and Associates) serves as the spectacular headquarters of the National Association of Home Builders. The first floor features an imaginative exhibit of U.S. housing.

14 Across the street, enjoy a drink in the lobby court of the 14-story atrium of the beautiful new **Vista Hotel.**

15 15th Street, NW, between L and M streets, has also been redeveloped privately during the past decade. Dominated by new office buildings, not unlike 13-story "boxes," the street is made more interesting by the huge **Washington Post** headquarters and the posh **Madison Hotel.**

16 The **Metropolitan African Methodist Episcopal Church*,** known as the National Cathedral of African Methodism by its followers, is a Victorian Gothic structure—a style popular in America in the 1880s. Completed in 1886, the building is known more for its importance to Black Washington as an influential church still prospering in central Washington than for its architectural style. The church is a Category II landmark listed in the National Register of Historic Places.

17 The Russians have outgrown this ornate **Embassy** on 16th Street, NW, and have built a huge complex on Wisconsin Avenue north of Georgetown. (Through a joint agreement, the U.S. is in the process of building a new embassy complex in Moscow.) Built in the 1920s as a home for the Pullman family, this structure was actually never occupied as a residence; it will remain as part of the Soviet complex.

18 Just to the north is the prestigious **University Club.** Formed in 1904 as a full-service private men's club, it has been in its present location since 1936. The existing building was designed by noted architect Harry Wardman in 1922 for the (now defunct) Washington Raquetclub.

19 The **Jefferson Hotel,** a small, quiet European-style hotel, offers visitors a pleasant and elegant contrast to the big convention hotel or chain motels. The lobby area is flanked by an interesting use of air shafts. A little-known restaurant within is a favorite of those who work in the area. Originally built as an apartment house and designed by Harry Wardman, the Jefferson has been a hotel for more than 40 years. It has been popular with artists and entertainers, including Victor Borge, Carol Channing, Vivien Leigh, and Van Cliburn.

20 Scott Circle is a good vantage point from which to view the **White House** (see Tour 4, The Mall—West). Together, the White House and the Washington Monument provide a teminal view to a great avenue—a typical feature of L'Enfant's city plan for Washington. North of Scott Circle, the street is lined with imposing churches, embassies, and mansions that rivaled the Massachusetts Avenue elegance during the early 20th century (see Tour 12, 16th Street/Meridian Hill).

21 The modern **National Geographic Society building** was designed by Edward Durell Stone in 1964. The first-floor **"Explorer's Hall"** museum is fascinating and worth a visit. The Society's original two-story structure on 16th Street, NW, was completed in 1903, with additions in 1914, 1916, and 1931. A new, third building, designed by Skidmore Owings and Merrill, lies between the two earlier structures.

22 The **Sumner School** (1872—Adolf Cluss) was one of the first public schools for blacks in the city and encompasses in its history a sense of the evolution of educational opportunity for blacks in the District of Columbia since the mid-19th century. Named for Charles Sumner, a major figure in the abolition movement, it has been nominated for the National Register of Historic Places.

23 The fanciful, rib-domed, brick edifice at the corner of Connecticut and Rhode Island avenues and M Street has been designated a Category III landmark status, protecting it from some of the strong development pressures near its site. The **Demonet Building** is the last of what once was a row of Victorian-style houses, constructed in 1880 by John Sherman, Jr., a local builder.

24 St. Matthew's Cathedral** (1899) is somewhat hidden by the large office buildings surrounding it, but good views of its dome are available from Scott Circle, the courtyard of the Iron Gate Restaurant off N Street, NW, and Jefferson Place. East of the cathedral is what remains of a row of elegant 19th-century townhouses that continued to 17th Street, NW. Half of the block was demolished to make room for the Metropolitan YMCA.

St. Matthew's Cathedral

25 N Street, NW**, between 17th and 18th streets, represents an almost contiguous block of beautiful 19th-century townhouses. The street retains its historic charm despite continual pressures for redevelopment to higher-density uses. This block is located in the Dupont Circle Historic District, which has been designated a Category II landmark and is on the National Register of Historic Places. This, plus a 1979 D.C. preservation law requiring an official review of demolition permits in the historic district, provides a limited measure of protection of this unique streetscape in Midtown.

26 The street contains two small European-style hotels. One of them, **Tabard Inn,** consists of three private residences built in 1860 and converted to a hotel in the 1920s. Edward Everett Hale wrote "The Man Without a Country" on the top floor in the 1860s.

27 Across the street from the Tabard Inn, tucked away in a courtyard, is an old stable turned into a restaurant—the **Iron Gate Inn*.** The stables were on the estate of Gen. Nelson A. Miles.

28 Dupont Circle** is Washington's largest circle park and one of its liveliest—at all hours of day and night. Located at the center of a cosmopolitan neighborhood, the Circle is surrounded by an area designated a historic district. The view from the Circle down busy Connecticut Avenue toward the White House is impressive (see Tour 13, Dupont Circle, for more information).

29 The **Euram Building*,** (21 Dupont Circle) was designed by a local firm, Hartman-Cox, and opened in 1970. This striking departure from the "Washington box" shows that imaginative design can be accomplished, even within a rigid zoning envelope. The inner courtyard is a pleasant surprise.

Euram Building

30 The Columbia Historical Society occupies the **Christian Heurich Mansion** (1892–94), a splendid example of Victorian architecture for which Washington is a treasure

Heurich House

house. Threatened by demolition to make way for an office building, a development-rights transfer was negotiated: the unused air space within the zoning envelope of the Heurich House site was sold to the adjacent site, permitting greater floor space in the office building. The proceeds of the sale are being used to restore and maintain the mansion and its properties, which include the park and small carriage house along Sunderland Place, as well as to support the scholarly activities of the society. An earlier home designed by Christian Heurich in 1887 is located diagonally across the street in a building now occupied by the Fleet Reserve Association.

31 The **Sunderland Building** (1969—Keyes, Lethbridge and Condon) is another example of good design possible within the confines of the city's height limit.

32 The Heurich Mansion and adjacent townhouses contain several small firms and professional offices. Notice how the **facades** of older structures along N street were retained in the new higher-density development.

33 Quiet **Jefferson Place, NW,** lined with 19th-century townhouses in office and retail use, frames a magnificent view of the dome of St. Matthew's Cathedral. As with many Dupont Circle area structures, the exteriors of several of its buildings are protected by voluntary conservation easements donated to the L'Enfant Trust.

34 An office building sports a **mirrored facade**—a mid-1970s building fad in D.C. More trivial: the building on the opposite corner is actually a multistory parking garage.

35 A walk along the south side of M Street, NW, toward Connecticut Avenue, leads you to the entrance courtyard of **1800 M Street,** a large office building opened in 1975. The ground level contains a shopping arcade and a landscaped open courtyard for dining and live music, relieving the monotony typical of many new office buildings in Washington.

36 Across the street, in a little triangular park, is a **statue of Henry Wadsworth Longfellow*.** Since 1909 he has gazed over his "neighborhood," which has completely changed from townhouses to high-rises.

37 A stroll down **Connecticut Avenue** will take you past some of Midtown Washington's most fashionable specialty shops and boutiques. Stop in to see the elegant marble promenade in the newly renovated Mayflower Hotel.

12/16th Street, NW, and Meridian Hill***

(elegant mansions, street of churches, active restoration area)

by Perry G. Fisher; 1983 update by John J. Protopappas

Distance: 1½ miles
Time: 2 hours
Bus: S2 and S4
Metro: Farragut North or Dupont Circle (Red Line)

Sixteenth Street, NW, is the most prominent of the numbered streets of Washington, and is laid out along the north-south center line of the White House, just slightly east of the central meridian of the District of Columbia. The impressive boulevard mounts a series of gentle terraces shaped in the glacial period. One of the highest terraces encircling the original City of Washington is that stretching across Meridian Hill and Mount Pleasant at an average elevation of about 200 feet; a terrace bisected by 16th Street in its route from Lafayette Square to Silver Spring, Maryland.

The lower 16th Street corridor and the Meridian Hill district occupy land that at the time of the establishment of Washington was part of three large estates stemming from 17th-century patents from Lord Baltimore. When L'Enfant submitted his plan for the City of Washington in July 1791, development in this section of the Territory of Columbia was rather typical of the tidewater region of the time. Minor plantation houses occupied the higher elevations overlooking the Potomac River. There were some widely scattered clusters of shacklike frame houses near the streambanks, which developed with the active milling enterprises along the large, swifter tributaries of the Potomac. Settlement was sparse despite a good deal of speculation and subdivision of land in expectation of a real estate boom to accompany the move of the federal government to Washington. However, most of 16th Street above K Street remained vacant throughout the first three-quarters of the 19th century. Before the Civil War, small cottages near M and 16th streets were built and occupied by semiskilled craftsmen and laborers. Many of these workers were black and were employed in the light-industrial and commercial business that depended on the streams flowing through the area.

Under the territorial form of government imposed upon the District of Columbia in 1871 and the ambitious public works programs of Alexander Robey Shepherd, executive officer of the Board of Public Works, the fortunes of 16th

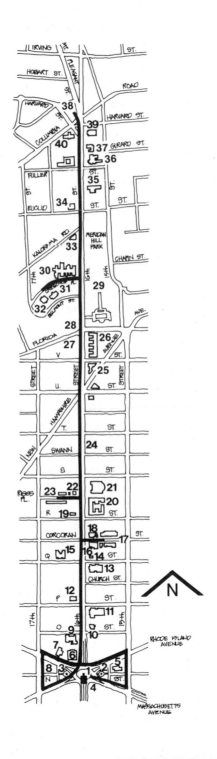

Street and Meridian Hill took a different direction. The foundations were laid for the impressive later development, which still sets the physical character of the street and district. Shepherd, as a successful local builder and real estate speculator, had a decided interest in the improvements of the West End of Washington. He began a program in the mid-1800s of deliberate cultivation of that section of the city as the most important residential and diplomatic quarter of the booming post-Civil War capital.

1 Scott Circle** (Massachusetts Avenue, Rhode Island Avenue, and 16th Street, NW) is one of the original federal reservations planned by L'Enfant, although Andrew Ellicott subsequently modified its configuration. It was not until the early 1870s that a park was laid out and an upper-class residential neighborhood developed. The park area has been eroded continuously until today there is no meaningful public gathering space in Scott Circle. The present chaos is a perfect illustration of the problems of adapting Washington's many multiple-street intersections to the demands of automobile traffic. The diagonal avenues and 16th Street are major commuting routes converging on this section of booming office construction. The automobile underpass along 16th Street was completed in 1942.

Scott Circle takes its name from the statue of Gen. Winfield Scott in the center of the space. The sculptor was Henry Kirk Brown and the figure was cast from a cannon captured in the Mexican War. The statue of Scott was first erected in 1874. (See Tour 11, Midtown, for more information on the area south of the Circle).

2 In the small triangular park just to the east is the interesting **Memorial to S.C.F. Hahnemann*** (1775–1843), founder of the homeopathic school of medicine. The memorial was designed by Charles Henry Neihaus and erected in 1900 by the American Institute of Homeopathy.

3 In the corresponding small triangular park just to the west of 16th Street is Gaetano Trentanove's **statue of Daniel Webster*** cast in bronze. The founder of the *Washington Post,* Stilson Hutchins, presented the statue to the city in 1900.

4 1500 Massachusetts Avenue Apartment House. This was the original **site of the Louise Home,** which was replaced by the present, bland apartment house in the early 1950s. The Louise Home was erected in 1871 through the generosity of William Wilson Corcoran, Washington banker, art patron, and philanthropist, as a refuge for "Protestant women of refinement and culture who have become reduced in circumstances in their old age."

5 1500 Rhode Island Avenue, NW—**National Paint and Coatings Association**.** The present 1912 exterior of this building is John Russell Pope's classical entombment for most of architect John Fraser's 1879 house for John T. Brodhead, wealthy Marine Corps officer from Detroit. In 1882 Brodhead sold the house to Gardiner Green Hubbard, founder of the National Geographic Society. Hubbard bought it for his daughter and son-in-law, Alexander Graham Bell, who lived there until 1889.

For an example of architect Fraser's great domestic commissions in Washington, one may still view the James G. Blaine mansion (1882) at 2000 Massachusetts Avenue, a building in all its essentials very much like the Brodhead-Bell mansion (see Tour 13, Dupont Circle). In 1889 Levi P. Morton, newly elected vice president, purchased the Rhode Island Avenue house.

6 1601 Massachusetts Avenue, NW—**Embassy of Australia Chancery*.** Built in 1965, this chancery firmly anchors Embassy Row at Scott Circle, despite the continuing move of embassies to the upper Northwest section of Washington. The undistinguished building by Australian architect Bates Smart McCutcheon is in no way an aesthetic contribution to an important crossroads. The Australian government recently doubled the size of the building to the rear, along 16th Street, after demolishing three fine row houses.

7 1619 Massachusetts Avenue, NW—The **Forest Industries Building*.**This is a much-praised work of the local architectural firm of Keyes, Lethbridge, and Condon. The order and polish, the dignified restraint in the use of materials, and the proportioning of the main blocks and elements of the facade have pleased both critics and laymen. A real understanding of the character of Washington and the design constraints it imposes is evident here.

8 The **vacant site** on the west side of Scott Circle, between Massachusetts Avenue and N Street, 17th Street, and Bataan Place, NW, awaits new construction. The distinctive turn-of-the-century row houses formerly on the site housed a long list of notable persons. But Scott Circle is an area that has been totally transformed in the years since the Second World War. The district is now overwhelmingly one of institutional and professional office uses.

A major factor in the changes that have taken place is the rezoning of the District of Columbia, which was prepared in 1954–56 by Harold M. Lewis of New York City, and which became effective May 12, 1958. (Dr. Lewis is now chairman of the District's zoning commission). Among the several zoning categories was the Special Purpose Category, a classification that has had particular importance for areas like Scott and Dupont circles, 16th Street, and the major diagonal avenues. The intent of the Special Purpose Zoning District was to stabilize areas of special architectural, historical, or functional character adjacent to districts of high-intensity commercial or Central Business District supporting uses. The conversion of existing buildings to chancery, nonprofit organization, or professional office use is a matter of right within an S–P zone, and this provision has resulted in the conversion of many former residences to handsome adaptive uses. However, within an S–P zone, a new hotel or apartment house of a height of 90 feet is also a matter of right. Construction of new 90-foot-high office buildings for chancery, nonprofit organization, or professional use requires the approval of the Board of Zoning Adjustment of the District of Columbia, and the board has been willing to grant such variances all too often. The result has been a continual erosion of row-house districts in Washington. The potential preservation benefits of Special Purpose Zoning are rarely realized.

9 Southwest corner of 16th and O streets, NW—**First Baptist Church.** This church building was designed in a pseudo-Gothic style in 1955 by Philadelphia architect Harold Waggoner. However, a different-style church once occupied the site. In 1890 architect W. Bruce Gray designed a red brick and sandstone church that combined Romanesque and Italian Renaissance styles. An impressive campanile, flanking the main church on the north, reached a height of 140 feet. A magnificent arched recess sheltered the main entrance to the building.

The First Baptist Church building of 1890 marks the period when many downtown congregations sought new sites in the developing 16th Street and Dupont Circle areas for their church buildings, in an attempt to escape the increasing commercialism of the older parts of downtown Washington.

10 1401 16th Street, NW—Ingersoll and Bloch (former **Gurley House**). This is a fortunate case of adaptive use in a Special Purpose Zone. The house was built in 1888 as a residence and was designed by one of the builders, Samuel and Charles Edmonston. This firm was responsible for the construction of two 16th Street houses designed by H. H. Richardson. The Edmonstons borrowed heavily from Richardson in their plans for the house, which has recently been put to use as law offices and the office of syndicated columnist Jack Anderson. Restoration costs proved cheaper than rental rates in newer speculative office buildings nearby.

11 Southeast corner of 16th and P streets, NW—**The Carnegie Institution*.** The Carnegie Institution is an internationally respected philanthropy devoted to research in natural science. The home of the institution is a rather uninspired beaux-arts design of the New York architectural firm of Carrere and Hastings. It was built in 1908 of Indiana limestone and the portico, at least, deserves some recognition for its impressive adaptation of the Ionic order and magnificent urns. It is an important structure, since it marks the spread of institutional uses to 16th Street in the early part of this century, and the growth of the scientific community in Washington.

12 Northwest corner of 16th and P streets, NW—**Foundry Methodist Episcopal Church*.** Foundry Methodist is from the period of 16th Street development in which the boulevard began to be referred to as the Street of Churches. Following the common pattern of wealthier congregations of the era, Foundry Methodist—founded by Georgetowner Henry Foxall, who operated the Foxall-Columbia Foundry on the Potomac—moved uptown from a downtown location. The present Foundry Methodist Church was built in 1903–4 on the plans of prolific and versatile Washington architect Appleton P. Clark, who was the man largely responsible for an important revision of the D.C. Building Code at the turn of the century.

Foundry Methodist has always been a socially active congregation, and has developed a wide variety of programs to serve the so-called "free community," that grew up in this area in the 1960s. It has worked well with the black population that increased dramatically in the post-World War II years. The congregation remains one of Washington's largest, even though most members actually live in the suburbs.

13 Southeast corner of 16th and Q streets, NW—**University of the District of Columbia Branch;** former **Jewish Community Center*.** It was quite an achievement in 1910 for the Jewish community in Washington (then centered in the old Southwest section) to be able to build an imposing building on 16th Street. The limestone structure—a work of B. Stanley Simmons—is in the classical manner, and perhaps its style and mass were inspired by the Carnegie Institution built two years earlier. The classical tradition was rarely employed in the design of the religious structures of Jewish people. The Jewish community in Washington has continued to move north in the District of Columbia and into the suburbs.

The University of the District of Columbia, which now occupies the building for one of its many temporary branches, is to be consolidated into a new campus. The future of the building at 16th and Q streets is uncertain.

14 1601 16th Street, NW—**C. C. Huntley House*.** This bracketed, stuccoed house is notable as one of the earliest examples of brick row houses on 16th Street and because its important stable building survives. The house was built in

C.C. Huntley House

1878 for C. C. Huntley, one of the principal owners of land along 16th Street.

15 1615 Q Street, NW—**The Cairo Hotel**.** This building was designed and built in 1894 by Thomas Franklin Schneider, who eventually built more than 2,000 structures in Washington, most in a very idiosyncratic interpretation of the Richardsonian Romanesque. Schneider here combines neo-Moorish and art nouveau elements in the facade of what is still the city's tallest nonmonumental building. Note especially the wonderful carved elephants.

The Cairo Hotel's 165 feet so shocked turn-of-the-century, row-house Washington that Congress imposed severe

Cairo Apartment House

height restrictions in 1910. The Cairo was opened as a first-class residential hotel, fell on hard times in the mid-20th century, and was restored as rental apartments in 1976. The sponsor of the restoration was the Georgetown Inland Corporation and the architect was Arthur Cotton Moore. Although the partial federal funding of the rehabilitation requires a percentage of low-moderate income apartments, only high-rent apartments were offered in the remodeled Cairo, a building located very close to the commercial core of Washington and in the center of an active restoration area. The structure was converted to condominiums in 1979.

16 Southeast corner of 16th and Corcoran streets, NW— **Church of the Holy City**.** Built as the Church of the New Jerusalem, and dedicated May 3, 1896, it is constructed of Bedford limestone, designed on the English perpendicular order, with a good deal of French Gothic influence. The gargoyles are worth a careful look. The tower is modeled after the one over the main entrance to the Magdalen College in Oxford, England. The architect of this fine church was H. Langford Warren, head of the Department of Architecture at Harvard University, and Paul Pelz of Washington was construction overseer.

17 The **1500 block of Corcoran Street, NW**,** immediately adjacent to the Church of the Holy City, is an interesting composite of late-19th-century domestic architectural styles in Washington row houses. A speculatively built "minor" street (originally an alley), Corcoran Street has been virtually totally restored within the last decade by young white professionals, reflecting the recent trend of black displacement from the row-house blocks near 16th Street.

18 1623 16th Street, NW—**Denman-Hinckley House*.** This is one of Washington's finer Romanesque revival houses and was built in 1886 for Judge H. P. Denman. The architects were Fuller and Wheeler of Albany, New York.

19 1601 R Street, NW—The Foxtrappe, former **Mulligan House*.** The house was built in 1911 for Navy officer Richard T. Mulligan and was designed by Jules Henri de Sibour, Washington's most gifted beaux-arts eclectic architect. The Mulligan House reflects the importance of the Georgian revival in the large-scale domestic architecture of early-20th century Washington. The building recently was converted to a somewhat elite black professional club—an interesting use for one of the many mansions along 16th Street looking for owners with ideas for adaptive uses.

20 1781 16th Street, NW—**The Chastleton Apartments.** The Chastleton opened in 1919 as an apartment hotel. It was built by Harry Wardman, the Britisher who came to the United States almost penniless in the 1890s and eventually built a Washington real estate empire. Wardman specialized in lavish apartment houses and luxury hotels, noted for the quality of materials and workmanship. It was Wardman who did much to introduce Washingtonians to apartment house living. The Chastleton, however, with its somewhat silly Gothic elements, is hardly noteworthy architecture.

21 1733 16th Street, NW—**Scottish Rite Temple***.** This is headquarters of the Supreme Council of the Southern Jurisdiction of the Thirty-third Degree of the Ancient and Accepted Scottish Rite of Freemasonry. The Scottish Rite Temple is one of the most architecturally significant buildings on lower 16th Street. John Russell Pope's design borrows from the famed Mausoleum of Halicarnassus. The cornerstone was laid in 1911 and the Temple was dedicated in 1915. The main space is beneath the ziggurat surmounting the Greek-temple base. Two sphinxes by A. A. Weimann flank the main entrance to the building and represent Divine Wisdom and Power. The symbolism of the Masonic order is displayed in many facets of the design. For example, the Ionic columns of the colonnade are 33 feet high, representing the thirty-third degree of Masonry. Despite the relation of architectural elements to the symbolism and work of the order, it is interesting that the Temple is but a version of Pope's design for the Lincoln Memorial site.

The wealthy Masons recently have angered the local community by using their tax-exempt status to aid in the purchase and demolition of much-needed residential units to the rear of the Temple building. The District of Columbia Council has introduced a controversial bill that would remove the real-property tax exemptions of organizations like the Masons, and thus partially prevent such city-destructive abuse of privilege.

22 1720 16th Street, NW—**Justice Brown House**.** The 1880s German Renaissance-style mansion of Associate Justice of the Supreme Court Henry B. Brown is a rare design in Washington. The wings and carriage house along adjoining Riggs Place are superb. Unfortunately, the buildings have not been kept up and have fallen into disrepair.

23 Riggs Place, NW**, one of Washington's more charming side streets, is largely a product of the speculative building activities of the 1890s. The stained glass and copper work of these modest row houses are worth noting.

24 Proceed north on 16th Street through an area that is a mixture of late-19th-century row houses and small early-20th-century apartment buildings. There is considerable deterioration of some of the properties in this vicinity, but considerable restoration as well.

Blocks to the east of 16th Street tend to house predominantly black population, while those to the west tend to be whiter and somewhat more affluent.

The 16th Street corridor in this area is zoned for medium-to high-density residential use (90 feet is the height limitation; 75 percent lot occupancy). Thus, from the realtor's standpoint, most of the existing structures are an underutilization of the land. At the present time there seems to be no intense developer interest in new high-rise residential construction along this stretch of 16th Street. The fact that the as yet unrebuilt 14th Street riot corridor is but two blocks to the east may be a factor in the static development situation.

As 16th Street crosses U Street, it enters the Meridian Hill district. The U Street intersection is poorly defined in terms of an architectural frame. Washington architect Chlothiel Woodard Smith has proposed raising the height limit at such key intersections to 25 stories in order to enhance the drama of entering the center of the city and to make a positive architectural statement more feasible where several very wide streets cross, as they do here.

25/26 2001 16th Street Apartment House and 2101 16th Street, NW, the **Roosevelt Hotel for Senior Citizens*.** These are two of Harry Wardman's mammoth residential buildings of about 1916. The Roosevelt was originally an apartment hotel for the well-to-do, but since the early 1960s has served as a home for senior citizens. Number 2001 has recently been renovated and sold as condominiums.

27 Florida Avenue, NW* (the original city limit of Boundary Street) marks the location of the Fall Line, which divides the older and harder Piedmont Plateau from the softer deposits of the Coastal Plain. Merchant and Mayor of Georgetown Robert Peter had assembled by 1760 a number of parts of a patent for land in this vicinity to form Mount Pleasant. His country farmhouse in the square bounded by 13th, 14th, W streets, and Florida Avenue, stood until the 1890s. Meridian Hill was originally referred to as Peter's Hill. In 1821 Columbian College (which grew into the George Washington University) built its first building on Meridian Hill, where it remained until moving to the downtown financial district in the 1870s. Another educational institution on Meridian Hill was the Wayland Seminary for the training of Negro Baptist preachers, which was built in the northeast corner of the present Meridian Hill Park in 1873.

The Meridian Hill area remained a combination of woodlots, orchards, and fields until after the Civil War. In 1867 Isaac Messmore subdivided Meridian Hill into building lots selling at 10 cents per square foot, but in those years there were few purchasers. Today land on 16th Street and Meridian Hill sells for an average price of $5 per square foot. Real estate values in this section of Washington peaked (with relation to the rest of the city) in the mid-20th century. In 1925, for example, so prestigious had the area become that the large houses on 16th Street itself sold for $250,000 and more. It was the extension of 16th Street north of Columbia Road along the true north-south line, and the bridging of Piney Branch Valley at the turn of the century, that prompted intensive development.

28 Northwest corner of 16th Street and Florida Avenue, NW—**Henderson Castle Tract**.** It was Mrs. Mary Henderson, wife of John B. Henderson (the Senator from Missouri who authored the Emancipation amendment and cast the deciding vote that saved Johnson from conviction in his impeachment trial) who began and maintained the cultivation of 16th Street as the premier residential and embassy boulevard of Washington from the late 1880s until her death in 1931. The Hendersons bought the tract in 1887 for about $31,000. The purchase was the first in what would be the eventual assembly by Mrs. Henderson of a real-estate holding of some 300 city lots in the Meridian Hill area. The wall is all that remains of the turreted, crenellated, red Seneca sandstone house built in 1888 and popularly known as Henderson Castle. J. E. Gardner was the architect of the pile and J. H. Lane the builder.

From her Meridian Hill tower Mary Henderson directed her architect, George Oakley Totten, in the upbuilding of 16th Street. She fought busses on the Avenue of the Presidents (she succeeded in having her street's name changed for one year) and Harry Wardman's apartment houses, which obstructed her view of the White House and degraded the capital city of villas. She also preached the evils of alcohol and oversaw the planning and partial construction of the great Meridian Hill Park opposite her home.

After many other plans and false starts, including proposals for a colony of homes for the elderly, the Henderson Castle tract has been developed into "colonial-style" townhouses in the $150,000 price range. The townhouse project has attracted the growing market of returnees from the suburbs and young couples already living in the city.

29 Meridian Hill Park***—east side of 16th Street between Florida Avenue and Euclid Street, NW. At the turn of the century, when the White House was in a bad state of repair, it was Meridian Hill that was seriously considered for a new presidential residence. Mrs. Henderson was one of the most vocal supporters of the movement. When it became clear that the presidential mansion would not be moved to Meridian Hill, Mrs. Henderson pressured Congress to buy the site for a public park. The purchase of the 12 acres that became Meridian Hill Park was authorized in 1910.

The park is one of the most important examples of formal garden design in the United States. Actual construction did not begin until 1917, and the lower part of the park was not opened until 1936. George Burnap was the original landscape architect and Horace W. Peaslee was responsible for the final plan and architectural design. The magnificent concrete work, in which aggregates were selected for varying sizes and colors, and the concrete was washed with muriatic acid quickly after it began to set in order to expose the aggregates, was begun as an experiment at Meridian Hill Park.

The use of massive retaining walls heightens the drama

of the natural topography. The upper two-thirds of the park is designed in the formal French manner with a large tapis vert bordered by promenades. The lower part of the park is inspired by the great Italian formal gardens of the 18th century. An artificial cascade of 13 waterfalls of graduated size, representing the location of the park on the Fall Line, is the principal feature of this section.

30 240 16th Street, NW—**Envoy Towers Apartments*.** The Envoy Towers opened in the early 20th century as Meridian Mansions, a very fashionable apartment hotel, and later acquired the name Hotel 2400. The enormous structure— some of the apartments of which have dining rooms that seat 24 people—changed hands a number of times in the early 1960s. After the 1968 riots, the District of Columbia leased much space in the building to house displaced victims of the 14th Street civil disturbances. The handsome structure's use as this kind of housing angered many of the nearby residents. Recently, it was totally renovated and turned into condominiums and rental units.

31 Crescent Place—White and Laughlin Houses**. On the high ridge between Belmont and Crescent places, opposite Meridian Hill Park, stand two of John Russell Pope's loveliest domestic commissions. Both repre-

Meridian House

sent departures from the usual ascetic classicism of Pope's work. **1624 Crescent Place, NW,** in something of a Georgian Revival mode, was built about 1912 for Henry White, ambassador to France, and was long the residence of Eugene Meyer, publisher of the *Washington Post*. The building, which takes such command of a fine site, is now part of the Antioch School of Law's Washington facilities.

32 1630 Crescent Place, NW, is a richly decorated limestone house in the manner of an 18th-century French pavilion. It was built for Irwin Laughlin, ambassador to Spain, in 1915. The manicured garden, with its beautiful canopy of pollarded trees, is a rare example of landscaping art. The house is now the Washington International Center.

33 2460 16th Street, NW—**Embassy of Ghana Chancery**.** This chancery was built through the joint efforts of Mrs. Henderson and her architect, George Oakley Totten. It was the first of 13 major mansions erected speculatively in order to attract embassies to Meridian Hill. Totten, adept beaux-arts architect though he was, never escapes the late Victorian exuberance, vitality, and curiosity that shaped his early career.

34 2600 16th Street, NW—**Inter-American Defense Board: The Pink Palace**.** A fanciful Venetian palace, built by the Henderson-Totten team in 1906, was first occupied by Oscar Straus, Theodore Roosevelt's Secretary of Commerce and Labor. Mrs. Marshall Field was another prominent occupant, and for a long time the pink stuccoed house was the headquarters of the District of Columbia Order of the Eastern Star.

35 2633 16th Street, NW—**Warder-Totten House**.** Originally constructed in the 1500 block of K Street for a prominent real estate developer, Benjamin Warder, the sandstone house is a product of H. H. Richardson's office. George Oakley Totten bought the shell of the house from the wrecker in 1902 and stored the parts of the building until he was able to reconstruct it as his own residence. The mansion makes a far better detached villa than part of a row-house block, which it originally was. The Warder-Totten House is now an element of Antioch College's Washington facilities.

36 2700 16th Street, NW—**former Embassy of Italy**.** Designed by the architects of Grand Central Station, Warren and Wetmore of New York City, 2700 16th Street is an especially fine adaptation of the Italian Renaissance palazzo. The interiors are rich in works of medieval Italian art and the walled garden to the rear is an elegant, formal outdoor space that creates the illusion of being in Italy.

37 2801 and 2829 16th Street, NW—**Embassy of Mexico**.** The former Spanish Embassy at 2801 16th Street was built for Mrs. Henderson and designed by George Oakley Totten in 1923. Mrs. Henderson had the mansion built in the hope that the federal government would purchase it as the official residence of the vice president.

2829 16th Street, the Mexican Embassy, was built in 1911 for Franklin MacVeagh, Taft's Secretary of the Treasury, by his wife as a Christmas present. The architect was Washington designer Nathan Wyeth. The Italianate house is one of the most elaborate in Washington and has perhaps the largest private dining room in the city: it will seat 250. The music room has an exact copy of the pipe organ at Fountainbleau. Beginning in 1934, Roberto Cuerva del Rio began his great series of murals within for the new owners, the Mexican government.

Together, these two great houses and the chancery buildings to the rear facing 15th Street form one of Washington's largest diplomatic complexes.

38 Harvard Square**—at the intersection of 16th Street, Columbia Road, and Harvard Street, NW—was originally planned as a circle in honor of Civil War hero Gen. George Meade. The pleasant landscaped area that actually developed just west of 16th Street is known, to however few, as Harvard Square. It was landscaped about 1915. Around the busy intersection are three important church buildings, erected during the years when the neighborhood was one of Washington's best residential neighborhoods. Columbia Road was here long before anything else manmade. It was an Indian route and later a post road to Georgetown from Baltimore.

39 Southeast corner of 16th and Harvard streets, NW—**All Souls' Unitarian Church**.** The architects of this skillful copy of James Gibbs's St. Martin's in the Fields, in London, were Coolidge and Shattuck of Boston. The church was constructed in 1924 at a cost of almost a million dollars.

Before the completion of the 16th Street church, the congregation was located downtown at 14th and L streets. Today the congregation is integrated and something of a status church among Washington blacks.

40 Southwest corner of 16th Street and Columbia Road, NW—**Mormon Washington Chapel**.** This is a very interesting architectural period piece designed by Ramm Hanson and Don Carlos Young of Salt Lake City, and completed in 1933. Young was the grandson of Brigham Young. Until September 1975, the Washington Mormons used the elegant Utah marble edifice for worship, but then decided to sell. A gleaming, gold-leaf-covered statue of the Angel Moroni, which rested atop the lovely spire until the Mormons vacated the building, was a landmark seen from all parts of Washington. The building is now a branch of the Unification Church.

13/**Dupont Circle*****
(mixed uses and historic preservation)

by Ruth Polan and Frederic Protopappas; original 1976
version by John Fondersmith

Distance: 2 miles
Time: 2 hours
Bus: 40,42,44,46,H-1 L-2, L-3, and L-9
Metro: Dupont Circle (Red Line)

Dupont Circle is a fascinating area offering a variety of
points of interest. It was the prestige neighborhood in
Washington at the turn of the century. The large mansions
built by the newly wealthy from across the country were a
reflection of Washington's increasing importance on the national and world scene. The mansions also reflect the
beaux-arts influence of the period and help give the neighborhood a special character. In addition to these great

houses are smaller townhouses and row houses along many streets, creating a more intimate scale.

With the stock market crash of 1929, Dupont Circle's fortunes began to decline, and by World War II the elegance and prestige that had been slowly diminishing virtually disappeared as the mansions were converted to boarding houses for government workers. When the war was over, society had changed: commercial interests were expanding and families were moving to the suburbs. This too was reflected in the Dupont Circle area as many proud old structures were razed to make way for modern office and apartment buildings. Other large townhouses were put to use as rental apartments.

Today Dupont Circle is an area in transition once again. Many large row houses and apartment buildings have been renovated and converted back to single-family homes or condominiums by people moving back into the city, again altering the demographic and economic balance. The area's accessibility to Metrorail contributes to pressures for very intense development. The major problem facing Dupont Circle now is how to retain historic quality, scale, vitality, and mix of residential and commercial activities while accommodating these pressures for more intensive land uses. The D.C. Office of Planning, in consultation with citizens and business people, is in the process of completing a neighborhood plan that will try to address these issues.

1 The tour begins at Connecticut and Florida avenues. (Until 1902 Florida Avenue was known as Boundary Street, because it formed the original northern boundary of the city of Washington.) **Connecticut Avenue** between Florida Avenue and Dupont Circle (as well as the block south of the Circle) has a bustling, cosmopolitan ambiance; its array of book stores, restaurants, cafés, antique stores, and other shops makes this one of the liveliest neighborhoods in the city. While many of the buildings along this stretch of Connecticut Avenue date from the late-19th or early-20th centuries, the zoning has allowed construction of such glaring incongruities as the 90-foot-high office building housing the Janus Theaters at 1666. Recently, however, the trend toward massive modern-style buildings has been modified. The D.C. Historic Preservation Office blocked the permit for an office building farther south on Connecticut Avenue, saying that "the primary standard must be that of the historic period."

2 The recently constructed building at **1718 Connecticut Avenue** demonstrates that it is possible to build attractive new buildings that do not clash with their surroundings. Designed by David Schwarz, it has been called the first really strong postmodernist building to go

1718 Connecticut Avenue

up in Washington. The facade features several interesting elements; the clock tower, gabled mansard roof, contrasting brick and limestone surfaces, and arched windows, all of which combine to create a modern structure that fits gracefully into its context.

3 Schwartz Drugstore, long a neighborhood institution, was stripped of its old-time soda shop atmosphere when its interior was renovated around 1980. Until then it was a congenial meeting place and popular hangout for Dupont Circle residents, street people, and assorted other regulars.

4 The corner of Connecticut Avenue and Hillyer Place is the site of **a new seven-story building** containing retail shops on the first floor and offices on the other six. Designed by GMR of Gaithersburg, Maryland, this structure features articulated stone entrances, window bays with keystones, and a cornice line with honed-down moldings; its style is thus architecturally consistent with its early 20th-century neighbors on the avenue. Its construction was the subject of much controversy and protest. The original design called for the structures on the site to be razed, including the building housing the historic Ben Bow (Ellen's Irish Pub), a popular neighborhood bar and gathering place. After months of petitioning and loud protesting, a compromise was reached: the facade of the Ben Bow was spared and is incorporated into the new structure. The bar itself, unfortunately, is gone.

Take time for a stroll down **Hillyer Place,** a short, quiet block lined with lovely trees and row houses.

5 The **row of buildings** on 20th Street between Q Street and Hillyer Place represents a successful effort at preservation of old structures. These turn-of-the-century townhouses are now occupied by offices, restaurants, and shops, and are an attractive feature of this part of the neighborhood.

6 On the southwest corner of 20th and Q streets, at 1520 20th Street, is the **Embassy of Colombia.** It was constructed around 1920 from a design by architect Jules Henri de Sibour, whose structures dot the Washington landscape. Built originally as a private residence, it was sold to the Colombian government in 1944. The house is designed in the style of a 16th–17th-century French country chateau. Its striking mixture of brick and limestone blocks on the facade and wrought iron and glass marquee above the entryway are among the features that make it an interesting contrast to the buildings around it.

7 Across from the embassy on Q Street is the northern entrance to the **Dupont Circle Metro station.** The precipitous descent through the circular entry into the station (this is the third deepest in the system, after Woodley Park/ Zoo and Rosslyn) makes this a dramatic highlight of Washington's Metro system for tourists and commuters alike.

8 At 2000 Massachusetts Avenue stands the **Blaine Mansion,** one of the oldest great houses to grace Dupont Circle. It was built in 1881 at a cost of $85,000 for James G. Blaine,

Blaine Mansion

one of the founders of the Republican Party and a three-time presidential candidate. Because it was originally designed for a different location, it seems somewhat misplaced on its present site. The dark-brick structure is an interesting combination of Victorian, Gothic, Romanesque, and Renaissance elements, with towers, seven chimneys, four skylights, and an elaborate covered carriage porch on Massachusetts Avenue.

9 Next to the Blaine Mansion at 2012 Massachusetts Avenue is the **Beale House,** a rather plain Renaissance revival house constructed in 1898. A similar building to the east was replaced by the modern headquarters of the American Home Economics Association, an only partially successful attempt to blend with its 19th-century neighboring buildings.

10 The **Indonesian Embassy,** the former **Walsh-McLean House** at 2020 Massachusetts Avenue, is one of Washington's truly great residences. It was designed in 1903 by architect Henry Anderson for Thomas F. Walsh whose wealth came from his discovery and development of one of the world's richest gold mines; it is rumored that a piece of gold from this mine is built into the foundation of the house. This ornate art nouveau mansion contains 60 rooms, some of which are the largest, most elaborate in Washington. Throughout its history, the house has been the scene of many lavish parties, attended by such notables as Alice Roosevelt Longworth and Admiral Dewey, among many others. Thomas Walsh's daughter, Evalyn Walsh McLean, who lived in the house until 1916, was the last private owner of the Hope Diamond. In 1951 the Indonesian government bought the mansion for $335,000 for use as its embassy. A modern addition to the old building has recently been completed so that offices can be moved out of the mansion itself. Set back from Massachusetts Avenue, the curving facade of the addition was designed to respect the undulating art nouveau exterior of the original structure. The back of the new portion, situated on P Street, affords a much more jarring view, consisting of a glass-and-brick box with a cylinder attached to one side.

11 Across Massachusetts Avenue, at 1600–1612 21st Street, is the gallery housing the **Phillips Collection,** one of the most outstanding private art collections in the United States. The original brownstone structure, built in 1897, was the home of Duncan Phillips, an avid collector of the contemporary art that now fills the rooms. The collection was opened to the public in 1918. The extension added in 1915, is stark and angular compared to the warmth of the old section.

12 To the west, at 2121 Massachusetts Avenue, is the **Cosmos Club,** one of the most prestigious clubs in Washington. The structure was built in 1901 for railway magnate Richard M. Townsend and his wife, who superstitiously insisted that it

be constructed around the shell of the home that formerly oc-
cuped this site.

13 Across the street, at 2118 Massachusetts Avenue, is the
Lars Anderson House, now the national headquarters of
the Society of the Cincinnati, an organization of descendants
of officers of the American Revolutionary Army. Constructed
in 1900, the beaux-arts residence was one of the largest and
costliest in the city, and is distinguished by its early-18th-
century English-style walled entrance court. The Society's
museum is open to the public.

14 The **Church of the Pilgrims,** on 23d Street, just south
of Massachusetts Avenue, is a landmark on the western edge
of the neighborhood. Across from the church in a triangular
park is an incongruous memorial to 19th century Ukrainian
national poet Taras Shevchenko. It consists of a modernistic
frieze next to a traditional statue of Shevchenko. The monument was erected in 1964 amid controversy as to the suit-
ability of a statue memorializing a Soviet national hero, but
its defenders see it as a tribute to oppressed people everywhere.

15 P Street west of Dupont Circle is an **active commercial strip** in the neighborhood, with many restaurants,
stores, art galleries, and other business establishments.
Many of the older buildings have given way to modern high-
rise apartments or hotels whose lower floors consist of commercial space, creating an architectural hodge-podge of this
busy street.

16 South of P Street, between 22d Street and New
Hampshire Avenue, are several **quiet, tree-lined blocks**
of older houses in varying stages of restoration and renovation. The residential character of this part of the neighborhood is a welcome respite from the high-rises and
commercial bustle of P Street and the large avenues.

17 Walk north on New Hampshire Avenue to **Dupont Circle.** In 1882 an act of Congress changed the Circle's name
from Pacific Circle (so called because it formed the western
edge of the city) to Dupont Circle, in honor of Civil War hero
Rear Admiral Samuel Francis Dupont. In 1884 a statue de-
picting Dupont riding a horse was erected here. Public dis-
satisfaction with this memorial, combined with the erosion of
its base, led to another congressional act in 1916 authorizing
its removal and the erection of a marble memorial fountain in
its place. Designed by Daniel Chester French (who also designed the statue of Lincoln in the Lincoln Memorial), the
fountain consists of three figures representing sea, stars, and
wind, traditional guardians of ships.

Over the years Dupont Circle has borne silent witness to
the social and political changes taking place around it. It is
frequently the starting point for political demonstrations and
marches, and on warm days it is filled with people splashing

in the fountain or relaxing on the benches around it. Permanent chess tables are located in the western part of the Circle and even on cold winter nights people congregate for spirited games.

Around the outside of the Circle are entrances, now closed and filled with debris, to tunnels once used by trolleys. The two tunnels, built in 1949 to relieve congestion on the busy streetcar line, have been closed since 1962, when the streetcars stopped operating. For a time they were used as fallout shelters. Now the District of Columbia government is soliciting plans for development of the tunnels, which are as wide as 26 feet in some sections, with 14-foot ceilings. Proposals that have been considered include a health and recreation club, a produce market, a retail mall with shops and restaurants, and a columbarium to house the ashes of the dead—an ironic suggestion since Dupont Circle is certainly one of the liveliest places in the city.

18 The **Hotel Dupont Plaza** is typical of a type of design, especially for apartments, that was popular after World War II. The hotel replaced the famous Leiter mansion, one of the most fabulous houses of the time, and was considered a notable example of modern architecture when it was built in 1949.

19 The Washington Club now owns the **Patterson House** at 15 Dupont Circle. This is one of only two mansions remaining on the Circle (the other is the Wadsworth residence, now Sulgrave Club—see below) and it was possibly the most flamboyant of them all. The original owner, Elinor Patterson, was a well-known socialite, journalist, and owner of the *Washington Times-Herald*. She used this house mostly for entertaining, which usually took the form of gala dinner parties. In 1927 Mrs. Patterson lent the house to President and Mrs. Coolidge while the White House was being refurbished, and they entertained the returning hero Charles Lindbergh there. Constructed in 1901–3, this building is an ornate example of neoclassical Italianate architecture. The face, of marble and glazed terra cotta, is replete with winged figures, fruit clusters, and other elaborate ornamentation. This unique structure gives the viewer some idea of what Dupont Circle must have been like in its heyday, before the encroachment of "redevelopment."

20 The **Embassy of Iraq,** formerly the Boardman House, at 1801 P Street, is considered one of the finest remaining Romanesque revival houses in the city. It was built in 1893 by Hornblower and Marshall.

21 The **Sulgrave Club,** at 1801 Massachusetts Avenue, occupies an entire block. One corner of the triangular building points to Dupont Circle, the back is on P Street, and the front is on Massachusetts Avenue; the building's unusual site was clearly an important factor in its design. It was built around 1900 as the residence of Herbert Wadsworth, and has been the home of the Sulgrave Club since 1933. This is one of the earliest beaux-arts mansions in the area, and features interesting terra cotta and cut-stone trim.

22 The National Trust for Historic Preservation now occupies the **former McCormick Apartments** at 1785 Massachusetts Avenue. Constructed in 1917, this monumental beaux-arts luxury apartment building originally contained six apartments, one on each floor, along with living space for 40 servants. It was considered the finest apartment building in the city, and was inhabited by numerous well-known personalities, including Secretary of the Treasury Andrew Mellon, who lived there while planning the National Gallery of Art. The building was declared a national historic landmark in 1977 when it was sold by the Brookings Institution to the Trust.

23 The **1700 block of Massachusetts Avenue** is a study in change. It is zoned "special purpose," a classification that allows for institutional buildings and apartments intended to serve as a buffer between the business district and residential areas.

24 The **Brookings Institution,** 1775 Massachusetts Avenue, is a noted national research center, but the building is architecturally undistinguished. Neighborhood residents often cite the Brookings building as a symbol of the kind of development they oppose. An addition to the present building, consisting of a mixture of commercial space on Massachusetts Avenue and residential space on P Street, has been proposed by Brookings. While its design is more in harmony with neighboring structures, this proposal has been received with mixed feelings by neighborhood conservation groups, who feel that it would constitute a dangerous commercial encroachment on a residential area. This is an excellent example of Metro-induced pressures on the residential character of this area.

25 The Moore Residence, at 1746 Massachusetts Avenue, is now occupied by the **Canadian Chancery.** Constructed in 1906–9 under commission of Clarence Moore (an investor who would later go down with the Titanic), this residence is considered to be one of the finest examples of Louis XV architecture in the city. Its granite exterior, wrought-iron bar grilles, and casement windows present an orderly and symmetrical appearance.

26 The section of **Massachusetts Avenue between 17th and 18th Streets** has been made part of a historic district. The buildings between the Canadian Chancery and the corner of 17th Street and Massachusetts Avenue exhibit a variety of architectural styles and periods that fit together harmoniously, unlike those across the street, which have little character and seem architecturally incongruous.

Located at 1724 Massachusetts Avenue, the headquarters of the **National Cable Television Association** is an example of a modern building that is nevertheless in keeping with its older neighbors. The southwest corner of 17th Street and Massachusetts Avenue is occupied by the **Chancery of Peru,** a classical Italian structure whose entrance faces the intersection.

27 Seventeenth Street, NW, between Massachusetts Avenue and S Street, is in a state of transition. Buildings long fallen into disrepair have been left empty in the expectation that development will turn them into small-scale retail shops and restaurants. Still other spots have already been restored and are useful additions to the area. Walking along this street one experiences a real feeling of community.

28 Church Street is another attractive block of townhouses. At 1742 is the **New Playwrights Theater,** which presents consistently fine productions of the work of young dramatists. Several of the houses on the west end of the block are used by small businesses and nonprofit organizations, yet the street retains its residential quality.

29 The **site of the original St. Thomas Episcopal Church** is now a park. The church, which was a splendid miniature Gothic cathedral, was destroyed by arson in 1970, but portions of the original altar and rear wall still stand at the back of the park. The congregation now attends services in a renovated parish house behind the original church. The carefully landscaped park is a popular gathering place for lunch-time picnics, summer sunbathing, and quiet contemplation. In the shadow of the destroyed altar, the park retains a churchlike atmosphere of peace and solitude.

30 The Weeks House, at 1526 New Hampshire Avenue, is now the home of the **Women's National Democratic Club.** Constructed in 1892, this turreted red brick house seems at the same time imposing and warmly inviting. It provides an interesting view to people waiting across the street for the L-2 bus. A totally incongruous modern wing has been added on the Q Street side, but is so inconspicuous that it does not have any negative effect on the character of the original structure.

31 The **row houses** on the 1700 block of Q Street provide us with an indication of popular residential architecture of the late 19th century. Built in 1889–92 and designed by Thomas Schneider (also designer of the Cairo Hotel—see Tour 12, 16th Street/Meridian Hill, no. 15), these stone houses are a lively mixture of different Victorian architectural features such as Richardsonian Romanesque arches, full turrets, and projecting bays. Each is different, yet taken together they form a coherent and unified whole.

32 The buildings on **Corcoran Street** were among the first in the neighborhood to be rehabilitated. Today this block is almost totally restored. Notice the care and attention to de-

SW corner of 17th and Q streets

tails reflected in the style and positioning of sculptures and reliefs in the houses on the south side of the street.

33 Occupying a triangular site at the intersection of 18th Street and New Hampshire Avenue is the mammoth **Belmont House,** one of the largest on this tour. It was built in 1909 from the design of E. Sanson and Horace Trumbauer (the designer of the Philadelphia Art Museum) by Perry Belmont, who was a U.S. congressman and minister to Spain at the time of the house's construction. Built in the Louis XVI style, it is massive and heavily ornamented, from the urns atop the eaves and the intricate wrought-iron balconies to the glass entrance doors. The Belmonts often held lavish parties in the exquisitely decorated rooms of this house. It was sold to the Order of the Eastern Star in 1935 and is the headquarters of that organization today.

34 From the corner of New Hampshire Avenue and R Street, walk west past the **Thomas Nelson Page House** at 1759 R Street. Built in 1897, it was designed in the Federal revival style by architect Stanford White. Farther west, between 18th and 19th streets, are the American Psychiatric Association and the International Student Center. Both of these buildings feature additions that were thoughtfully designed to blend with the character and scale of the original buildings.

35 The final stop on the tour is at the northeast corner of 20th and R streets. The restaurant Fourways is located in the **Fraser Mansion,** a registered historic landmark that has housed a string of restaurants and clubs since the 1930s. It is sometimes referred to as the Scott-Thropp House because it was incorrectly thought to have been built by Thomas A. Scott, Assistant Secretary of War under Abraham Lincoln. The Italian Renaissance mansion was actually built in 1898 by Hornblower and Marshall for New York merchant George S. Fraser. In 1901 Fraser's widow sold it to Scott's daughter, Miriam Thropp—hence the misnomer. Marshall was probably the designer of the spectacularly ornate interior, which has recently been restored to its original grandeur, complete with beautiful carved-wood panelling in many of the rooms.

14/**Shaw School Urban Renewal Area* and Logan Circle Historic District****

(new and historic structures—residential, commercial, and institutional)

by Thurlew Tibbs, Jr.;
original 1976 version by Audrey Parkinson

Distance: 2¼ miles
Time: 1¾ hours
Bus: 70 (7th Street/Georgia Avenue); 62 (Howard and Georgetown Universities–P Street)
Metro: Gallery Place (Red Line); transfer to 70 bus on 7th Street

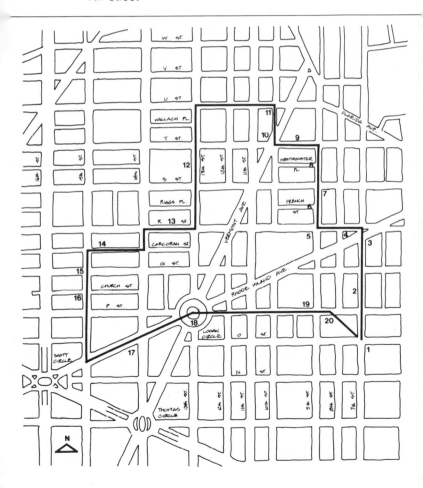

Shaw, located immediately north of Downtown, is a large part of the District's Model Cities Neighborhood. Largest of the urban-renewal areas in the city, with 675 acres of land, Shaw contains 33,000 residents.

The area derives its name from Shaw Junior High School, which became a symbol of the area's redevelopment through new construction in the 1960s and 1970s. New construction for both public facilities and private residences has been completed, along with a substantial number of rehabilitation projects—primarily involving the older red brick housing stock.

1 The tour begins at 7th and O streets, NW, scene of the 1968 civil disturbances along the 7th Street corridor. The Urban Renewal Plan for Shaw was adopted in 1969 to eliminate blight and renew and rehabilitate housing for low and moderate-income families.

The 10-story, 137-unit **Immaculate Conception Apartment Building,** designed by Bryant & Bryant, was sponsored by the Immaculate Conception Community Partnership. This was the first limited dividend partnership to sponsor housing in Shaw. Twenty percent of the units are under the Rent Supplement Program. **Gibson Plaza,** a 10-story, 217-unit building, was sponsored by the nearby First Rising Mount Zion Baptist Church. The open space, with trees and benches adjacent to the building, is used by residents. The **John F. Kennedy Adventure Playground** was one of the first projects in the area. Children use the park on Sundays when they climb and swing on the large replicas of a space ship and bus. The small size of the park and the blacktop surface of the playground leave much to be desired as a place for children to play. The Recreation Department of the District of Columbia runs the playground. The **O Street Market*,** built in 1886, has been designated a Category III landmark worthy of preservation. Its restoration was completed in early 1980. A visitor to the market will find delicacies, fruits, vegetables, fish, and poultry displayed in stalls, while lazy ceiling fans stir the rich aromas.

2 The **Samuel Kelsey Garden Apartments** offer a more intimate scale to the housing built in the area. Sponsored by the Deliverance Church of God in Christ and financed under Section 236 of the Housing Act of 1968, this housing is for families with moderate incomes.

3 The **Old Shaw Junior High School,** at 7th Street and Rhode Island Avenue, NW, has recently been renovated into housing for the elderly, under the sponsorship of Asbury Church, and renamed the Asbury Dwellings. Rehabilitation of older buildings such as this one is more commonplace in Shaw today. It is particularly satisfying to see an underused public structure given new life.

O Street Market

4 Named for Watha T. Daniel, civic leader and first chairman of the D.C. Model Cities Commission, this **library*,** the first in the Shaw area, was dedicated in September 1975. The design complements the triangular site and it deserves a look inside.

5 The new **Shaw Junior High School**** represents years of active citizen participation in the decision-making process. "Shameful Shaw," as the old school was known, was a central issue in the area long before the civil disturbances of 1968. The present site was selected after consideration of the number of households, buildings, nonresidential establishments, and owner-occupied houses required to be removed in clearing the site. Building the Shaw Junior High School was the uniting factor in the Shaw School Urban Renewal Area. This accomplishment represents a continued interest and involvement of many area residents.

6/8 An increasing emphasis on home ownership for low- and moderate-income families is evident in Shaw. Neighborhood conservation and stabilization has been partially realized in the **French-Westminster Area*.** Houses in this four-block section have been rehabilitated and sold to individual owners, as well as to the National Capital Housing Authority under the Section 235 program for moderate- and low-income families. The character of the area has been enhanced by new brick sidewalks, fencing, and street paving.

7 The new **New Bethel Baptist Church,** at 9th and S streets, is the home church of the Reverend Walter Fauntroy, D.C. delegate to Congress. This structure, along with the ad jacent high- and low-rise mixed-use development, is a church-sponsored project intended to revitalize the area.

9 The four new townhouses located in the 900 block of T Street, NW, amid older structures, have solar panels as part of their building technology—a first for the Shaw area.

10 The **Evans-Tibbs House,** located at 1910 Vermont Avenue, NW, is a historic landmark that houses an extensive collection of Afro-American art, as well as materials on the development of Washington. The hours are by appointment and can be arranged by calling (202) 234–8164. The structure was the home of pioneer educator Wilson Bruce Evans and his daughter, opera and civic leader Lillian Evans (Evans-Tibbs).

11 The **Masonic Temple,** erected in 1921–22, was part of a group of substantial commercial structures then rising along U Street to form the financial and social hub of Washington's Afro-American community. Other important structures along this corridor include the Bohemian Caverns, a famous jazz spot of the 1940s and 50s, and the industrial bank— both at 11th Street. The Lincoln Theater, near 13th Street, has been the site of many famous concerts.

12/13/14/15 Homes along 13th, R, Corcoran, and 15th streets point to the **rich architectural heritage** of the Shaw area and are the finest examples of molded-brick construction in the city.

16 St. Luke's Church was designed by John Langford in the 1880s and is a historic landmark housing one of the city's oldest Afro-American Episcopal congregations.

17 The cityscape along Rhode Island Avenue between 15th and 13th streets shows the **diversity of building scales** where pressures for high-rise apartments and, in particular, hotel developments are in direct competition for land on which housing already exists.

18 The **Logan Circle Historic District**** is a unique assemblage of 132 Victorian buildings. The importance of this district has been recognized by both federal and local governments. The Logan Circle Historic District is now listed on the National Register of Historic Places. A basic part of the original L'Enfant geometry for the city, the Circle, is a Category I landmark on the National Capital Committee of Landmarks list. The district itself is a Category II landmark and the statue of **Gen. John A. Logan*** is Category III.

By the late 1880s most of the houses now standing in the Logan Circle area had been built, and the neighborhood had become a racially mixed group of professionals and middle-class business people. Today, a third of the buildings in the Logan Circle Historic District have been designated for rehabilitation, and these private restoration efforts are expected to bring medium- and high-income residents into the district. The rehabilitated building at 1318 Vermont Avenue,

Logan Circle row houses

NW, housing the National Council of Negro Women, serves as headquarters for the **Bethune Museum.**

19 The **Shiloh Baptist Church** and **Family Life Center** at 9th and P streets offers a broad range of social services in a recently dedicated building that adjoins the beautifully restored 100-year-old church structure.

20 The new Giant store adjacent to the historic O Street Market provides the area with the largest food-chain store in the renewal area. Originally in partnership with the city, the Shaw development project successfully satisfies that partnership through liberal financial and careful market planning.

The Other Washington

15/**Kalorama** ***
(embassies, beaux-arts mansions)

by Perry G. Fisher; 1983 update by John J. Protopappas

Distance: 1½ miles
Time: 1½ hours
Bus: N2, N4, or D2, D4, D8 on Q Street
Metro: Dupont Circle (Red Line); transfer to above bus
routes or walk to Sheridan Circle

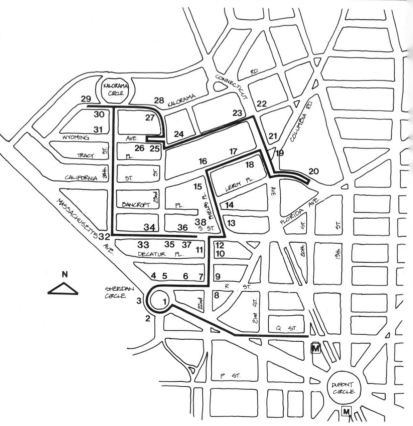

Kalorama is the center of the foreign diplomatic community and contains one of the finest collections of beaux-arts-inspired mansions in the United States. Handsomely developed, richly treed, and topographically varied, Kalorama is a pleasant island of quiet urbanity near central Washington.

For almost a century after the founding of Washington, D.C., much of the elegant district was part of a large estate of great natural beauty. Superbly sited, the estate looked out over the Potomac, northern Virginia, and the infant capital city. The estate bore the same name as the modern neighborhood, and was noted for its fine manor house, which stood until 1888. Kalorama was carved out of the widow's mite, a colonial patent of approximately 660 acres granted in 1664 to John Langworth by Lord Baltimore.

Kalorama, well known for the concentration of embassies and chanceries in its large mansions, is a phenomenon of the early-20th-century expansion of Washington. Its evolution into a beautiful and sophisticated neighborhood is closely related to several important developments: the termination in 1890 of the distinction between the City of Washington and the County of Washington (i.e., the area of the District of Columbia outside Florida Avenue); the extension of Massachusetts Avenue beyond Florida Avenue in the same period; the new bridges across Rock Creek; the commitment made in 1890 to preserve the Rock Creek Valley as a scenic and recreational resource; the proximity of Kalorama to established wealthy neighborhoods like Dupont Circle; and the filling up of older portions of the city in the dynamic post-Civil War years.

From the outset, it was intended that Kalorama become a prime residential area. Intelligent and aggressive real estate promotion, very attractive building sites, and the astounding growth of the colony of wealthy people in Washington who wanted the most fashionable town residences, made Kalorama. These developments provided an opportunity for architects working in the beaux-arts influenced styles of the general classical revival period following the Chicago World's Columbian Exposition of 1893.

1 Sheridan Circle*** (Massachusetts Avenue at 23d Street, NW). In November 1886 the Commissioners of the District of Columbia held public hearings to discuss plans for the extension of Massachusetts Avenue and a circle in honor of Stephen Decatur. The widow of George Lovett, last private owner of the Kalorama estate, protested the proposed improvements affecting her property. However, a New York real estate firm paid the Lovett heirs $354,000 for the remaining 60 acres of the estate. At $5,900 an acre (in 1887!), subsequent development by owners of the planned Kalorama Heights subdivision had to be either for a very wealthy population or for a very high-density population. It is clear to anyone standing in Sheridan Circle today that the former type of development turned out to be the actual case.

Decatur Circle became Sheridan Circle in 1890, when the Officers of the Army of the Cumberland received authorization to commission a statue of Gen. Philip H. Sheridan,

Civil War hero who died in 1888. Gutzon Borglum (sculptor of Mount Rushmore) was commissioned, and the model of his equestrian statue of Sheridan was accepted in January 1908. The statue was erected the following year. In the past, the statue has been compared to a traffic cop stuck in mud, but the harshness of critical opinion of the work has lessened since. Mrs. Sheridan, of course, loved it instantly, and in fact had built 2211 Massachusetts Avenue in 1905 in order to be close.

Sheridan Circle is perhaps the only one of Washington's circles that has maintained its grand residential character. It was the earliest part of the Kalorama neighborhood to develop and the Circle was a natural focus for neighborhood growth. Sheridan Circle is enclosed by a group of marvelous early-20th-century mansions whose mass, detailing, and styles are appropriate to the wide, baroque boulevards of L'Enfant's original plan for the capital city.

A number of foreign embassies are now located in these buildings. Around the circle one can see the Greek, Korean, Rumanian, and Turkish embassies as well as a number of others.

2 The Alice Pike Barney Studio House**, at 2306 Massachusetts Avenue, NW, is now owned by the Smithsonian Institution, and is next to the Korean Embassy (on the right). It was built in 1903 by Alice Pike Barney, a wealthy playwright and painter, for her many artistic pursuits and informal entertainments. The wonderful house, influenced by the mission style of architecture, was designed by Waddy Butler Wood of Washington. It includes studio and stage facilities and an interesting collection of 17th-century Spanish furniture. The Barrymores, Caruso, and James Whistler were among those Alice Barney entertained here.

3 The **Edward H. Everett House,** now the **Embassy of the Republic of Turkey**,** is located at 1606 23d Street, NW. It was built by Edward H. Everett, a multimillionaire cap-

Turkish Embassy

italist-industrialist. Much of his fortune was the result of his patenting of the modern fluted bottlecap. The architect of the Everett mansion was George Oakley Totten, Jr. Begun in 1910, the house was not completed until 1915. As in so many of Totten's buildings, classical details are combined in a totally personal and idiosyncratic manner. Totten was too aware of architectural developments in America to remain uninfluenced by the pioneering work of Midwestern and California architects that was contemporary with the full-blown beaux-arts. This native influence shows in features like the trellised roof garden on the Q Street side of the house. Similarly, the impact of Totten's time in Turkey shows in such features as the elaborate interior carving. It is hardly surprising that the Turkish government admired this house and has occupied it since late 1932.

4 The **U. A. R. Interests Section of the Egyptian Embassy** is located at 2301 Massachusetts Avenue, NW, in the **Lieutenant Joseph Beale House**.** The gently curved facade of this magnificent 18th-century Italy-inspired palazzo contributes a beautiful transition from R Street to Massachusetts Avenue. The architect of the detached house was Glenn Brown, who from 1899 to 1913 was Secretary of the American Institute of Architects. The austerity of the exterior of the limestone and stucco mansion is not matched within. Instead, the interiors display some of the most remarkable and elaborate plaster work of any Washington building still standing.

In 1928 Egypt acquired the Beale House for its ambassadorial residence. The house now serves as the home of the ambassador of the United Arab Republic.

5 The **Embassy of the Philippines,** at 2253 R Street, NW, is located in the **Gen. Charles Fitzhugh Residence** (1904). The scale of the building is somewhat smaller than most of the houses around Sheridan Circle, but the Fitzhugh residence holds its important position by clarity of form, plain surfaces, clearly articulated openings and basic horizontality. Waddy Butler Wood, the architect, used strong Mediterranean and even Wrightian influences; the unusual use of segmentally arched windows under the eaves is a typical Wood curiosity.

6 Of the **row of three houses** at 2225, 2223, and 2221 R Street, NW**, the central building was first constructed. It was built in 1904 for Alice Pike Barney, who just a year earlier had opened her studio house on Sheridan Circle. In 1931 Chief Justice of the Supreme Court Charles Evans Hughes purchased the house and lived there until his death in 1948. The government of Burma has been the owner since. George Oakley Totten, Jr., was the architect of all three dwellings in the group. The smaller houses flanking the Barney residence were constructed in 1909. They are stuccoed, and in general harmonize well with the Fitzhugh residence just down the street. The repeating porte-cocheres add great charm to the street.

7 The **Gardner Frederick Williams House****, now the **Embassy of Pakistan Army, Navy, and Air Attachés Office,** is located at 2201 R Street, NW. This imposing, straightforward, clean-lined house was built in 1906–7 for Gardner Frederick Williams, a mining engineer who had been associated with Cecil Rhodes in Africa. George Oakley Totten was the architect. The house was once known for its lovely garden along R Street, but today the entire garden and virtually all of the surrounding property are given over to diplomatic parking. The site is an eyesore. In recent years, the citizens of Kalorama have consistently fought the continuing spread of embassy office uses to Kalorama, because the problems of traffic and parking in the area's narrow streets are insurmountable.

8 The **Palmer House,** at 2132 R Street, NW, is a handsome Georgian row house, and was the home of A. Mitchell Palmer while he served as Wilson's Attorney General. Palmer was one of the chief figures in the "Red Scare" paranoia that swept the country after World War I; he saw Communists everywhere. On June 2, 1919, an unidentified terrorist tossed a bomb into the Palmer home and in the process destroyed himself. Palmer was in the house at the time, but was uninjured. Police presence in quiet Kalorama has been notable ever since.

9 The **Franklin D. Roosevelt Residence,** now the **Embassy of Mali,** at 2131 R Street, NW, is where Franklin Roosevelt lived from 1917 to 1920, while serving as Assistant Secretary of the Navy. The house has 17 rooms and 6½ baths, and was well-suited to the needs of the growing Roosevelt family. Now painted an inappropriate mustard color, the house serves as the residence of the Ambassador of Mali.

10 In 1906 wealthy Boston spinster Martha Codman built her magnificent Washington home at 2145 Decatur Place, NW. The designer was New York society architect Ogden Codman, a relative of hers. The **Codman House** is especially attractive because of its cherry-red brick and beautifully dressed stone. Although 18th-century England is the architectural inspiration, the approach to the house reminds one of a Parisian hotel. The superb garden terraces and the block of the mansion itself act as massive retaining walls for the Decatur Terrace slopes. The Codman House became the Louise Home in about 1950, when the original Louise Home for poor but genteel Southern Protestant ladies was demolished to make way for the apartment house at 1500 Massachusetts Avenue, NW.

11 Designed and constructed by the Office of Public Buildings and Grounds in 1911–12, the delightful **Decatur Terrace Steps and Fountain**,** at 22d Street between

Decatur Place and S Street, NW, solved the problem of linking Decatur Place with much higher S Street, and did so in favor of the pedestrian. It is a rare occurrence in an American city when a street becomes a staircase, and Washington's example is unknown to many residents.

12 The home located at 1743 22d Street, NW, was built in 1904–5 for **Charles D. Walcott,** Secretary of the Smithsonian Institution and an active real estate promoter in northern Washington. The architect was George Oakley Totten, in partnership with Laussat Rogers. The house has been modified and altered, but was originally a beautiful Italianate-mission-style home that took command of its fine site.

13 Closer to Connecticut Avenue, the character of Kalorama changes. As early as 1873, streetcars ran along Connecticut Avenue from 17th Street to Florida Avenue. In the blocks of Kalorama adjacent to this major diagonal avenue of L'Enfant's plan, one notices speculative row house development typical of a streetcar suburb; 1801–1809 **Phelps Place** is a good example of the pattern. The row was built in 1896 by William Alexander Kimmel, an active speculator and building contractor responsible for 17 Washington churches in addition to countless houses. Most of the Phelps Place buildings now serve foundation or educational purposes. The row houses of the nearby blocks of S Street near Connecticut Avenue, Bancroft and Leroy Places have long been popular with government officials. There was an especially heavy concentration of prominent New Deal personalities in this section of Kalorama. Most of the pleasant row houses in this favored district were built between 1900 and 1915.

14 The **Conrad Miller Residence*,** now the **Office of the USSR Agricultural Counsellor,** is located at 1823 Phelps Place, NW. It was designed by Washington architect Thomas Franklin Schneider for Conrad Miller, celebrated lecturer and publisher, and his wife, Anna Jenness Miller, author and lecturer. It was constructed in 1896–7 and displays all of Schneider's full-blown mannerisms.

15 At the southwest corner of Phelps Place and California Street, NW, is the **St. Rose's Industrial School,** now the **Mackin Catholic High School for Boys*.** Organized originally in a downtown location in 1872, St. Rose's Industrial School (for the training of orphan girls in home economics and "feminine" manual arts) was built in about 1904 in what was then open country. Later the building became the St. Ann's Infant Asylum. In the 1960s it was the Cathedral Latin School, and today is the Mackin Catholic High School, whose enrollment is mostly black and nonresident in this section of Washington. The impressive Roman brick and brownstone structure is one of the few buildings in Kalorama not intended as a residence. A structure of this size would not be permitted in the area if built today.

16 The **2100 and 2200 blocks of California Street, NW***. At California Street, Connecticut Avenue, and Columbia Road is the only concentration of large apartment houses in the Kalorama district. At the turn of the century the heights above Florida Avenue attracted massive apartment house development, which aroused the ire of many residents who felt that such structures were alien to the character of the city.

In the 1960s these enormous buildings—some of which had been neglected and overcrowded during the war years—received the overflow of the nearby Spanish-speaking immigrant population. Some of the structures continued to deteriorate, but in recent years condominium conversion, and the attraction of the large, well-built apartments for young professionals able to pay higher rents, have resulted in the removal of a good portion of the Latino population.

17 Typical of the grander apartment houses of about 1905, **California House,** located at 2205 California Street, NW, has very large, handsomely appointed apartments. Justice Louis Brandeis resided here for many years.

18 The **Westmoreland Apartment,** at 2122 California Street, NW, was built in 1905. It is a fine example of Washington's "apartment-house baroque" architecture.

19 Connecticut Avenue and Columbia Road, NW—**equestrian statue of Maj. Gen. George B. McClellan.** The completely personality-less bronze statue of the commander of the Army of the Potomac was designed by Frederick MacMonnies in 1907 and rests on a base designed by James Crocroft. MacMonnies had attracted worldwide attention and praise with his sculpture for the World's Columbia Exposition in 1893, but so had some atrocious architecture at the same fair.

From the vantage point of the Lothrop house site (see no. 21, below), one can imagine what a wonderful view the early houses on Kalorama Heights must have had. The commanding view from Kalorama was possible until the development of the Washington Hilton Hotel site across Columbia Road from the Lothrop mansion.

20 At Columbia Road and T Street, NW, is located the **Washington Hilton Hotel-Universal Office Building.** The large tract of land occupied by the Washington Hilton Hotel and large office buildings directly south was long called Oak Lawn, after the huge and ancient oak tree that stood there. In the 1920s the site was proposed to accommodate a National Masonic Memorial, which resulted in the submission of an interesting scheme by Frank Lloyd Wright. If constructed, this would have been a far better work of architecture and site design than the hideous, gleaming Washington Hilton Hotel. The erection of the hotel in the early 1960s totally upset the fabric of this neighborhood.

21 At the northeast corner of Connecticut Avenue and Cal-

Alvin Mason Lothrop House

ifornia Street, NW, is the **Alvin Mason Lothrop House**,** now part of the **USSR Embassy Complex.** This 40-room, Italianate, limestone mansion was built in 1901 for Alvin Mason Lothrop, partner in the dry-goods firm of Woodward and Lothrop (now Washington's largest department store). The architects were Joseph Hornblower and James Rush Marshall.

22 Of all the mammoth luxury apartment buildings erected on this stretch of Connecticut Avenue in the early 20th century, the **2101 Apartments**** is perhaps the most impressive. Built in 1928 by the same firm that built the Shoreham Hotel, it has only 66 apartments. All have at least seven rooms with three baths and three exposures. Of special interest are the sculptured parrot gargoyles and lion's-head medallions above the entrance portals. On the roof are eight atlantes. Some of Washington's most prominent people have long been housed here. In its art deco decorative flair and in its excess of elegant spaciousness, the building might be considered the last gasp of the truly lavish and significant phase in grand apartment-house construction in Washington. Just compare it to Watergate, for example—a recently constructed "luxury" apartment building.

23 The **Mortimer J. Lawrence House**** (1907), at 2131 Wyoming Avenue, NW, was built for Mortimer J. Lawrence, the publisher of *The Ohio Farmer, The Michigan Farm-*

er, and *The Pennsylvania Farmer.* He was a Cleveland bank president as well. The house was Lawrence's wedding gift to his bride, Carrie Snyder. Both were infatuated with Italy and had their architect, Waddy Wood, model the house after a Tuscan villa. Throughout, there is fine marble and mosaic work; barely a surface, interior or exterior, is wood. Note the beautiful copper soffiting.

24 Now part of the **UAR Embassy complex,** the **William Howard Taft House**** was the home of ex-President Taft from the time he returned to Washington as Chief Justice of the Supreme Court, in 1921, until his death in 1930. Mrs. Taft lived on in the house until her death in 1944. Taft purchased the large, Georgian revival-style house from Massachusetts Congressman Alvin Fuller. The building was constructed about 1904.

25 The **Anthony Francis Lucas Residence**,** now the **Embassy of Zambia,** is located at 2300 Wyoming Avenue, NW. The cost of this delightfully pretentious house at the time of its construction in 1913 was an incredible $20,-000. The architect was Clark Waggaman, a local resident, who during his short career specialized in large suburban homes for the wealthy. Undoubtedly, this house is one of the most unusual in the city—so closely is it tied to the products of Italian mannerism, particularly the work of an architect like Giulio Romano. The most important space in the building is the two-story room behind the loggia on 23d Street. It is roofed with groin vaults and splendidly articulated. The dining room is noteworthy for its richly carved oak paneling.

26 The **Warren G. Harding Residence*,** at 2314 Wyoming Avenue, NW, is where Harding lived as senator from Ohio from 1917 until becoming President in 1921. The house is more important for its historical than for its architectural values. However, the use of a side entry is unusual in Washington, and the interesting use of classical elements and overall sculptural quality make the building more intriguing than a first glance might acknowledge.

27 The **Royal Thai Legation*,** at 2300 Kalorama Road, NW, is one of the few Kalorama buildings built for a foreign mission. The Royal Thai Legation dates from about 1915. Note the Eastern symbolism incorporated in the concrete work: for example, the garudas (mythological bird that was the vehicle of Vishnu) atop the pilasters of the Kalorama Road facade.

28 The **W. W. Lawrence House***** is now the **Embassy of France.** Located at 2221 Kalorama Road, NW, it occupies a dramatic and beautiful site high above Rock Creek, and is the largest house in Kalorama. It was built in 1911 for W. W. Lawrence, whose fortune was in mining. The government of France purchased the house in January 1936 for about $400,000, including furnishings and household equipment. The Kalorama Road mansion has served as the residence of the French ambassador ever since.

The architect of the splendid Tudor house was Jules Henri de Sibour, born in France in 1872 but raised in the United States. De Sibour, who studied architecture at the Ecole des Beaux-Arts, had an extremely successful Washington career. He worked most often in eclectic borrowings from French classicism, and thus, the house for W. W. Lawrence marks an unusual venture into the Tudor country manor house heritage. The mansion is actually perfectly symmetrical, but creates the impression of a rambling asymmetry, because it is impossible to approach head-on from any of the surrounding streets.

29 The Lindens*—2401 Kalorama Road, NW. The section of Kalorama west of the French Embassy dates entirely from the period since 1925. Kalorama Circle is unusual among the circles of Washington in that it was planned for development, rather than as a public park. None of the houses on the Circle is especially good architecture, but the overall quality of development, the superb **views across Rock Creek Park,** and the cut-off, quiet character of the neighborhood keep this one of the city's most expensive and

The Lindens

prestigious sections. By way of comparison over time, the two charming Tudor, or Norman, stone houses at 33 and 29 Kalorama Circle were designed by Horace Peaslee and built in 1926 for Leslie F. R. Prince for a combined price of $45,000. And the decade of the 1920s was a period of extreme inflation!

In this neighborhood of recreated historical styles, the Lindens is an example of the real thing—or almost. The Georgian house was actually built in 1754 in Danvers, Massachusetts, for Marblehead merchant Robert Hooper. The Lindens served as the summer home of Thomas Gage, the last royal governor of Massachusetts, and for this reason is sometimes known as the Gage House. The Robert Hooper mansion was moved to Washington by Mr. and Mrs. George Maurice Morris in 1936. At the time, they were searching for a suitable home for their antiques, and by acquiring the Lindens, the Morris's spared the house from planned destruction. Walter Macomber, resident architect of Williamsburg, directed the disassembly of the building, which was carried out by Williamsburg workmen.

30/31 The **Devore and Stewart Residences**,** 2030 and 2000 24th Street, NW, respectively, were built for two sisters whose father, Canadian-born Wisconsin lumber magnate Alexander Stewart, had in 1909 built the family's first Washington home at 2200 Massachusetts Avenue, on this site of the Kalorama estate cemetery. In 1931, 2000 24th Street was built. The architect was New Yorker William L. Bottomley, who has been described as the "master of the old new house," and the Devore residence justifies his reputation. It is a limestone demipalace in the style of a French hotel of the Louis XV period. In 1961 G. Howland Chase offered 2000 24th Street to the U.S. government as a permanent home for the Chief Justice of the Supreme Court, along with an endowment to maintain it. The government refused the gift offer. A minor scandal erupted two years ago when the public learned that the Roman Catholic Diocese of Washington planned to buy the home for its bishop. The building was recently purchased as a conference-reception center for a "Christian businessmen's" organization.

In 1938–39 the other sister built 2030 24th Street, next door. The architect was Philadelphian Paul Cret. Again, France is the source of the design, although in the Stewart house there is a sort of Norman country house inspiration. The stonework and detailing are exquisite throughout. This building is probably the last great home of Kalorama.

32 Proceed south on 24th Street and take note of the many embassies along the way. When you reach S Street, NW, you will see to your right the **Robert Emmett statue,** located at the corner of 24th and S streets near Massachusetts Avenue. Emmett was an Irish revolutionary who looked to America as a guide to his country's independence. The Hon. Victor J. Dowling, chairman of the Emmett Statue Committee, presented this statue to the Smithsonian Institution on June 28, 1917, in the presence of President Wilson. It was erected on this site on April 22, 1966, the 15th anniversary of Irish independence.

Quote on the back of the statue:

"I wished to procure for my country the guarantee which Washington procured for America. I have parted from everything that was dear to me in this life for my country's cause. When my country takes her place among the nations of the earth then and not until then let my epitaph be written."—Extracts from Emmett's speech from the DOCH. Sept. 19, 1803.

33/34 Next, proceed east on S Street and visit the **Woodrow Wilson House**** (2340 S Street, NW) and the **Textile Museum*** (2310–30 S Street, NW). Both are open to the public and are well worth seeing.

Wilson House

35 The **William A. Mearns residence*,** at 2301 S Street, NW, was built in 1906 for Mearns, a banker and president of the Washington Stock Exchange. The architects were Frost and Granger of Chicago. The house seems too informal for the location.

36 The **Gales-Hoover House**,** 2300 S Street, NW, now the **Embassy of Burma,** is one of the earliest houses built on Kalorama Heights. This house was originally the home of Major Thomas M. Gales, who was connected with the realty firm that developed the Kalorama section. The Gales House was built in 1901–2 and the architect was Washingtonian Appleton P. Clark. It is unmistakably a late-19th-century house trying desperately to become Georgian. It is far more famous as the home of Herbert Hoover, who moved here in 1921, when he was appointed Secretary of Commerce by Harding, and who returned here after serving as President. Precisely in front of the Hoover House, in the middle at S Street, was the Kalorama mansion that stood until 1888, when it was demolished to accommodate the building at S and 23d streets.

37 Mitchell Playground** and the site of **Kalorama Square** development (north side of S Street between 23d and 22d streets, NW). The land for Mitchell Playground was donated to the city by Mrs. E. N. Mitchell in 1918. She and her husband had planned a large residence there, but his death terminated the project. The only proviso of Mrs. Mitchell's generous bequest was that the city care for the grave of her pet poodle, Bosque, perpetually. The dog's grave still remains, surrounded by a white chain fence, in the middle of the play area.

The fortresslike Kalorama Square townhouse project represents the most recent chapter in the long story of Kalorama. The pseudo-Georgian dwellings are the enterprise of a Kalorama resident, architect Walter Marlow. A landscaped central mall covers the parking area between the rows of houses.

38 The **Frederick A. Delano House*,** now the **Embassy of Ireland,** is located at 244 S Street, NW. Georgian revival architecture dominates the upper portions of Kalorama. It was the leading style of domestic design in early-20th-century Washington. Waddy Wood designed this house for Frederick A. Delano, an uncle of Franklin D. Roosevelt and president of the Wabash and several other midwestern railroads.

This is the last house on the tour. If you now travel back to Massachusetts Avenue through the western part of Kalorama, you see the houses becoming quite a bit more modest. Until the mid-1920s, most of this area was woodlands. Frances Hodgson Burnett, author of *Little Lord Fauntleroy,* was a major property owner. The land was rather rugged and not as attractive as property west of Rock Creek, which was more accessible from Massachusetts Avenue and thus was developed somewhat earlier. Much of Kalorama is a far younger community than many people think, and it is a community of greater diversity than is commonly assumed.

16/**Adams-Morgan****

(grand apartment houses, ethnically diverse neighborhood)

by Anthony Hacsi and Susan Harlem

Distance: 1¾ miles
Time: 1½ hours
Bus: 42, 44, 46, H-1, L-2
Metro: Zoo and Dupont Circle (Red Line)

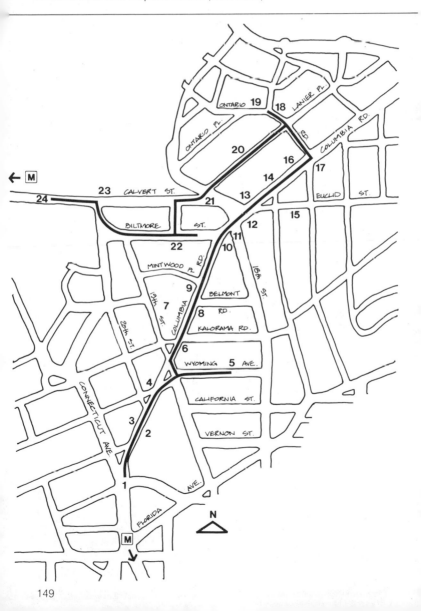

Adams-Morgan is now Washington's most ethnically and economically diverse neighborhood, but it started as a community for the wealthy. A hundred years ago the area was mostly rural. With cool breezes and good views of the city, its location on a hill made it attractive, but before the extension of streetcar service in the 1890s, it was not practical for many to live so far from the city. Around 1900 construction began on large apartment houses and roomy row houses, and most of the buildings now in the area were in place by 1920. What in the 1950s would come to be called Adams-Morgan then consisted of handsome subdivisions known as Washington Heights, Lanier Heights, Meridian Hill, and Cliffbourne. For the first half of the century the area was known for its elegance and its many politically or socially prominent residents.

With the Great Depression and later the World War II housing shortage, the area began to decline. Townhouses were made into rooming houses, and large apartments were split into smaller units. In the postwar years, middle-class flight to the suburbs was coupled with an increase in lower-income residents. The new people found the area a good place to live but, along with long-time residents, they became concerned about further decline. Although local citizens' organizations had been active since before the turn of the century, cooperation between the racially segregated groups failed, and a new integrated organization was formed in 1955. Taking the names of two elementary schools in the area, the then all-white Adams and all-black Morgan, it was called the Adams-Morgan Better Neighborhood Conference. It marked the beginning of an era of increased neighborhood activism, and it created a new name for the area. An urban-renewal plan that evolved from the citizens' concerns was debated through the early 1960s, but was never adopted. Its rejection was due largely to fear of the kind of displacement that had resulted from other urban renewal projects, particularly in Southwest Washington.

During the 1960s Adams-Morgan became known as the Hispanic center of Washington. Unlike Hispanic enclaves in other American cities, Washington's is heterogeneous, with representation from the Caribbean, Mexico, Central America, and South America. (At one time a plan was proposed to develop a highly commercial "Latin Quarter" here.)

The 1970s saw the arrival of another group of "immigrants"—young middle-class whites. In a pattern repeated in inner cities across America, they found the close-in, low-cost housing very attractive. With higher demand, widespread renovation, and real estate speculation, prices soared. The displacement of the poor, feared in the 1960s as part of organized urban renewal, has become a reality as a consequence of the gentrification that began in the 1970s. Shoppers frightened away from Adams-Morgan by its proximity to the 1968 riots have returned. New stores and restaurants, often appealing to the middle class, are opening with increasing frequency. Merchants are advertising Adams-Morgan as Washington's "Village," and many Washingtonians are predicting, as often as not with regret, that it will become another Georgetown. The main question concerning Adams-Morgan's future is whether it will retain its "Unity in Diversity" (the area's motto) or will return to the posh district it was in its early years.

1 Columbia Road was an Indian footpath before the District of Columbia was established and then an early post road between Georgetown and Baltimore. In the early 19th century it was known as Tayloe's Lane, when it led to a popular race track near 14th Street where Col. John Tayloe (for whom the Octagon was built) and others ran their horses. It has always been Adams-Morgan's main thoroughfare, and has become a major commercial street for the area. As you walk up Columbia Road, to your left is Kalorama Triangle (its other two sides are Connecticut Avenue and Calvert Street—see Tour 15, Kalorama), Adams-Morgan's wealthiest section and one that has remained largely all white.

2 The Wyoming**, 2022 Columbia Road (1905, 1909, 1911—B. Stanley Simmons). Dwight and Mamie Eisenhower and their son John lived here in apartment 210, and then 302, from 1927 to 1935. This was their longest stay anywhere except the White House and their farm in Gettysburg. Twenty-four members of Congress and 70 high-ranking military officers have also lived at the Wyoming, and four countries have maintained their legations here. This large apartment house was constructed in three parts: the southern portion in 1905, the northern part and entrance pavilion in 1909 (you can see how the original entrance has been bricked up), and a rear addition in 1911. The monumental entrance pavilion has Corinthian columns and limestone ornamentation (note the lion's head). The original revolving doors were replaced long ago, but the pavilion retains its iron marquee. The lobby features white Italian marble walls and stairways, a tobacco leaf motif in the ceiling moldings, and mosaic tiled floors designed to simulate Oriental carpets. The largest of the 106 apartments include five bedrooms, parlor, library, reception hall, and trunk room.

Until the Washington Hilton Hotel was constructed in the early 1960s, the Wyoming enjoyed an exceptional view of the city. In 1980 this building and two adjacent apartment houses were threatened by a proposed expansion of the Hilton, but neighborhood groups protested, and the plan was disapproved by the city zoning commission. The Wyoming was converted to condominiums in 1982.

Middendorf/Lane Gallery

3 Middendorf/Lane Gallery*, 2009 Columbia Road
(1889—William L. Conley). The oldest building on this tour
was designed as a single-family home and was used as
such until 1947. For a while it was split into apartments and
was once used as a dance studio. Since 1979 it has been an
art gallery and home for the owners, who commissioned extensive renovations. The eclectic design combines formal elements with a homey front porch. Notice how the first-floor
columns and pediment are imitated on the third floor. These
classical elements are mixed with Victorian hooded windows.

4 The Altamont*, 1901 Wyoming Avenue (1915–16—
Arthur B. Heaton). Col. George Truesdell, a commissioner of
the District of Columbia 1894–97, lived on this property for

many years in his mansion, Managasset, before he had the Altamont built. It was designed in the Italian Renaissance style and has a tile roof with twin towers, a loggia, vaulted frescoed ceilings in the entrance halls, an Italian carved-stone mantel and fireplace in the reception room, and patterned tile floors in the public hallways. The original tenants were offered an exceptional array of amenities: fireplaces, wallpapered bedrooms, copper cooking utensils, garbage incinerators, sitz baths, some oval and circular rooms, and sweepers in each apartment connected to the vacuum-cleaning plant in the basement. The upper floors contained only three apartments each: one with three rooms plus bath, and two with 12-13 rooms plus five baths and sleeping porch. Many of the large apartments were divided into smaller and less expensive units during the Depression. The seventh floor originally had a Palm Room, a café opening onto the loggia, and additional kitchens for entertaining. These spaces, along with the former billiard room in the basement, have been converted to apartments. The Altamont has been a cooperative since 1949.

The **Adams Elementary School,** the source of half the name of this community, is located south on 19th Street at California Street. It was named for John Quincy Adams. The former **Morgan Elementary School,** now the Marie Reed School, is at 2200 Champlain Street. Thomas P. Morgan was a commissioner of the District of Columbia 1879–83.

5 Admiral Peary Residence, 1831 Wyoming Avenue (1913—George N. Ray). Admiral Robert E. Peary, who led the first expedition to reach the North Pole, bought this house in 1914 and died here on February 20, 1920.

6 The Alwyn, 1882 Columbia Road (1910—Merrill Vaughn; 1913 (northern addition)—Appleton P. Clark, Jr.). To the casual observer it may not be apparent that the Alwyn was designed in two stages by two different architects. This is because Appleton Clark's addition has the same scale, wall surface, and roof style as the original. But while Merrill Vaughn's portion has squared corners and many oval and circular windows, Clark's has a rounded corner and only squared windows. Clark also added wrought-iron balconies, decorative carving, and a corner tower. The "K" on the tower refers to the 1913 owner, William Pitt Kellogg, a U.S. representative, senator and governor of Louisiana.

7 Kalorama Park, with its fine old oak trees, is all that remains of the woods and farms that once covered the entire area from Florida Avenue to Rock Creek. In 1828 Anna Maria Thornton, wife of architect of the Capitol William Thornton, sold two large farms to Christian Hines and his brother, Matthew. They planned to cultivate silkworms on the property and planted a grove of mulberry trees for this purpose. The venture was not successful, however, and the mulberry trees were eventually removed. Members of the Hines family were buried in a plot in what was then an oak grove in the northern section of their land, and is now the rear of stores at 2440–2444 18th Street. The Hines brothers sold their property to John Little in 1836. "Little's Woods," as the area was known, became smaller and smaller as parcels were sold during the next hundred years. This last remaining section was considered for development in the 1940s, but citizen pressure to make it a public park prevailed. Every summer Kalorama Park is home to Washington's Latino Festival.

8 The Norwood, 1868 Columbia Road (1917—Hunter & Bell), was known only by its address until 1974, when the residents voted to name it in honor of long-time resident manager, Kathryn M. Norwood. Actress Tallulah Bankhead lived here 1918 to 1921, when she was a teenager. Her father, William B. Bankhead was a U.S. representative at the time and later became Speaker of the House. Her grandfather was a U.S. Senator while he lived there from 1918 to 1922. William Edmund Barrett, author of *Lillies of the Field,* lived here in the 1970s. The Norwood's facade is extremely elaborate, with extensive white terra-cotta decoration and an ornate classical portico with flanking entrance lanterns. Above the front columns and the second floor are ram's heads. Note also the swan's neck pediment above the third floor, and the brickwork above the fifth floor.

9 The Woodley*, 1851 Columbia Road (1903—Thomas Franklin Schneider). This was the first apartment house on Columbia Road. It was designed and built by Thomas Franklin Schneider, architect of the Cairo Hotel. Schneider used light brick extensively, to simulate stone. This gives the building a heavy, solid look, reinforced by the massive porte-cochère. There is less stone simulation on the upper floors, where a lighter look is desired. Note the two-story gallery and the highly decorated frieze. On the roof, though difficult to see from most vantage points, is a cupola. The original six apartments on each floor have been broken up into efficiencies and one-bedroom units, and in 1976 were converted to condominiums.

10 SW corner, 18th Street and Columbia Road**
(Perpetual American Federal Savings—1979—Seymour Auerbach). This is the site of the worst disaster in Washington's history. On this corner stood the Knickerbocker, an elegant movie palace built by Harry M. Crandall in 1915 as part of his prestigious chain of theaters. The Knickerbocker had a full orchestra, which played during intermissions, and patrons often attended in formal dress. On the evening of January 28, 1922, during the city's heaviest recorded snowfall, the roof of the Knickerbocker collapsed onto a full house, under the weight of 50 tons of snow. Rescue operations involving the fire and police departments, the Marines, and the Walter Reed Hospital Corps continued through the night, greatly

The Woodley

hampered by the snowstorm. The final toll was 97 dead and 127 injured. Although investigations determined that the building contractor had failed to follow the design specifications, architect Reginald Geare, his career ruined, committed suicide five years after the accident. Harry Crandall hired Thomas Lamb to redesign the ruined building, and the Ambassador, another fine movie theater, opened in 1923. It was demolished in 1969 after several years of diminishing business.

The site remained vacant for the next decade. During the 1970s, community groups were successful in preventing the construction of a gas station on this prominent corner. The present branch of Perpetual American Federal Savings and Loan was constructed after months of negotiations with citizen groups who fought for and won the right to community involvement in the bank's loan policies. An open-air market, which had blossomed on this corner before the bank's construction, continues on the plaza. On Saturdays, the busiest day for this community market, you can buy fresh fruits, vegetables, cheeses, breads, and flowers, shop at a flea market, and enjoy an occasional concert by local musicians.

11 The **intersection of Columbia Road with 18th Street*** is considered the "heart of Adams-Morgan." The community's commercial section began here in the early 20th century; the 18th and Columbia Road Business Association has been active since the 1920s. Some of Washington's businesses opened their first stores near here, including Ridgewell's Caterers, Dart Drug, Toys-R-Us, and the General Store. Eighteenth Street is now a colorful shopping strip, with restaurants, cafés, and shops representing many cultures—Salvadoran, French, Mexican, West African, Jamaican, Italian, Ethiopian. There are also galleries, picture-framing shops, and antiques and second-hand stores. Angle parking has replaced parallel parking here to make room for more cars and to create a more informal atmosphere. The D.C. Office on Latino Affairs is located at 2409 18th Street.

12 SE corner, 18th Street and Columbia Road
(1899 [original structure]—Waddy B. Wood). Architect of the Department of the Interior Building and many large homes in the Kalorama neighborhood (including the Woodrow Wilson house), Waddy Wood designed this building as a single-family residence. Within four years after it was constructed, the commercial potential of this site was exploited by conversion of the first floor to a pharmacy. It continued as a pharmacy until 1969 (from 1922 to 1969 it was a Peoples Drug Store), and since then it has been a McDonald's. Note the steeply pitched roof with shed dormers.

13 NE corner, Columbia and Adams Mill Roads
(1915—B. Stanley Simmons; 1920 addition—B. Stanley Simmons and Charles S. Holloway). You should have no difficulty here (now the home of the Transcentury Corporation) in differentiating between the original building and its addition. The older tapestry-brick section was built to house shops on the ground floor and apartments on the upper floors. The newer section, with its classical facade of limestone and granite, was added as the home of the Northwest Savings Bank. From 1949 to 1969 Gartenhaus Furs was located here. The original bank vault is still in the building and has been used as a tiny auditorium for theatrical productions. Notice that the clock still works!

14 Avignone Freres*, 1777 Columbia Road (1928—Frederic B. Pyle). When this neighborhood was a home for wealthy people who entertained, there were several catering and confectionary establishments in the area to serve their needs. Avignone Freres, in business since 1918 and at this location since 1928, is the sole survivor of that era and is probably the oldest continuously operating business in the community. The quality of the ice cream here attracted the children of Presidents (Margaret Truman and Caroline Kennedy were two), but after the riots in 1968 the restaurant part of the operation was closed. Its reopening in 1978 was one of many indications of the area's renewed commercial health. Inside, there are many original fixtures and wooden cabinets, as well as a confectionery, bakery, and delicatessen. The ice cream is still available, and the bakery is noted for its large, buttery croissants. The center stairs lead to a balcony with tables overlooking the main floor.

15 First Church of Christ, Scientist, 1770 Euclid Street (1911—Marsh & Peter and E.D. Ryerson). This classic-style church with its colonnade entrance porch is constructed of brick and limestone. There are regularly scheduled services in Spanish.

16 1743—51 Columbia Road. In 1906–7 Harry L. Wardman, the most prolific Washington developer of his time, built six small apartment buildings on this site. They were designed by his chief architect, Albert H. Beers. Wardman named them the Derbyshire, the Hampshire, the Cheshire, the Wilkshire, the Yorkshire, and the Devonshire. In the early 1950s, they were replaced by a Safeway and Giant (recently renamed Save Right). The Safeway expanded eastward in 1981, building on its parking lot. While resulting in a roomier store with a greater variety of merchandise, this enlargement has also exacerbated the parking shortage.

17 The Beverly Court, 1736 Columbia Road (1914–15—Hunter & Bell). For years many artists have lived and worked in this building, with its large and unusual spaces well-suited for studios. After the death of the Beverly Court's owner in 1977, the tenants formed an association to purchase the building. They became the first tenants' group in Washington to finance the rental-to-cooperative conversion through private lending institutions. Also in the Beverly Court is Ayuda, a nonprofit organization offering legal services to low-income residents.

18 2809 Ontario Road (1909). Paul Pelz, architect with John L. Smithmeyer of the original Library of Congress building, designed this house for Henry Park Willis, a Secretary of the Federal Reserve Board and a framer of the Federal Reserve Act of 1914. Note the unusual rounded end walls, the arched dormers and entrance, and the lion's-head rainspout.

19 The Ontario**, 2853 Ontario Road (1903–4 and 1905–6—James G. Hill). Archibald M. McLachlen, founder of Washington's McLachlen National Bank, gave up his home on this property to build the Ontario. Although designed as a whole, it was constructed in two stages: the western portion in 1903–4 and the eastern, larger portion, in 1905–6. (The smaller of the two entrance porticoes served as the original entrance). Constructed in a part of Washington still quite rural, the building had an unobstructed view of nearby Rock

Creek Park and the new National Zoological Park.

Some of the Ontario's special features are the decorative keystones above the windows, cast-iron entrance doors and balconies, and a turret crowned by a cupola. Inside, there are brass mailboxes, tile-bordered floors in the lobby and hallways, and rare cast-iron staircases with marble stairs. The 20 apartments on each floor range from two to nine rooms, with 10-foot ceilings, gas-burning fireplaces, and extensive wood trim.

Architect Hill, former supervising architect of the Treasury Department, lived here from the time the building opened until he died in 1913. Other notable residents have included Gen. Douglas MacArthur, Sen. Robert LaFollette, Adm. Chester Nimitz, and more recently, author Nora Ephron and Watergate journalist Carl Bernstein.

20 Engine Company No. 21**, 1763 Lanier Place (1908—Appleton P. Clark, Jr.). When this site for the fire-

Engine Company #21

house was announced in 1906, some in the neighborhood objected to it not only because it was on a narrow street in a residential neighborhood, but also because it was not centrally located for its area of service. The justification given was that the only nonresidential street was 18th Street, which was on a hill (difficult for the horses), and the price of land there exceeded the appropriation. Another factor may have been that from this northern high ground, the horses could run downhill to fires. This stuccoed-brick building looks more like a Spanish mission than a firehouse. The tower was needed for drying hoses, but in this context it looks as if it should house bells. Notice how the design incorporates the rainspouts.

In 1925 the *Washington Evening Star* began an annual competition among fire stations to see which could most quickly get its fire engine out of a station. Engine Company 21 set a "world record" of six seconds the following year. Architect Clark lived on this block at no. 1778 from 1905 until his death in 1955. His home has been replaced by condominiums. Al Jolson's parents also lived on Lanier Place, at no. 1787, and the Stafford (1911—Hunter & Bell), at no. 1789, was one of the first two cooperatives in the city.

21 Calvert Street. From Lanier Place you reach Calvert Street (called Cincinnati Street until 1905) where it intersects Adams Mill Road (so named because it once led to a flour mill owned by John Quincy Adams). The **Beacon,** on the northwest corner of Calvert Street and Adams Mill Road at 1801 Calvert (1911—J.J. Moebs) makes maximum use of its triangular lot. The **mirror-image duplex** at nos. 1847–49 was designed by Arthur Heaton. Notice how the right facade has been changed. At no. 1855, the **Cliffbourne** (1905—N.R. Grimm) has an unusual variety of window heads, while next door at no. 1915, the **Sterling** (1906—Appleton Clark) has Palladian windows and a loggia on the fourth floor. On the southwest corner of Calvert Street and Cliffbourne Place, **2516 Cliffbourne** (1901—Waddy Wood) is a charming house with tile roof, shed dormers, two open porches, and a second floor balconet.

22 Biltmore Street** is one of Adams-Morgan's loveliest residential streets. Named Baltimore Street until 1905, it was once known informally as Generals' Row because of the many military officers who lived here. Coming from Cliffbourne Place, your first view is of four large row houses, nos. 1848-50-52-54, each with its own distinctive facade. Down to the left is the duplex, nos. 1822-24 (1906—Albert H. Beers). When its building permit application was filed, the question, "Will the roof be flat, pitch, or mansard?" was answered by "All kinds." Toward the other end of Biltmore Street, at no. 1940, is the tapestry-brick **Biltmore** (1913—Claughton West) with its balustraded roof and overhanging Italian cornice. There are only four apartments to a floor, and each apartment has its own fireplace. The hearths are ar-

Biltmore Street

ranged so that by pulling a slide the ashes drop through a metal chute to a bin in the cellar.

23 Trolley turnaround. On this site was a trolley turn-around known for many years as the Rock Creek Loop. Streetcar service, which spurred the development of what is now called Adams-Morgan, came to the area in September 1892. The first line ran north on 18th Street, then west on Calvert, across the bridge, and north on Connecticut Avenue to Chevy Chase Lake, Maryland. In 1935 the section of the run from here to Chevy Chase was replaced by bus service, and Rock Creek Loop became the end point of the streetcar line. Streetcar service continued here until Washington's last trolleys were replaced by buses on January 28, 1962. Buses now use this loop to turn around, and a small structure from the streetcar days remains.

Another streetcar line began to serve the area in 1897, coming up Columbia Road as far as 18th Street. In 1900 that line was extended east on Columbia, then north on what is now Mt. Pleasant Street to Park Road. It was replaced by bus service in December 1961.

24 "Duke" Ellington Memorial Bridge* (1934–35—Paul Cret). As a requirement of its streetcar charter, the Rock Creek Railway built a 125-foot-high steel trestle bridge on this site in 1891. In 1911 it became shaky and had to be reinforced and narrowed. Finally, in 1934, construction of a replacement bridge was begun. Traffic here was too important to interrupt, so the old bridge was moved 80 feet downstream to be used as a detour until the new one was completed. To do this, the bridge's footings were put on rollers on top of parallel rails. The bridge was then moved by machinery powered by horses. Auto traffic resumed the same day, and streetcar traffic was interrupted for less than 48 hours. The new Calvert Street Bridge, as it was called for many years, was constructed of concrete faced with Indiana limestone. It was renamed in the 1970s for Washington native Edward Kennedy "Duke" Ellington. The abutments are embellished by Leon Hermant's relief panels representing four modes of travel: ship, train, automobile, and airplane. This bridge has a reputation as the favorite Washington bridge for people seeking to leap to their death.

A pleasant way to end this tour is to stop in at the nearby Calvert Restaurant for some Middle Eastern food, or retrace your steps to the many interesting cafés to be found on both 18th Street and Columbia Road.

17/**Woodley Park**** and **National Zoo****

(early-20th-century apartments, National Zoo, prestige residential area, Rock Creek bridge)

by Floy Brown (1976); 1983 update by Lindsley Williams and Charles Szoradi

Distance: 1½ miles
Time: ¾ hour
Bus: L-2, L-4, L-6, L-8 (on Connecticut Avenue) and 91, 92, 94 (on Calvert Street)
Metro: Woodley Park/Zoo (Red Line)

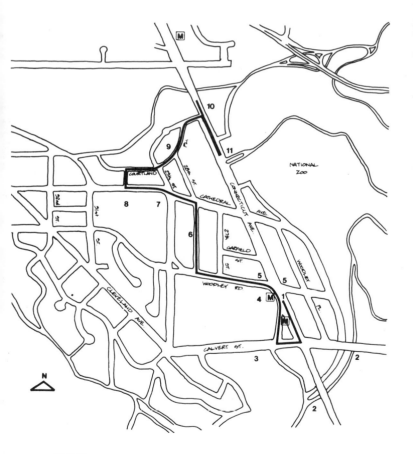

Woodley Park was originally part of a 1,000-acre tract of hilly, wooded land purchased by Gen. Uriah Forrest shortly after the American Revolution. Around 1800 the

general transferred 250 acres to a wealthy Georgetown lawyer named Philip Barton Key, uncle of Francis Scott Key. The house that Key built was known as Woodley House, named after the old bachelor hall in Mrs. Elizabeth Gaskell's novel, *Cranford*.

Natural topographical borders locate Woodley Park on the peak of land that rises from the valley of Rock Creek, extends northward for a mile, and then slopes downward to a spring branch of the creek. The altitude and cooler summer temperatures made the area a desirable summer retreat from the city during the 19th century.

In the 1890s Woodley Park was purchased by Sen. Francis G. Newlands of Nevada, owner of the Chevy Chase Land Company. Newlands was also principal owner of the newly chartered Rock Creek Railway of the District of Columbia, a line that would connect Chevy Chase with downtown Washington. Put into operation in 1892, the streetcar route opened the area to suburban development.

1 Proceed south along Connecticut Avenue. Reflective of the heterogeneous residential character of Woodley Park, the shops and restaurants along Connecticut Avenue include everything from the neighborhood drugstore to international haute cuisine. Numerous **sidewalk cafés*** provide congenial resting places.

2 The original steel-deck truss bridge crossing Rock Creek Valley at Calvert Street has long since been replaced by the existing concrete structure, now known as the **Duke Ellington Memorial Bridge*** (see Tour 16, Adams-Morgan, no. 24). The "million dollar" **Connecticut Avenue Bridge*** opened in 1907. At that time it was the largest concrete bridge in the world, and its name and presence highlighted the appeal of Woodley Park.

3 Proceed west along Calvert Street. The **Shoreham Hotel*,** constructed in 1930 by Harry Bralove, proved a worthy rival to the Wardman Park. It has been said that the Shoreham attracted so many prominent Washingtonians that one could ring a bell there anytime and summon a quorum of senators.

4 Proceed north along 24th Street to Connecticut Avenue. At the corner of Connecticut Avenue and Woodley Road stands the **Wardman Tower*,** now part of the Washington Sheraton Hotel. Harry Wardman, the master builder of Woodley Park, constructed the 1,500-room luxury hotel in 1918. Washingtonians called it "Wardman's Folly," little realizing that a hotel in the suburbs could prove to be so popular. Now primarily a residential wing of the larger complex, the tower has served as home to many of the nation's Vice Presidents and other VIPs. The tower portion of the hotel was built in 1928 by Doskned Mesrobian and is a Category I historic landmark. (The original "crescent-

Wardman Tower

shaped" main building was demolished in the late 1970s and replaced with the present structure.)

Turn left at Woodley Road. Adjoining the original Wardman Tower at the corner of Connecticut Avenue, the complex now includes 16 acres of landscaped grounds, large convention facilities, and the only first-class post office in an American hotel.

5 The **apartment buildings** at 2700 and 2701 Connecticut Avenue and extensive Cathedral Mansions at 3000 Connecticut Avenue are also Wardman's work. By constructing reasonably priced houses and apartments along the streetcar line, Wardman converted rural property into comfortable town living.

6 Turn right onto 28th Street. The neo-Georgian brick townhouses, many of which have been modernized to contemporary standards, are characteristic of the Wardman subdivision south of Cathedral Avenue, known as Woodley Park. No longer a suburb, the area is desirable now to old and young alike, offering a variety of lifestyles.

7 Turn left on Cathedral Avenue. Proceeding down Cathedral Avenue away from Connecticut Avenue, one passes **Single Oak*,** now the home of the Swiss ambassador, which was built in the mid-1920s by Sen. Francis G. Newlands of Nevada as residence for a married daughter.

8 High on a hill behind a row of stately oaks stands elegant **Woodley Mansion*.** The white-stucco Georgian house served as the summer home of four 19th-century Presidents, including Van Buren, Tyler, Buchanan, and Cleveland. Henry L. Stimson lived there while serving as Secretary of State for President Herbert Hoover and Secretary of War for Franklin D. Roosevelt. The building is now owned and operated by the private Maret School.

9 Turn right at the alley and cut through to Cortland Place. Take another right on Cortland Place and proceed past the playground that adjoins Klingle Creek Valley to Devonshire Place. Many of the homes in this mixed residential neighborhood were part of the exclusive Wardman subdivision north of Cathedral Avenue known as **English Village.** The crescent-shaped streets give a picturesque effect.

At the intersection of Connecticut Avenue and Devonshire Place, decide whether you want to take in the National Zoo or not. The Zoo is to the south, about 500 feet. To the north is Cleveland Park (and the nearest Metrorail station). Or you can take the Cleveland Park Tour (no. 18) in reverse.

10 Notice the **Kennedy-Warren** apartment building, 3133 Connecticut Avenue, at the east side of Connecticut Avenue where it intersects Devonshire Place. It was built in the early 1930s in art deco style. Notice also the bridge of the same era and style, including eight **bridge lights** that were illuminated until a reconstruction in the late 1970s.

Kennedy Warren

11 At the crest of the hill is the entrance to the **National Zoological Park**.** Designed by the famous landscape architect, Frederick Law Olmstead, the world-renowned, 175-acre Zoo recently celebrated its 80th birthday. It exhibits nearly 3,000 animals of more than 800 species and subspecies, many of them rare and not exhibited elsewhere in the country. The Zoo's most famous residents—the giant pandas Hsing-Hsing and Ling-Ling—were a gift from the People's Republic of China following former President Nixon's visit there in February 1972. The Zoo contains many well-marked paths that are not included in this guide (nor are the mileages).

18/**Cleveland Park**** and **Washington Cathedral*****

(turn-of-the-century residences; huge Gothic cathedral)

Cleveland Park segment by Kathleen Sinclair Wood;
Washington Cathedral segment by Charity Vanderbilt
Davidson

Distance: 2 miles
Time: 2¼ hours
Bus: L-2, L-4, L6, L8, H-2, and H-4
Metro: Cleveland Park (Red Line)

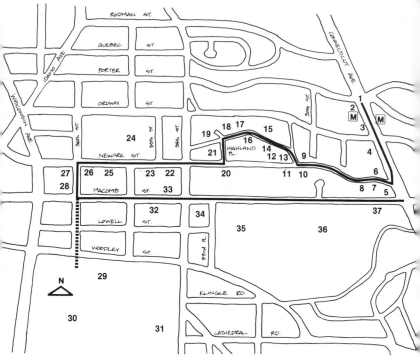

Cleveland Park is significant as a neighborhood with a strong sense of community and a unique architectural quality. With its tree-lined streets, brick sidewalks, and large frame houses, it has successfully retained much of its late-19th/early-20th-century atmosphere. Many of the architectural styles that gained popularity in the late 19th century are represented in Cleveland Park's houses.

Cleveland Park and the Close of the Washington Cathedral (officially known as the Cathedral Church of St. Peter and St. Paul) were originally part of about 12,000 acres purchased about 1790 by Georgetown merchants Benjamin Stoddert (who was also the first Secretary of the

166

Navy) and Gen. Uriah Forrest (former mayor of Georgetown, friend of George Washington, and representative from Maryland in the U.S. Congress). Forrest bought Stoddert's share in the property, and in 1794 moved with his family to the house he built and named Rosedale after his ancestral home in England (see no. 24, this tour). The area remained rural until the late 1880s when it became a fashionable retreat from Washington's hot, humid summers. Wealthy Washingtonians, including President Grover Cleveland (from whom the area derived its name after he established his summer White House at Oak View in 1886—demolished in 1927—see no. 26) built large rambling summer "cottages" of which Twin Oaks (no. 35) is the sole surviving example.

In 1892 streetcar service began on Connecticut Avenue, connecting Chevy Chase to the city center. Cleveland Park was one of the chief beneficiaries and quickly became a desirable area for year-round residence. Housing starts mushroomed in the years between 1894 and 1920. The Cleveland Park Company, formed in the early 1890s with John Sherman as its president, was responsible for the most varied and interesting houses in this "streetcar suburb." John Sherman was an enlightened developer, who hired local architects to design his houses and provided certain amenities (a streetcar waiting lodge, stables, and a fire station), to make Cleveland Park life more attractive to his prospective residents. The residential development of Cleveland Park was virtually complete by 1920. At that time, residential and commercial development along Connecticut and Wisconsin avenues intensified to provide services for the residents who previously rode the streetcar into the city to purchase all of their provisions.

Cleveland Park has remained a popular in-town residential area with a touch of rural atmosphere because of the open space that has been preserved. Its residents consistently have been professionals (especially lawyers), high-level government officials, academicians, and journalists.

1 Cleveland Park Metro Station was designed by the office of Harry Weese Associates and opened in December 1981. Turn left after ascending the long escalator. At the top of the second escalator, walk straight ahead.

2 Fire house #28 opened December 1, 1916, making it the second building on this strip of Connecticut Avenue. It was designed by Snowden Ashford, who was appointed the first municipal architect in 1909. This was a progressive fire station when it opened, with motorized equipment replacing the less efficient horse-drawn engines. Notice the handsome stone arches and angle quoins as well as the red brick with white trim, especially the central Swan's

Neck Pediment with a pineapple as a centerpiece. All are details of the Georgian revival style, recalling the early plantation houses along the James River. Reverse your direction and walk south on Connecticut Avenue.

3 3520 Connecticut Avenue (apartment building 1919); **3500-3518 Connecticut Avenue** (unified series of townhouses of 1920). These were the first residences to be built along this stretch of Connecticut Avenue. Harry Wardman built them before the Wardman Towers in Woodley Park.

4 The art deco **Uptown Theater** joined the commercial strip in the early 1930s, providing a new kind of entertainment. Notice the art deco details: decorative features in stone and brick, etched glass, and the marquee with its decorative use of lights and color.

5 Cross Newark Street and notice the **library** built in 1952. This site was designated in 1898 by John Sherman, president of the Cleveland Park Company, to be the location of an architect-designed stone-and-stucco lodge in which early residents could wait for the streetcar in warmth and comfort. It was also used for various community meetings and activities. It burned about 1910 and was not rebuilt. Today the library serves a similar function as a focal point for the community. Turn right and walk up Newark Street.

6 2941 Newark Street (1898—Robert Head). A local architect, Robert Head designed at least 17 houses for Cleveland Park from 1897 to 1901 in a variety of styles ranging from the informal Queen Anne, which this house represents, to the more formal Georgian revival. Notice the turret, the tall, ribbed chimney that joins the two distinct parts of the house, the variety of roof forms and window shapes, and the first use by Head of the rope dipped in plaster motif on a gable on the west side of the house.

7 2940 Newark Street (1903—architect-developer John Sherman). This is one of the first houses built by the Cleveland Park Company after John Sherman had ceased employing architects. The change probably was due to the imminent bankruptcy of Thomas Waggaman, who appears to have been the primary landholder and financial backer. This house was the residence of the famous arctic explorer Commander Robert Peary, who discovered the North Pole in 1909.

8 2960 Newark Street (1899—Robert Head). This Georgian revival house was the residence of O.T. Crosby, who founded PEPCO in 1896. Notice that the house serves as a visual focal point as you ascend the hill. Also note the classical details.

9 3035 Newark Street (1898—Robert Head). This magnificent Queen Anne-style house has a commanding view of the city. Notice the twisted columns and sunray motif on the porch, the swags in the frieze area, the varied roof forms, including a central, bell-shaped turret, and the window forms, including leaded and stained-glass windows.

10 3038 and 3042 Newark Street (1903—John Sherman). Notice the use of rope dipped in plaster and applied over the entrance of no. 3042 as a decorative motif.

11 3100 Newark Street (1897—Waddy Wood). Notice the varied windows, including an eyebrow window in the roof, and the decorative effects achieved by the cut shingles and the rope dipped in plaster in the arched shape above one window.

12 3121 Newark Street (1903—Ella Bennett Sherman, the wife of the developer of Cleveland Park). Notice the two oriel windows on the east side of the house, the rope dipped in plaster motif, and the handsome brackets supporting the central third-story balcony.

Turn around and retrace your steps to Highland Place, where you turn left.

13 3100 Highland Place (1896—Frederick Bennett Pyle). Notice the Palladian window in the dormer, the elliptical oculus window by the front door, and the varied shape of the porch, including a porte-cochère.

House on Highland Place

14 3138 and 3140 Highland Place (1901—Robert Head). Two of the last houses designed by Head exhibit a Japanese influence in the sticklike brackets under the overhanging eaves and in the gentle upward flare of the roof on the central dormer of no. 3140.

15 3141 and 3155 Highland Place (1895–6—Robert I. Fleming). These "twin houses" were the first to appear on Highland Place. They were built on the unsubdivided portion of Cleveland Park, which was still considered to be agricultural land. The irregular course of Highland Place seems to derive from a property line.

No. 3155 is significant as the home and first office for the W. C. and A. N. Miller brothers, who formed their real estate company as very young men just after their father died. W. C. and A. N. Miller is still an active real estate development firm in Washington today.

16 3154 Highland Place (remodelled 1906—William Dyer). This early house has received its distinctive appearance through successive renovations. Early photographs show it as a simple frame house until the shingled pagoda-style porch was added in 1906, and then it was further modified in 1916, when the shingles were replaced by the red tiles you see today.

17 3209 Highland Place (1905—Hunter and Bell). This was the first brick house built in Cleveland Park. Notice the formality and symmetry of this Georgian revival house and the use of darkly glazed bricks similar to those found in Williamsburg.

18 3225 Highland Place (1898—Robert Head). This represents Head's first attempt at a Georgian revival house with the Ionic columns on the porch and the Palladian window motif on the side. Once again, the house has a commanding presence on the street.

19 3301 Highland Place (1912—B. F. Meyers for W. C. & A. N. Miller). This is one of the earliest houses constructed by the W. C. and A. N. Miller brothers, who lived down the street and employed B. F. Meyers to design many of their early Cleveland Park houses. They are representative of the second wave of developers active in Cleveland Park after the demise of the Cleveland Park Company in 1909.

Turn left at 33d Place and walk to Newark Street where you should turn right.

20 3300 Newark Street. The present house of 1920 was built on the site originally occupied by a frame building that housed the chemical fire engine and the police office. This was provided by the Cleveland Park Company in 1901 for the comfort and safety of the early residents.

21 3301 Newark Street (1895—Pelz and Carlyle). This modified Italian villa-style residence was the first house built on the east side of 34th Street. Pelz (one of the architects of the Library of Congress) and his partner, Carlyle, were the first architects hired by John Sherman. The site of this house marks the beginning of the subdivided area of Cleveland Park, which was laid out by 1894 in a regular grid pattern from Wisconsin Avenue to 33d Place on Newark Street. The area you have just walked through was unsubdivided agricultural land; consequently, the large, irregularly shaped lots were determined by the developer or prospective owners, and the curvilinear streets owe their charming character to property lines and the natural contours of the land. You will notice the increased regularity of lot sizes during the remainder of your tour.

Cross 34th Street with extreme caution and continue on Newark Street.

22 3410 Newark Street (1895—Pelz and Carlyle). Notice the tower rising out of the west side of the house as you walk by. Look back to catch a glimpse of the Palladian window beside the tower, which lights the landing of the stairs.

23 3418 Newark Street (1982—Sam Dunn). This recently completed house is sensitively designed of wood to carry on the traditional building material of the neighborhood. Architect Sam Dunn said he wanted to create a "1982 Cleveland Park House" with a creative flair of its own.

24 Rosedale, 3501 Newark Street (1794). This eight-acre tract is all that remains of the large acreage Gen. Uriah Forest originally owned in the 1790s. It can be entered from the drive near the corner of Newark and 36th streets. A stone building on the property (referred to as the "old Kitchen") is believed to have been built in 1740, while the weatherboard farmhouse, typical of the 18th century, was built by Forrest about 1794. The Forrests made this their permanent residence, and George Washington is believed to have been a guest at Rosedale while the new capital city was being built. Pierre L'Enfant, also a personal friend, is rumored to have helped design the original gardens.

In 1796–97 Forrest mortgaged Rosedale (420 acres and the house) to obtain a loan from Maryland so that the new government could complete construction of the Capitol. Forrest then lost most of his money when the Greenleaf real estate syndicate collapsed in 1797. His brother-in-law, Philip Barton Key, who built Woodley House (Maret School), bailed him out by buying all of his land at auction, paying off the mortgage, and then dividing the land into generous parcels, which he sold. He conveyed the farmhouse and 126 acres to Mrs. Uriah Forrest, who was the sister of Key's wife.

Rosedale remained in the family until 1920, when Avery Coonley, a Chicago philanthropist, and his wife purchased it. Frank Lloyd Wright visited his former clients at Rosedale and is reported to have proclaimed it "honest architecture."

In 1959 the Coonleys' daughter and her husband, Waldron Faulkner, sold the house and eight acres to the National Cathedral School for Girls. The brick buildings that now surround the farmhouse (1968—Waldron Faulkner) were intended as dormitories and faculty housing for the school. In 1977 the property was sold to Youth for Understanding, an international student-exchange organization, which uses the modern buildings for its offices and classrooms while preserving and restoring the 18th-century farmhouse. Architect Winthrop Faulkner designed the three white brick townhouses on 36th Street at the entrance to Rosedale, which is a Category II landmark.

25 3512 Newark Street (1895—Pelz and Carlyle). Notice the Palladian window on the side of the house as you approach it, and then look back as you walk by to see the oriel on the west side of the house, which rises and has its own terminating roof form.

26 The **stone wall** that you encounter just after passing 3518 Newark Street, with its distinctive Hugh Jacobsen renovation, is all that remains of Grover Cleveland's summer home, Oak View. In 1886 President Cleveland purchased an 1868 stone farmhouse and hired architect William M. Poindexter to wrap fanciful wooden Victorian porches around it, giving it a totally new appearance. This was to become the summer White House for the President and his new bride, the handsome young Frances Folsom, who was the daughter of his former law partner. This set a precedent for the area; prominent Washingtonians followed his example and established summer homes nearby. Cleveland's home deteriorated and was eventually razed to make way for the present brick house, built in 1927 for a descendant of Robert E. Lee. The stones from Cleveland's house were used to build this wall.

27 3320 36th Street—stable for 3601 Macomb Street (1900—Sherman & Sonneman). You will pass on your right a most interesting Palladian window motif, which replaced the large opening in the upper story of the stable that had provided easy access for the storage of hay for the horses. The former stable, built out of Rock Creek granite, makes a very attractive little house.

28 At this point you can continue on 36th Street to reach the Washington Cathedral (see no. 29, this tour) or you can turn right on Macomb Street to reach Wisconsin Avenue, where you will find restaurants and public transportation. To continue the walking tour of Cleveland Park, turn left on Macomb Street and begin to descend the hill. Most of the houses in the next two blocks were not built until the second decade of the 20th century, when developer Charles Taylor was at work with architect R. G. Moore.

29 The Cathedral Church of St. Peter and St. Paul*** (also known as the National Cathedral and the Washington Cathedral). Late in 1891, a group of Washingtonians interested in planning a cathedral in the city met at the home of Charles Carroll Glover, a prominent local banker and the prime mover in an effort to establish Rock Creek Park. Two years later, in 1893, Congress chartered the Protestant Episcopal Cathedral Foundation to oversee the con-

National Cathedral

struction and operation of such a cathedral and to carry out an educational program. Mount St. Alban, rising above the flatlands of the city, was selected as the site, and in 1906, Bishop Henry Yates Satterlee and the Cathedral Chapter decided on the Gothic design submitted by George Frederick Bodley, then England's leading Anglican church architect. Henry Vaughn, a prominent American proponent of the neo-Gothic style was selected as the supervising architect. More than 20,000 people attended the laying of the foundation stone in 1907. The Bethlehem Chapel, opened in 1912, was the first section completed. Construction was halted during World War I, and was resumed in 1922, under the supervision of Philip Hubert Frohman of Frohman, Robb & Little. Frohman, the cathedral architect for more than 50 years, modified the original design of the nave and the central tower. The choir, apse, and north transept were opened in 1932, the south transept in 1962, and the 301-foot Gloria in Excelsis tower (with its magnificent carillon and ring of bells) in 1964. The west front (Frederick Hart, sculptor) was dedicated in 1982. If work continues at the present rate, the west towers will be completed in another six to eight years or so. As the first dean, G. C. L. Bratenahl, once explained, "it will be finished when enough people care enough to give enough to finish it."

The funerals of such famous Americans as Woodrow Wilson (who is also buried there) and Dwight D. Eisenhower were held at the Cathedral. Dr. Martin Luther King, Jr.'s last sermon before going to Memphis in April 1968 was preached here.

The Pilgrim Observation Gallery, high above the west facade, is open from 10 a.m. to 3:15 p.m. (admission charged) and offers a unique view of the city and suburbs.

The Cathedral itself can be entered from the north or south transepts or from the west end. The Cathedral Foundation conducts 30–45 minute guided tours of the interior, Monday through Saturday, 10:00 a.m. to 3:15 p.m.

Leave the Cathedral by either the south transept or the west front and follow the stone wall to the entrance to:

30 The Bishop's Garden** (1928–32—landscape design by Mrs. G. C. F. Bratenahl). Turn right through the Norman arch. The Bishop's Garden actually consists of several gardens, including a rose garden and a medieval herb garden, connected by boxwood-lined, stone-paved walkways. With its pools and ivy-covered gazebo, it is among the city's most pleasant and peaceful places.

Return to the main roadway and continue east to the Pilgrim Steps and the equestrian statue of George Washington (Herbert Haseltine, sculptor). Those wishing to, should descend the 40-foot-wide steps, cross Pilgrim Road, and follow the:

31 Woodland Path*. This curvilinear walk, which is maintained by local garden clubs, leads either to St. Alban's School or to a lower section of Pilgrim Road. The branch to Pilgrim Road includes a large wooden foot bridge (1961—Walter Dodd Ramberg); the bridge is particularly noteworthy for its composition, the size of its members, and its overall character. Cross the foot bridge to Pilgrim Road and then walk south on Pilgrim Road to Garfield Street, NW, to the St. Alban's Tennis Club (1970—Hartman and Cox). This small, well-ordered building is notable for its varied, but dignified facade.

Return to the main road. Beyond the Pilgrim Steps and the deanery (1953—Walter G. Peter) is the Greenhouse, which offers a great variety of herb plants for sale (catalogues are available on request).

The low, modern building (1964—Falkner, Kingsbury & Stenhouse) to the right of the Greenhouse is Beauvoir, the Cathedral elementary school (founded 1933). Other structures on the western end of the Close include buildings for administration, the College of Preachers, the Cathedral Library, and canons' housing (all 1924–29—Frohman, Robb & Little).

Retrace your steps past the south transept entrance and Pilgrim steps and walk west toward Wisconsin Avenue. The Herb Cottage on your left, one of the earliest buildings on the Close, was originally built to house the Cathedral's baptistry, but now serves as a gift shop. Continue around to the left past the Episcopal Church House (1913—Henry Vaughn) and notice the panorama of Washington stretching before you from the Peace Cross (dedicated 1898). The buildings in this section of the Close house St. Alban's School For Boys (founded 1903) and St. Alban's Parish (consecrated 1855; substantially altered, early 1920s).

You can leave the Close via Wisconsin Avenue and/or Massachusetts Avenue, both of which are served by major bus routes, or return to the Cleveland Park tour, using the entrance at 36th Street.

32 3426 Macomb Street (1897—S. A. Swindell). This little house set so far back from the street is the oldest house on Macomb Street and represents the cottage style popularized by A. J. Downing. Notice the change in the sidewalk at this point as you leave the early subdivision of Oak View and enter Cleveland Heights (Macomb and Lowell streets from this point to 33d Place). This house stood alone for almost 20 years before W. C. and A. N. Miller and George Small built some neighboring houses in Cleveland Heights.

33 Macomb Playground appeared on the real estate maps as early as 1937. In 1954 the neighborhood mothers raised $1,000 in one week to pay for trees and sod to beautify the playground.

34 John Eaton School (west wing: 1911—Appleton P. Clark, Jr.; east wing: 1923—Arthur B. Heaton; auditorium: 1931; renovation: 1981–82—Kent Cooper Associates). As you cross 34th Street, you are looking at the rear of the school, which opened in 1911. From here you can see the oldest wing with the entry from the playground marked for boys and the tall chimney designed by Heaton. The newly enlarged and landscaped playground is particularly appreciated by the school and the community.

35 Twin Oaks, 3200 Macomb Street, rear entrance; main entrance is 3225 Woodley Road (1888: Francis R. Allen). This is the only remaining example of a house designed to be a summer home located in the Cleveland Park area. Twin Oaks is an extremely early example of a colonial (Georgian) revival house—perhaps the earliest one surviving in the United States. It bears a close resemblance to McKim, Mead, and White's H. A. C. Taylor House of Newport, Rhode Island, of 1886 (demolished, 1952). Gardiner Greene Hubbard, a Bostonian, hired architect Francis Richmond Allen from his native city to design his summer home, which resembles the large rambling New England frame seaside summer houses. Hubbard was the founder of the National Geographic Society and also was the chief financial backer for Alexander Graham Bell, which made possible the establishment of worldwide telephone service. Twin Oaks was the summer gathering spot for the entire Hubbard family, including Alexander Graham Bell, who was married to Hubbard's daughter, Mabel, and Charles Bell, president of American Security and Trust Bank, who was married to another Hubbard daughter, Grace.

Twin Oaks remained in the possession of this family until it was sold in 1947 to the Republic of China. It then became the residence of the Chinese ambassador. In 1978, with the U.S. recognition of the People's Republic of China, Twin Oaks became the property of the Friends of Free China. It is private property and therefore not open to the public, but the house, its wooded site, and rolling lawns are visible from the lower ends of both driveways. A decision on Twin Oaks' landmark status is pending review.

36 Tregaron (formerly The Causeway), 3100 Macomb Street (originally the rear entrance); 3029 Klingle Road (original entrance). The entire estate, including buildings and grounds, is a Category III landmark. This 20-acre portion of Gardiner Greene Hubbard's 50-acre estate was sold in 1911 by Alexander Graham Bell to James Parmelee, an Ohio financier. The estate was designed in 1912 by Charles Adams Platt who was then the nation's foremost country house architect. Landscape architect Ellen Shipman assisted him. Platt's brick neo-Georgian mansion sits on the crest of the hill surrounded by sloping meadows and landscaped rustic woodland areas, including bridle paths. The property was acquired by Joseph E. Davies (ambassador to the Soviet Union 1934–38) and his wife, Marjorie Merriweather Post. It was renamed Tregaron after the ancestral home of Davies's mother in Wales. Davies, who occupied the house until his death in 1958, added the Russian dacha (cottage).

In 1980 the property was sold and divided into two parcels. The six acres at the top of the hill, which include all of the present buildings, belong to the Washington International School, which holds classes there. The remaining 14 acres are owned by the Tregaron Development Corporation, which applied for permission to construct 120 townhouses that would have wrapped around the existing mansion on three sides. This proposed development was considered by various city agencies, including the Joint Committee on Landmarks, which was concerned that such intense development would damage the integrity of this historic landmark. In January 1983, the D.C. Zoning Commission unanimously rejected the proposed development, but encouraged the developer to return with a more imaginative plan that would preserve more of the character of this unique site. Tregaron is also a privately owned site to which public access is limited.

Both it and Twin Oaks are visible from the surrounding streets through the trees after they have shed their leaves.

37 As you complete your tour of Cleveland Park by walking down Macomb Street to Connecticut Avenue, you will be passing through the final phase of development completed by the Cleveland Park Company between the years 1905 and 1909. Notice **3031 Macomb,** at the corner of Ross Place, with its Palladian window decorated with a fan shape in the arch and a rope dipped in plaster motif. This house with its large arch set in the main gable of the house is repeated at **2929 Macomb.** You may also remember it from Newark Street. As you approach Connecticut Avenue you can probably pick out the other Sherman frame houses with their expansive porches, flaring roof eaves, and commanding positions above the street. You will also walk past the location of the **Cleveland Park Stable** (2932 Macomb).

When you reach Connecticut Avenue you can turn right and proceed on the Woodley Park Walking Tour (no. 17) in reverse or you can go to the National Zoo. If you turn left, you can return to the Cleveland Park Metro Station.

19/**Howard University***
(major black university)

by Deborah A. White; 1983 update by Bob Campbell

Distance: 2 miles
Time: 1 hour
Bus: 70
Metro: Gallery Place (Red Line); transfer to 70 on 7th
　　　　Street, NW

For more on black Washington's heritage, you may wish
to visit nearby LeDroit Park (Tour 20) and Shaw School

Urban Renewal Area and Logan Circle (Tour 14). A visit to all three areas is recommended.

1 The **administration building** houses the office of the president and vice presidents. Howard has been described as America's most cosmopolitan and integrated educational community. Among the more than 10,000 students and 4,600 faculty and staff members are individuals from all 50 states and more than 90 foreign countries. Their varied customs, cultures, ideas, and interests contribute to the university's international character and vitality. The main campus occupies 75 acres, with buildings representing a variety of architectural styles from Georgian to contemporary.

Administration Building, Howard University

The university is made up of 17 colleges and schools. Some trace their history to the university's founding and others have opened within the past year. There are 57 undergraduate majors and 33 advanced-degree programs. Classroom visitation during tours is prohibited.

2 Howard Hall is considered a historical landmark on campus. It was the original building where classes were first held in 1867.

3 Cramton Auditorium, with a seating capacity of 1,500, is the scene of concerts, plays, dance workshops, lectures, and other university-wide programs throughout the year.

4 IRA Aldridge Theater, a part of the Fine Arts School, offers dramatic productions by the Howard Players and other groups. Behind Cramton Auditorium on 4th Street, NW, is WHUR–93.6 FM radio station and Howard University students' radio station WHBC–830 AM. These stations afford students practical experience in radio production.

5 The first floor of the Fine Arts School includes **art galleries*,** which present individual and group shows. Most notable is the James V. Herring Gallery, which features African sculpture bequeathed to the university by Dr. Alain Locke. Works by art students, exhibitions from the university's permanent collection, and work by outside artists are also featured. To the left of the Fine Arts Building is the new University Center, which features many modern facilities for the enjoyment of the entire university community. Under construction on the corner of Fairmont ahd 6th streets, NW, is the building that will house the school of business.

6 Frederick Douglass Memorial Hall is a liberal arts classroom building.

7 Locke Hall, another liberal arts building, houses the University Computer Center.

8/9 The **School of Education** and the **Center for Academic Reinforcement.** The latter program was begun in 1975 to supplement the education of the student with English and mathematics deficiencies.

10 The University Libraries System encompasses **Founders Library*** and 11 branch libraries in the colleges and schools. Founders, the main library, has more than 360,000 volumes, and the combined holdings of the

Founders Library, Howard University

university libraries exceed 750,000 volumes. Founders Library houses two collections of particular interest. The Channing Pollock Theater Collection spans the development of theaters around the world and is acquiring additional materials related to the black contribution to the dramatic arts. The Bernard B. Fall Collection is one of the finest collections of materials on Southeast Asia, particularly North and South Vietnam. It includes books, microfilms, periodicals, and writings accumulated by the late Dr. Fall, a professor of government at Howard and a recognized author and expert on Southeast Asia. The world's most comprehensive collection of materials on Africa and persons of African descent is found in the Moorland-Spingarn Research Center. The center's collections focus on black life, literature, and history, and include works by black authors from the 16th century to the present.

11 Rankin Chapel holds interdenominational services every Sunday, often featuring guest speakers from around the country.

12 The **Biology Greenhouse,** along with the College of Pharmacy, Chemistry, and Physics buildings, are located in "The Valley" or "Death Valley." Across 4th Street from the "Valley" are women's dormitories.

13 The **College of Allied Health Sciences** is at the corner of College and 4th streets, NW. Part of the former Freedmen's Hospital, which was replaced by the new Howard University Hospital, is also on this street. The buildings of the old hospital will be used as office space for the university and as training laboratories for medical students.

14 At 4th and Bryant streets, NW, is the Graduate School of Arts and Sciences. Housed in this building is WAMM–TV Station, which serves the Washington metropolitan area and allows students to train in television production. Also, a student computer center is in this building.

15 At 6th and W streets, NW, are the **Colleges of Dentistry and Medicine.** The latter is connected by a glass enclosed corridor to the Howard University Hospital.

16 The 500-bed **Howard University Hospital,** facing Georgia Avenue, was erected on the site of the old Griffith Stadium. This modern facility, with its four-fold emphasis on teaching, research, education, and patient care, replaces Freedmen's Hospital. The new hospital is a major component of the university's Center for Health Sciences, including the Colleges of Medicine, Dentistry, Pharmacy and Pharmacal Sciences, Allied Health Sciences, and Nursing. The Cancer Research Center is also planned for construction on the hospital grounds.

17 The **School of Architecture and Planning,** on 6th Street, prepares its students to become active in the search for solutions to the major problems facing urban communities in this country and throughout the world. The **School of Social Work** is across from this building.

In addition to the main campus, other points of interest not included in the tour are the 19-acre Dunbarton Campus near Rock Creek Park, acquired by the university in 1974. This campus houses the School of Law, Howard University Press, several of the institutes, and the administrative offices. The beautifully landscaped grounds provide a setting of unusual serenity in the midst of the bustling city. This campus can be reached by a shuttle bus leaving from the Founders Library every hour on the half hour.

The university also owns a 108-acre site at Beltsville in Prince Georges County, Maryland. Plans call for its development as a campus for research in the life sciences and training in veterinary medicine.

18 The Howard Inn, facing Georgia Avenue, NW, formally known as the Harambee House, has 150 rooms, three conference rooms, one large ballroom, a restaurant/lounge, indoor swimming pool, and health spa. This facility serves as a training center for hotel/motel management for Howard's students.

19 Lewis K. Downing Hall, on 6th Street, houses the School of Engineering, which offers curricula in electrical, mechanical, civil, and chemical, and computer-systems engineering.

20/**LeDroit Park****
(historic black residential area, Howard Theater)

by Suzanne Ganschinietz

Distance: 1½ miles
Time: ¾ hour
Bus: 92, 94, 96, 98, 62, 64, and 66
Metro: No convenient station open

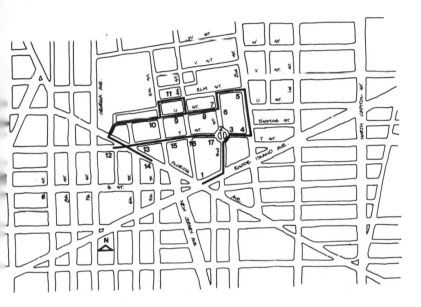

For more on black Washington's heritage, you may wish
to visit nearby Howard University (Tour 19) and Shaw
School Urban Renewal Area and Logan Circle (Tour 14). A
visit to all three areas is recommended.

    LeDroit Park is a Category II landmark of the National
Capital and is listed on the National Register of Historic
Places. It is a small, unified subdivision built during the
1870s. More than 60 detached and semidetached houses
in the district were designed by James H. McGill, a well-
known local architect, in the Calvert Vaux cottage tradition.
The area, which was adjacent to the boundaries of Washington when built, was advertised as offering the advan-
tages of city living with the open space of the country. No
fences were erected between the homes, although the entire area changed in the 1880s and 1890s as developers
sold the remaining land within the district for the erection
of row houses. An additional change occurred near the turn

of the century as the area became a predominantly black community.

For many years the area has been the home of a number of prominent black citizens. Located between Howard University and Howard Theater, two nationally significant black educational and cultural centers, the neighborhood has served as an important cultural and political center for the entire city of Washington.

Today LeDroit Park retains much of the same scale and character and most of the architecture that it had at the turn of the century. Many of the original detached houses scattered among the slightly later brick-and-frame row houses are still standing. The row houses, constructed in the late 1880s and 1890s, are primarily low-rise brick structures with fine terra-cotta and decorative brickwork. They have rooflines frequently accented with turrets, towers, pedimented gables, and iron cresting that combine to provide a varied and rhythmic pattern to the streets. Many of the detached and row houses retain decorative iron-work fences and balustrades. Unique in Washington are the twisted porch columns found in the row houses on 3d Street near the circle.

1 301 Florida Avenue, NW (Safeway). This site was the residence of David McClelland, one of the original owners and developers of LeDroit Park. The site, now used by an Elk Lodge and Safeway store, marked one of the major entrances to LeDroit Park.

2 3d Street, NW. The developers of LeDroit Park were responsible not only for the architecture and the landscaping of the subdivision but also for the design of the streets and sidewalks (which remained in private hands until 1901). The **circle on Third Avenue*** was part of the original street pattern, although the rationale for it is not entirely clear. The circle was recently redesigned and landscaped to resemble its original appearance and has been named **Anna Cooper Memorial Circle.** One of the early advertisements for the park referred to Harewood Avenue (3d Street) as a projected main thoroughfare for trolleys from the city out to the Soldier's Home farther north. Early maps, however, show that this throughway did not develop and that 3d Street terminated just above Elm Street. It may be that the designers wished to imitate the L'Enfant plan with its monumental circles. Indeed, we know that the houses envisioned for Harewood Avenue were to be the most lavish and the most expensive in the park. The original vista of 3d Street was quite different from the present-day view, since most of the McGill houses have disappeared. Despite this change, the Circle remains a strong identification and orientation point for LeDroit Park. Although the street has retained its relatively low scale, the openness and sense of "refined elegance" envisioned by the developers is gone, replaced by the long mass of modern brick construction on the east, row houses on the west, and the new elementary school at the end.

3 1901–1903 3d Street, NW*. The large white-and-gray house on the northwest corner of the circle was a **McGill-designed house** and belonged to Gen. William Birney and Arthur Birney. It is virtually unchanged from its original state.

4 201 T Street, NW**. This was the **home of Dr. Anna J. Cooper,** who graduated from Oberlin College in 1884 and came to Washington to teach high school. She later received an honorary master's degree from Oberlin and a doctorate from the Sorbonne in Paris. She became associated with Frelinghuysen University, founded by Dr. Jesse Lawson in 1906, to provide evening education classes for employed blacks. When the university needed a permanent home, Dr. Cooper donated her house, which remained the location of the school until it closed in the early 1960s.

Birney House (McGill-designed)

5 Vista at Elm and 2d streets, NW. At the northern end of LeDroit Avenue, nonconforming buildings such as the elementary school and the Howard University dormitory facility are examples of recent intrusions that have changed the original residential character of LeDroit Park.

6 1900 block of 3d Street, NW. At 1915 3d Street, the

present site of the Howard University dorms, was the house of James H. McGill, the architect for many of the LeDroit Park houses. McGill enjoyed a brief but prolific architectural career. At 19 he joined the office of Henry R. Searle, a Washington architect, and during the next six years he climbed from draftsman to architect. He opened his own office in 1872 and was soon associated with A. L. Barber in the development of LeDroit Park. In addition to the homes in the park, he designed 60 other homes, five churches, two markets, a roller-skating rink, and four major office buildings, including the LeDroit Building, still a downtown Washington landmark. He moved out of the LeDroit Building in 1881, advertising both as an architect and a building-supply salesman. He left architecture altogether the next year, and for the next 25 years ran a prosperous building supply business.

Also on 3d Street was the house (now demolished) of A. L. Barber, the builder of most of the McGill-designed houses in LeDroit Park. Amzi L. Barber, like his father, was trained for the ministry at Oberlin College. He came to Washington in 1868 to head the normal department at Howard University. He was later elected to a professorship of natural history and, at age 29, was appointed acting president of Howard. He left the university to spend full time developing LeDroit. His business interests included the building and management of the LeDroit Building and other real estate interests. During the 1880s he developed Columbia Heights, north and west of LeDroit Park, constructing Belmont, which he rented to Chief Justice Fuller of the U.S. Supreme Court. Barber's major interest changed in the mid-1880s to the Barber Asphalt Paving company, which made him a very wealthy man.

7 1938 3d Street, NW. This house was the **boyhood home of former Sen. Edward W. Brooke** of Massachusetts.

8 1910 3d Street, NW. This house, a McGill-designed building, is the former residence of J. J. Albright. A prominent Washington businessman and a dealer in coal, Albright also owned the St. Cloud Building (now demolished), which was designed by McGill.

9 400 block of U Street, NW. This is the **only remaining block in LeDroit Park original to the 1870s** development and containing no intrusions. All the houses in this block were designed by architect McGill.

406 U Street, NW. This is the home of Garnet C. Wilkinson, educator and assistant superintendent of Colored Schools until 1954, then assistant superintendent of the integrated system. Dr. Wilkinson was a graduate of Oberlin College.

414 U Street, NW. Clara Taliaferro, a pharmacist and daughter of John H. Smyth (appointed minister to Liberia in 1890 and a lawyer and educator), lived in this double house.

419 U Street, NW. Oscar DePriest lived here while serving in Congress. When elected in 1928, DePriest was the first black Congressman since 1901.

400 block of T Street, NW

10 500 block of U Street, NW. Howard University (see Tour 19, Howard University) and LeDroit Park have traditionally had a close relationship. Howard University was founded in 1867 by Gen. Oliver O. Howard, head of the Freedman's Bureau, to provide an institution that would welcome all students, including freedmen. A. L. Barber, developer of LeDroit Park, came to Washington to head the Normal Department at the school and later served as acting president of the university. Faculty members, administrators, and students have always lived and worked in the area. The growth of the school, however, now represents one of the major threats to the park. This threat is dramatically visible in the new medical building, which looms over the district north of U Street.

11 400 block of Elm Street, NW. Nos. 406, 408, 410, 411, 2022 4th Street, 414 Elm Street, 416–420 Elm Street are known as the "4 Elm Street" project. They were restored by a combination of matching grants from the Department of the Interior, the homeowners, and the Department of Housing and Community Development.

Nos. 407, 409, 417, 431, 429, 427, 419, 415 Elm Street have been restored by matching grants between the Howard University Hospital and the Department of the Interior.

12 Howard Theater, 620 T Street**. LeDroit Park housed many of the entertainers who performed at Howard Theater, which is located just across Florida Avenue from the neighborhood. The Howard Theater, along with the Apollo in New York City, the Pearl in Philadelphia, and the Uptown in Baltimore, provided the stage on which many of the most prominent entertainers in the past half-century made their debuts. Segregation created barriers that made it difficult for black artists to develop and receive recognition, and the Howard thus played a very important role in the development and promotion of black talent. The theater not only played host to the big names and big bands but introduced new talent by its amateur-night contests. Winners of these contests included Ella Fitzgerald, Billy Eckstein, and Bill "Ink Spots" Kenny. The Howard not only was host to stars like Pearl Bailey, Sarah Vaughn, Lena Horne, Sammy Davis, Jr., Billie Holliday, and Dick Gregory, but moved in the 1950s and 1960s into rock and roll and the Motown sound. The Platters, Gladys Knight and the Pips, Smokey Robinson and the Miracles, James Brown, the Temptations, and the Supremes (who made their first stage appearance at the Howard) all appeared at this theater. The Howard is quiet now, but money is being raised to reopen the building as a viable Washington cultural institution.

13 Vista—T Street, NW: 525 T Street*. This house, complete with stable, is one of the **finest remaining houses** in the historic district designed by James McGill. **517 T Street*:** This finely detailed and well-preserved house is another good example of McGill's work.

517 T Street, NW

14 519 Florida Avenue, NW, has been restored with matching Interior Department funds and will soon serve as the home of the LeDroit Park Preservation Society.

15 Vista—400 Block of T Street, NW. 420 T Street: Professor Nelson Weatherless, an early advocate of equal rights, a teacher and an activist lived here. His daughter still resides in the house. 418 T Street: This was the home of Dr. Hattie Riggs, a black woman from Calais, Maine, who taught at the M Street High School. Although she earned a medical degree, she never practiced medicine. 408 T Street: (Maple Avenue)*is the **home of Washington's first elected mayor, Walter Washington.** It was the family home of his wife, Bennetta Bullock Washington, daughter of the Reverend George O. Bullock, a prominent minister and social worker.

16 Vista—4th Street, NW. Fourth Street (formerly Linden Street), the only north-south thoroughfare in LeDroit Park that was aligned with the street pattern to the north, was the first area to be subdivided. The northwest corner of Florida Avenue and 4th Street is shown on an 1887 map as having been divided into 12 small lots. The large, red-painted brick building on this corner is one of the oldest post-McGill buildings in LeDroit Park. Today much of 4th Street has been filled in with row house development.

17 300 block of T Street, NW. **330 T Street, NW:** Fountain Peyton, one of the first 10 black lawyers in Washington, resided here. His daughter, Esther Peyton, still lives here. **326 T Street*:** This was the **home of Mary Church Terrell,** a woman of great importance to the black community, who was active in the women's suffrage movement and was the first black woman appointed to the D.C. Board of Education. This house has been designated a National Historic Landmark.

21/**Old Anacostia****

*(black residential area, late-19th-century buildings,
Anacostia Neighborhood Museum)*

by Sam Parker; 1983 update by Peter Fuchs

Distance: 1½ miles
Time: ¾ hour
Bus: 92 (best), 94, A2, A4, A6, A8, B2, and B4.
Metro: Eastern Market (Blue and Orange Lines), transfer
to 92 Garfield bus on 8th Street, SE

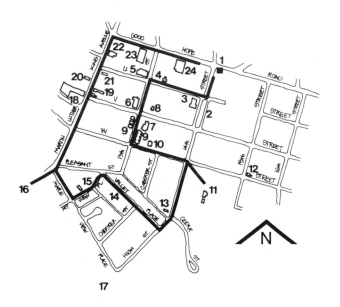

Incorporated in 1854 as one of Washington's earliest residential subdivisions, Old Anacostia retains considerable
historical, architectural, and environmental appeal. The
area had evolved from an ancient settlement of the
Nacotchtank ("Nacostine") Indians to rich farmland. By the
latter half of the 19th century, a subdivision called Uniontown developed into a working-class neighborhood and
encompassed other minor subdivisions. Though the composition of its residents has changed over the years, many
of its social and physical resources endure and continue to
influence the community. Old Anacostia derives its distinctive sense of place from its rolling area, its views to downtown Washington, the charm and human scale of its
buildings, and an appealing neighborhood environment.
    Old Anacostia has a positive and readily identifiable

character. The cohesive quality is apparent in the physical evidence of a pleasant and remarkably intact low-density, late-19th-century neighborhood.

1 The tour begins at 14th Street and Good Hope Road, SE. Old Anacostia first began to develop as a residential community after 1854, when John W. VanHook and two other men purchased 240 acres of farmland from the Chichester Tract for development into a residential subdivision. The original grid of streets laid out by the Union Land Association has survived to the present day and is framed by **Good Hope Road** to the north, **15th Street** to the east, **W Street** to the south, and **Martin Luther King Jr. Avenue** to the west. Known initially as Uniontown, the development was aimed at the middle-class employees of the nearby Washington Navy Yard across the Anacostia River.

2 At 14th Street between U and V streets, SE, is the striking **Old Market Square***, a block long and 40 feet wide. It was part of the original layout for Uniontown and was the prime focal point of the community.

3 The belfry of the **Anacostia Methodist Church** provides an interesting visual reference along the square.

4 The houses at 1312 and 1342 U Street, SE, represent two of the **early dwellings** still remaining. No. 1312 U Street features an elaborate bracket cornice, window pediments, and a handsome cubical cupola. This striking residence stands in pronounced contrast to the later houses around it.

5 Though dilapidated, the houses at 1230–1250 U Street, SE, called **"Rose's Row,"** are potentially handsome. Their form and detail are remarkably well integrated. The architectural character of Old Anacostia is in many ways unique when compared to other communities in the Washington area. Nowhere else does there exist such a homogeneous collection of late-19th-century small-scale frame and brick buildings. The pleasant environment of Old Anacostia is less the product of outstanding architecture than the result of average buildings working together with remarkable success to create a cohesive and expressive whole.

6 The Victorian Gothic is represented by two churches at diagonally opposite corners of V and 13th streets, SE. **St. Teresa's Catholic Church*** was designed by E. Francis Baldwin, partner in the Baltimore firm of Baldwin and Pennington, and was built by Isaac Beers in 1879. A stucco building of simple form, the church is embellished by a large rose window on the front facade, decorated with a simple circular tracery.

7 Emmanuel Episcopal Church*, by contrast, is more irregular in form. Erected in 1891, the building employs rustic stonework with varied earthen brown tones. Its highly picturesque massing adds considerably to the building. The massive corner belfry, with its tall spire and spreading eaves, makes Emmanuel Church one of the most prominent visual landmarks in Old Anacostia today.

Emmanuel Episcopal Church

8 At 1308 V Street, SE, is **Neighborhood Housing Services,** a private nonprofit organization made up of area residents, representatives of financial institutions, businesses, and the District of Columbia Government, working together for neighborhood improvement. NHS provides long-term, low-interest loans to property owners to repair code violations. Visitors are welcome at the NHS office.

9 A walk along 13th between V and W streets, SE, shows an attractive streetscape with its canopy of trees, row of brick duplexes set off by white frame porches and iron fences, and picturesque churches and church yards. The exteriors of the frame houses in Old Anacostia were embellished, often interchangeably, with varying degrees of cottage style, Italianate, or mansard details of the period. The decoration of these buildings was simplified from that of the more elaborate brick townhouses built elsewhere in Washington at this time. Yet these small houses, with their repetitive rhythm of regularly spaced porches, windows, and doors, succeeded in achieving great expressiveness and neighborhood homogeneity. These buildings provided the setting for lively and interesting streetscapes and a community environment of great pride and appeal.

10 The duplex at 1310–1312 W Street, SE, is an example of the prevalent worker's cottage built after the turn of the century. Notice the rooflines, which reinforce a strong geometrical appearance.

11 Cedar Hill**, 14th and W streets, SE, built around 1855, was the home of Frederick Douglass, a noted black anti-slavery editor and leader of the abolitionist movement. The handsome brick house, with its commanding **view of Washington**,** is listed in the National Register of Historic Places. It is open to the public from 9:00 a.m. to 4:00 p.m.

Cedar Hill

12 From the front of the Douglass home notice the Queen Anne house at 15th and W streets, SE, built between 1887 and 1894.

13 The house at 2217 14th Street, SE, was remodeled with the assistance of NHS, as was the house at 1342 Valley Place SE.

14/15/16 An interesting walk down **Valley Place** and **Mt. View Place** will take you to the **Anacostia Neighborhood Museum**,** 2405 Martin Luther King Jr. Avenue, SE. The growth and development of the museum represents a successful experiment in community involvement. The museum includes an educational department, which serves schools, churches, and hospitals, and has a series of changing exhibits. Call (202) 287-3306 for information about current exhibits. The museum is open weekdays from 10:00 a.m. to 6:00 p.m.; Saturdays and Sundays 1:00 p.m. to 6:00 p.m.

17 If a car is available, stop at Our Lady of Perpetual Help School, 1602 Morris Road, SE. It offers one of the most beautiful **views of Washington**.** From 1854, what are now called Martin Luther King Jr. Avenue and Good Hope Road were earmarked for commercial development. The first establishments, which included the legendary Duvall's Tavern and George Pyle's Grocery, tended to concentrate at the intersection of these two streets.

18/19 Two later additions include an interesting **art deco building** at 2122 Martin Luther King Jr. Avenue and the **colossal chair** of the old Curtis Brothers Furniture Store. Although an architectural eyesore, the chair has become a neighborhood landmark.

20 The first home of the Anacostia Bank, 2021 Martin Luther King Jr. Avenue, was built between 1903 and 1913 and is a marvelous expression of the **Georgian revival** mode.

21 The monumental building at Martin Luther King Jr. Avenue and U Street is an example of **neoclassical revival** built between 1913 and 1927 as the second home of the Anacostia Bank.

22 Three storefronts at 1918–1922 Martin Luther King Jr. Avenue highlight a new treatment of commercial buildings that appeared between 1936 and 1943. Notice the pediments over each store. The unit at 1922 retains the original window-sash panels, revealing the richness of the initial composition. Notoriety was brought to Good Hope Road in 1865, when **John Wilkes Booth** used it as an escape route after he assassinated President Lincoln.

23 Several of the two-story commercial buildings, such as **1227 Good Hope Road,** may be converted residences. Though heavily modified on the first floor, the upper portion of the building remains substantially intact, revealing handsomely proportioned brick detailing in the corners and arches crowning the windows.

A number of structures have been built in Old Anacostia over the past 25 years. In that time, the commercial area has undergone changes of varying scope; sometimes as minor an an addition of updated and often tasteless signs, at other times as major as the replacement of existing buildings with new ones. Many of the new buildings, unfortunately, are unarticulated structures that add nothing positive either to the streetscape or to the community as a whole. Some of them at least make an effort to maintain the scale and setback of the surrounding buildings.

24 Perhaps one of the most offensive of the new buildings is the **C & P Telephone building,** which displays an alarming mediocrity of design and disregard for its surroundings. Notice the parking lot that cuts a hole in the residential block on U Street.

22/**Georgetown*****

(historical residential district, specialty boutiques and restaurants, C & O Canal, Georgetown University)

by Mickey Klein and Barry Steeves;
1976 version by Robert H. Cousins

Distance: 3½ miles
Time: 2¼ hours
Bus: 30, 32, 34, 36 (on Pennsylvania Avenue)
Metro: Foggy Bottom (Blue Line), then walk to
Pennsylvania Avenue and 28th Street, NW

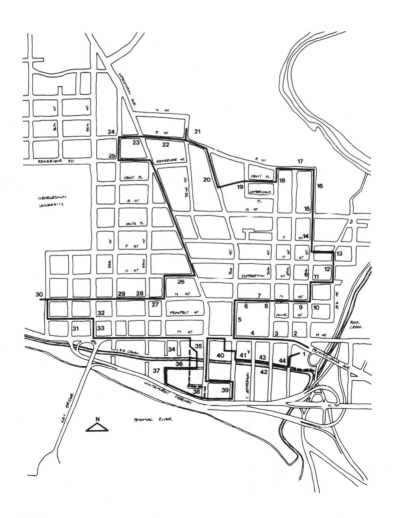

n 1751 the Maryland Assembly founded what it called
Georgetown and drew up a plat for the land south of the
present-day N Street, NW, to the river. However, there is evidence that a grant of land, comprising what is now known
as Georgetown, was awarded much earlier to Ninian Beall
in 1703. In the 1740s, tobacco from nearby Maryland
growers was being inspected, crated, and shipped from
warehouses along the Potomac River at Georgetown. Then
in 1791, Georgetown was included in the area selected by
President Washington to be the seat of government. By this
time, work had started on the Chesapeake and Ohio Canal
(1785) much farther west, even though this important artery
was not completed through Georgetown itself until the
1830s.

By the beginning of the 19th century, the people who
were making money in commerce and government were
building their fine residences in the area north of N Street
(Dumbarton Oaks and Evermay were built in 1801, and
more modest but handsome Federal houses still standing
in the 3300 block, the 3100 block, and the 2800 block of N
Street were built in the period between 1813 and 1820).

Georgetown declined in importance as a major tobacco port in the early part of the 19th century, as steam navigation made deeper ports more desirable. In 1871
Georgetown was joined with the City of Washington and
became part of the District of Columbia. For the next 50
years, it was not the fashionable place to live that it is today, but speculators continued to add Victorian row houses
next to formal Federal mansions, on their gardens or on
subdivided land, and Georgetown took on its urban village
character. Bounded by Georgetown University on the west,
Rock Creek on the east, large houses along R and S streets
as well as by Montrose Park, Dumbarton Oaks, and Oak
Hill Cemetery on the north, and the Potomac River on the
south, Georgetown today has grown within its "borders."
Because of its proximity to Downtown, its village and pedestrian scale, the beauty of its neighborhood streets filled
with historic houses of all sizes, and its lively and convenient shopping area, it is at the top of the list of desirable
places in Washington in which to live. In fact, it is so desirable and such an economic magnet that it is constantly in
danger of being overbuilt and overrun with traffic.

Georgetown today is an urban, cosmopolitan neighborhood of contrasts. On relatively quiet, tree-shaded residential streets, with brick sidewalks, fine old Federal
homes with walled gardens are set next to Victorian workers' houses, only 12- to 14-feet wide. Entrances and setbacks vary; facades, doors, and trim are painted in subtle
colors to blend with the architecture and neighboring
houses. Montrose Park and Dumbarton Oaks on the north
offer landscaped breathing space, as does the peaceful
C & O Canal on the south, edged with a brick path for
strollers and galleries, shops, and historic houses. Along

the commercial streets of Wisconsin Avenue and M Street, on the other hand, there is continual bustling activity. Restaurants of all nationalities, shops, vendors, movie theaters vie for attention from pedestrians on crowded sidewalks.

Within this historic neighborhood, the battle of preservation and compatible development is never ending. As new shops, hotels, townhouses, and apartments are added on old parking lots, gas station sites, and on subdivided large lots, and as the waterfront develops, traffic congestion and citizen concern become increasingly intense. Although bus service is adequate, there is no subway stop and more autos pour in with each new development.

The "Old Georgetown Act," passed by Congress in 1950, defined the historic district, which was added to the National Register of Historic Places as a National Landmark in 1967. The Old Georgetown Act also calls for Commission of Fine Arts review of all new development and of exterior modifications of existing developments. In most cases, the review has helped to maintain a harmony of materials, architecture, and scale and has restrained commercialism. No neon signs are allowed in Georgetown, for example. However, the Fine Arts Commission review is only advisory and can be overruled by the city.

One of the latest developments is a crescent-shaped, mixed-use project on the waterfront (see no. 39, this tour), with a small public park nearby. With the waterfront's redevelopment, the area below M Street is becoming densely developed with townhouses, apartments, restaurants, shops, and offices. It is as if a new community has been added to the old, yet Georgetown continues to hold its charm and to be one of the most fascinating parts of Washington.

1 The Georgetown tour begins at the southwest corner of 28th Street and Pennsylvania Avenue, with the **Four Seasons Hotel,** designed by the Washington office of Skidmore Owings and Merrill. The rectangular, brick structure includes hotel, office, and retail uses. It is contemporary in design, but its materials and simplicity relate to its more venerable neighbors. The building wraps around the 19th-century row of shops known as Diamond Row on Pennsylvania Avenue and M Street, and its back doors connect to the Chesapeake and Ohio Canal and towpath. The brick courtyard, with a pedestrian arcade and a semicircular driveway, is highlighted by a dramatic clock tower facing Pennsylvania Avenue and currently is enlivened by life-size sculptured figures by J. Seward Johnson. Standing next to the clock tower, one can observe the push and pull of styles in the redeveloping commercial area on M Street. Nineteenth-century Victorian houses, modest brick infill contemporaries, art deco and neocolonial structures, and a postmodernist bank all fit into the scene.

2 Two banks: at 2901 M Street, the **National Permanent Savings and Loan;** at 29th and M Streets (SE corner), the **Madison National Bank.** The National Permanent building was built in the early 1970s, imitating the Federal style. Reflecting a different approach, the whimsical Madison National Bank, designed by Martin and Jones and built in 1982, is an example of postmodern contextual architecture. Its paned windows with their arches are similar to those of the National Permanent Bank building across 29th Street. Its classical columns relate to the decorative columns of the art deco Biograph Theater next door. The Madison National Bank won an AIA Preservation Award in 1982.

3 3001–3009 M Street, NW. This **row of four houses*** (now retail uses on the ground floors) shows the common three-bay facade typical of the Federal period. The two houses on the right are dated about 1790, the two on the left a little later. The group was carefully restored in 1955.

4 3051 M Street, NW. The **Old Stone House**** is believed to date back to about 1766. Regardless of the exact date, it is generally accepted as the oldest building in the District of Columbia and is now the property of the National Park Service, which maintains it as a public museum.

5 1221 31st Street, NW. Now the Georgetown branch of the U.S. Postal Service, this Renaissance revival building, designed in the manner of an Italian palace, was originally a **custom house** for the bustling port of Georgetown. It was designed by Ammi B. Young and was constructed in 1857–58.

6 3038 N Street, NW. This fine old Federal house was built in 1816 and has been the home of elder statesman **W. Averell Harriman.**

7 3017 N Street, NW. This is the house **Jacqueline Kennedy** bought and occupied for a short time after becoming a widow. She complained of hordes of sightseers who came by and invaded her privacy, and subsequently moved to a more anonymous, high-rise apartment building in New York City.

8 3014 N Street, NW. This large house was built in 1799, but with obvious later additions. It is notable for its nicely detailed round-top windows on the first floor. Supposedly, President Lincoln's son lived here for a time.

9 2806, 2808, and 2812 N Street, NW. These three houses make one of the most outstanding groups of fine **Federal architecture*** in the Georgetown area. They were all built between about 1813 and 1817. Nos. 2806 and 2808 are almost identical except that they are mirror images. No. 2812 is larger—and symmetrical. It is referred to as the Decatur House because it is said that the Commodore's widow lived here after his death.

10 2726 N Street, NW. In the rear yard of this house, there is a brick wall against the neighboring house on 28th Street that contains a large colored **mosaic*** designed by Marc Chagall. The artist, reportedly a friend of the residents of the house, decided, during a visit, that the spot was perfect for some alfresco art. The best place to see the mural is from the southwest corner of the street intersection and it is best seen in the winter.

11 2716 Dumbarton Avenue, NW. The **Roman Catholic Church of the Epiphany** has masses in French and is very popular with the embassy crowd. The little church was once highly favored by Jacqueline Kennedy.

12 1350 27th Street, NW. The **Stephen Trentman House*,** built in 1968, was designed by Hugh Jacobsen, a prominent Washington architect. This house represents an excellent alternative to the "fake-federal" style found elsewhere throughout Georgetown as new infill houses were added in the 1950s and 1960s. Its scale and materials fit in well with the Victorian neighborhood.

13 1411–1419 27th Street, NW. These townhouses were built in 1954 after a revision to the zoning regulations required off-street parking at the rate of one parking space for each dwelling unit. Although parking is required to be provided, it is not required to be used (note the subsequent conversion of garages to other uses). On the other hand, Georgetown residents can purchase an inexpensive yearly sticker, which allows them to park on the street all day, while visitors are restricted to two hours.

14 2805 P Street, NW. This was once the home of **Dean Acheson** and his wife. The Achesons were among the vanguard of the Georgetown restoration movement in the 1930s. The restoration of Georgetown was popular with the New Dealers of the Roosevelt administration, many of whom, like Harry Hopkins, lived there.

15 2813 Q Street, NW. This house was doubled in size and redone by Hugh Jacobsen in 1968, in one of the first attempts by this architect to renovate in a manner combining contemporary ideas and materials with more traditional themes.

16 1623 28th Street, NW. **Evermay,** designed by Nicholas King, is one of the showplaces of Georgetown and is the scene each year of a tea at the end of the Georgetown Garden Tour. It was built in 1801, was greatly modified over the years, and finally was carefully restored to its original Georgian splendor.

17 R Street at 29th Street, NW. **The Renwick Chapel*** of Oak Hill Cemetery, built in 1850, is one of only four structures designed by James Renwick still standing in the District of Columbia. Its simplicity is in strong contrast to other Renwick

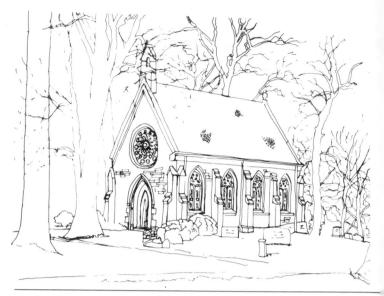

Renwick Chapel

buildings, such as the original Smithsonian Museum on the Mall (see Tour 3, The Mall—East) or the Renwick Gallery next to Blair House (see Tour 8, White House) on Pennsylvania Avenue.

18 2920 R Street, NW. This has been the home of **Katharine Meyer Graham,** chairman of the board of the *Washington Post.*

19 1600 Avon Place, NW, is the residence of **Arthur Cotton Moore,** architect of the Canal Square project (see no. 41, this tour) and the remodeled Cairo Hotel (see Tour 12, 16th Street/Meridian Hill), and many other projects in the city. The house was built in the late 1960s on a difficult, sloped site, and is notable for its arrangement to insure family privacy.

20 1644 31st Street, NW. This great house, **Tudor Place,** was built in 1815. The architect was William Thornton, the winner of the original competition for the design of the U.S. Capitol.

21 R Street at 31st Street, NW. **Dumbarton Oaks***** is worth an afternoon visit. This magnificent 16-acre estate is now owned by Harvard University, but reflects the generosity and interests of its benefactors, the late Robert and Mildred Bliss. Mrs. Bliss was a very accomplished horticulturist and landscape architect. Note the extensive gardens, ranging from a formal pebble mosaic pool to a romantic rustic pool shaded by lindens. Mr. Bliss was a former Foreign Service officer and ambassador to Argentina. He collected pre-Columbian works of art, which are now housed in a handsome **museum**** designed by Philip Johnson. It is open to the public during designated hours and is reached from the 32d Street side of the property. Not to be overlooked is the great Georgian mansion, which was the original house at The Oaks and was built in 1801.

22 3238 R Street, NW. The **Scott-Grant House*** was built in 1858 and was once occupied by President Ulysses S. Grant as a "Summer White House." The property, which is quite large for Georgetown, has been subdivided.

23 3304–3310 R Street, NW. This row of houses was a single house called Friendship, occupied by the late **Evalyn Walsh McLean,** socialite and one-time owner of the Hope Diamond.

24 3402 R Street, NW. This was the home of H. R. Haldeman, close aide to former President Nixon. He was living here during the Watergate revelations. There were reports that a neighbor directly across the street hung a hugh "Impeach Nixon" banner just opposite Haldeman's front door.

25 1686 34th Street, NW. This large house, which until recently occupied an entire city block, was built in 1820 and has been the home of **Roger L. Stevens,** chairman of the Board of Trustees of the Kennedy Center for the Performing Arts.

Now proceed down Georgetown's main commercial strip, Wisconsin Avenue, to O Street, NW.

26 Potomac and O Streets, NW—**St. John's Episcopal Church*** (1809). This lovely old church is also attributed to William Thornton, the architect whose design for the Capitol building was the foundation for many subsequent modifications. Like the Capitol, this church has undergone many modifications; evidence of the last, the Victorian, is seen along Potomac Street.

27 N Street between 33d and Potomac streets has a row of **six Federal houses** that were built by Walter Clement Smith in 1815 and have remained in their original form since then.

28 3307 N Street, NW. **John F. Kennedy** and his wife lived here at the time he was elected President. Mute testimony to the prominence of this house in the days just before the inauguration is evidenced by a plaque on the house across the street (the side wall of 3302) expressing appreciation from grateful members of the press for comforts received there.

29 3327–3339 N Street, NW. This group of five houses, known as **Cox's Row*,** named after the owner-builder, a former mayor of Georgetown, was built in 1817. The handsome

Cox's Row

doorways, dormers, and facade decorations are characteristic of the Federal period. The houses have been converted into condominiums.

30 37th and N streets, NW. The relatively new **Lauinger Memorial Library, Georgetown University**,** was the subject of prolonged and impassioned debate among the Fine Arts Commission, the Citizens Association of Georgetown, the National Capital Planning Commission, the university, and others. The result, designed by John Carl Warnecke & Associates and completed in 1970, now seems worth all the effort. Its fanciful profile and sympathetic color, texture, and massing combine to make this addition a welcome one. It was named after Georgetown University's first graduate killed in the Vietnam War.

31 3508 Prospect Street, NW—**Prospect House*.** Erected in 1788, this house in the late 1940s was the home of the late James E. Forrestal, the first Secretary of Defense.

32 3425 Prospect Street, NW. This handsome house is known as **Quality Hill*** and was built in 1798.

33 "Old Georgetown Falls Street," 35th Street, from Prospect to M streets, NW. This street has a special pavement treatment that came about after months of work by local citizens with help from the city. It is an excellent example of a self-help project in an urban environment.

Walk down this street and proceed east to Potomac Street and the Market House.

34 The **Market House** at M and Potomac streets was restored by Clark, Tribble, Harris, and Li as a miniature food emporium. It was originally built in 1864 as a public market and was used for that purpose until the 1930s. After some years as an auto parts store, the building was restored in the late 1970s. The city intends to return it to a public market.

35/36/37 On M Street between Potomac Street and Wisconsin Avenue is **Georgetown Park,** designed by Lockman Associates and opened in 1981. It is an intriguing preservation project: it retains the exterior facades and scale of the 19th-century buildings, while inside it is a multilevel, neo-Victorian, skylit shopping center. Enter through the main doorway and you will find an array of elegant shops, small cafés, and a central plaza with a fountain, seating, and plants. The development includes apartment houses above the stores.

Georgetown Park

From here you should leave Georgetown Park from one of the two south exits on level 2. These exits lead to bridges that cross the C & O Canal. Pause on the bridge and you may see one of the summer tourist boats on the canal.

The bridge will then lead you to Conran's, a British contemporary home-furnishings store housed in a beautifully restored warehouse. A welcoming public courtyard has been created at the east entrance to the building. The warehouse was restored by Lockman Associates in 1979.

You may proceed west on Grace Street to the next station or you may want to wander a little around this area, taking a look down Cecil Place to Cherry Hill Lane, where you will find a group of well-restored townhouses. Across Cecil Place is the Papermill, a large residential project that combines rehabilitation of a warehouse with newly constructed "mews houses"—and that is worth a look too.

38 Tucked in between the Canal and K street (Water Street), just west of Conran's on Grace Street, is the **Flour Mill,** designed by Peter Vercellis. The reuse of the old Washington Flour Company building (about 1840) for offices and the new brick apartment building, with more than 70 units, was completed in 1981. A waterfall and a small plaza are among its attractions. Walk in and go through the building to Grace and Water streets. Then proceed east along Water Street. The open area along the river is slated for conversion to a waterfront park.

Waterfront Center

39 At the corner of Wisconsin Avenue and K Street (Water Street), NW, is **Waterfront Center*,** a 90-foot-high office/retail building designed by Hartman-Cox. The rebuilding of the waterfront area has been the subject of bitter debate for more than a decade. The disagreement has been over height, density, and even use. The permit for this structure was obtained before recently adopted new zoning (the result of years of study) took effect and reflects what the old industrial zoning would allow. Integral in its design is the preservation of the old brick warehouses located at the corner of Wisconsin Avenue.

Traffic on the elevated Whitehurst Freeway (constructed in the late 1940s) can be heard inside the building. The city has studied alternatives to the elevated structure to improve its aesthetic and environmental relationship to the area.

Now proceed east along K Street and you will see a large open parking lot along the Potomac River. After a tremendous amount of debate and conflict between Georgetown residents, the city government, and developer interests, this area will shortly be developed as a riverside park. At

31st Street turn left and you will be at the next station. Across K Street at this point will be Washington Harbour, a mixed-use waterfront development, designed by architect Arthur Cotton Moore.

40 The **Old Georgetown Incinerator,** about 1930, is a four-story art deco industrial structure with a towering smokestack. It sits on an acre of land and is slated to be redeveloped in the near future. The primary bid proposal would make it into a 375-seat dinner theater.

A plaque on the site attests to its history. Suter's Tavern once stood here, from 1783 to 1795. On March 30, 1791, George Washington is said to have met neighboring landowners in Suter's Tavern and negotiated the purchase of lands required for the Federal City, later called Washington. Suter's Tavern was also used by Major Pierre Charles L'Enfant, who is said to have completed the original plan for the capital city there in 1791.

41 Canal Square**, 1054 31st Street, NW, is a lively and innovative office and specialty-shop complex, which successfully incorporates some old warehouses along the C & O Canal into the project and is built around an inner court. It was designed by Arthur Cotton Moore and was completed in 1971. Between Thomas Jefferson and 31st streets, along the canal's towpath, is a group of small houses built on speculation in 1870. They were originally lived in by artisans and workers. Since that time they have been converted to a festive retail atmosphere.

You may also notice here one of the canal locks that is still in working order and is being used by the reconstructed tour boat to demonstrate its original operation.

42 1058 Thomas Jefferson Street, NW. The current office use is an example of the continuing use of old structures for changing purposes over a period of time. This little structure was built originally as a Masonic hall in about 1810.

43 1055 Thomas Jefferson Street, NW. Like Canal Square, this new building, called **The Foundry*,** uses red brick, combines its new construction with the preservation and adaptation of a landmark structure (an old foundry), and is oriented to the canal. The landscaped areas on both sides of the canal offer pleasant sites for summer concerts and the terminal for canal boat tours.

44 CFC Square is a contemporary red brick building, designed by architect Arthur Cotton Moore, that blends with restored warehouses. It is located at the northwest corner of 30th Street and the canal and extends through to 29th Street. It was completed in stages between 1975 and 1983. From here you may continue along the canal towpath to Rock Creek Park or proceed north on 19th Street to station 1, where the tour began.

Nearby Historic Ports

23/**Old Town Alexandria, Virginia*****

(18th-century port city, specialty shops and restaurants, Torpedo Factory Art Center)

by James L. Wilson

Distance: 1⅓ miles
Time: 1¼ hours
Bus: 6B, 9, 10, 11, 12, 14, 15, 25A, 29K, and 29N
Metro: King Street (Yellow Line), transfer to Alexandria City bus.
Auto: Immediately after crossing the 14th Street Bridge, follow signs to Old Town Alexandria southbound via the George Washington Memorial Parkway alongside the Potomac River. The Parkway becomes Washington Street in Alexandria. Market Square is two blocks east of Washington Street; however, no left turn is allowed at the intersection of King and Washington streets.

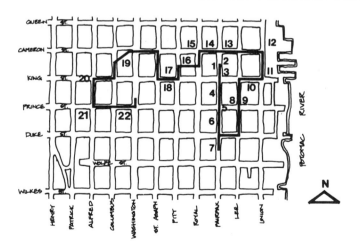

Founded by John Alexander, a Scottish merchant, Alexandria was incorporated in 1749 by an act of the Virginia General Assembly. It became a flourishing seaport and trading center, surpassing the port of New York and rivaling Boston in shipping activity. George Washington was intimately involved with Alexandria from teenage surveyor to first President of the United States. Many colonial sites still exist here in excellent condition and most are open to the public. Major waterfront improvements and development have occurred during the past decade, making Alexandria both a historic and a modern city.

From 1791 to 1847 Alexandria was part of the District of Columbia, and was once considered as a site for the U.S. Capitol Building. During the Civil War, Union soldiers occupied this Confederate City. With the advent of railroads, the economy of Alexandria declined. Warehouses and wharves along the Potomac deteriorated. Housing also became dilapidated.

A six-block commercial urban renewal program called the Gadsby Project was completed in May 1981, 20 years after it was begun. This project rekindled the spirits of Alexandrians and led to renovations throughout much of Old Town. Formerly dilapidated warehouses are now fashionable shops and restaurants. Brick sidewalks, colonial street lamps, and street trees were extended for 19 blocks along King Street.

1 Our tour begins at the fountain in **Market Square**,** which was the first block completed of the Gadsby Urban Renewal Project, dedicated in 1967. The historic City Hall steeple continues to count minutes, hours, and centuries. British troops paraded in front of Market Square during the French and Indian Wars. Each November a reenactment of colonial events is held next to Market Square in front of Gadsby's Tavern.

2 The **Carlyle House**** was built in 1752 by John Carlyle, a wealthy Scottish merchant. This house served as the meeting place for General Braddock and five British governors when they proposed the Stamp Act of 1755, taxation without representation, the spark that ignited the American Revolution. The Northern Virginia Regional Park Authority restored the Carlyle House in 1976, making it one of very few urban parks in Northern Virginia. Formal gardens behind the house, with fashionable brick walks, were completed in 1982.

3 The **Ramsay House*,** Alexandria's oldest house, was built in 1724 as a home for the city's first Lord Mayor, William Ramsay, another Scottish merchant and city founder. Today the house is restored and serves as Alexandria Tourist Council Visitor's Center. Dozens of free flyers and a short movie about Alexandria are available here.

4 The Stabler-Leadbeater **Apothecary Shop*** was founded in 1792. It served continuously as a drugstore from 1792 until 1933. Today it is a museum and antique shop with a remarkable collection of authentic apothecary furnishings.

5 The former Green Steam Furniture Works was a downtown garage for the repair of Mercedes Benz automobiles until the late 1970s. Today **200 South Fairfax Street**** serves as condominium homes for wealthy urbanites. This building typifies reuse of old buildings, a strong trend during the past decade in Alexandria.

6 The restored residence at **215 South Fairfax Street*** further typifies the private improvements to Alexandria that have come about during the past decade. Public improvements such as brick sidewalks and street trees have motivated private investments in restoration and new infill townhouses, adding to a current boomtown psychology. Restored in 1982, this house had an assessment of slightly over $400,000 in January 1983.

7 The **Old Presbyterian Meeting House*** was built in 1774 by Scottish founders of Alexandria. The interior is well preserved. A cemetery behind the church holds the Tomb of the Unknown Soldier of the American Revolution. Memorial services for George Washington were held here in December 1799, when icy, muddy roads made the journey to Christ Church impossible. Step inside and push the button for a tape recording of the church's history.

8 Gentry Row**, the brick-paved 200 block of Prince Street, is lined with homes of early merchants and many important Alexandria patriots of the American Revolution. Cobblestoned **Captains Row** contains homes of colonial sea captains. Only a few streets and alleys in the city still sport cobblestone pavement; most of these rough riverstone rock surfaces have been covered with asphalt.

9 The Athenaeum* is one of Alexandria's two surviving examples of Greek revival architecture. Built in 1852 as a bank, the structure later became a Methodist Church. Today it serves as an exhibit hall for the Northern Virginia Fine Arts Association with art shows open to the public several times each year. The pumpkin color is original!

10 Lower King Street***, the 100 block, includes many unique shops and an unusual variety of restaurants. This highly successful commercial area was made even more successful by the 1983 restoration of the Torpedo Factory. The small park at the waterfront end of King Street typifies the recent city council philosophy of public acquisition of the waterfront, changing the land from private industrial to public uses. Upper King Street, to the west, has begun to benefit from a public improvements project completed in August 1982 along the entire 19 blocks of King Street from the waterfront to the new Metro station. The project included brick sidewalks, colonial lamp posts, street trees, and putting telephone and power lines underground. At a cost of $600,000 per block, both sides, this project is sparking a rebirth of deteriorated upper King Street and is expected to pay back the city many times by generation of increased tax revenues.

11 The **Torpedo Plant complex***** was built during World War I. Used as a federal records center for many years, the four buildings in the complex were purchased in 1970 by the city of Alexandria. In 1982 the major building (no. 10) was demolished to make way for a much-needed public parking garage with more than a hundred private condominium units above. Buildings no. 1 and no. 3 along the waterfront were renovated and converted to offices, retail shops, and a permanent home for the **Torpedo Factory Art Center*** and City Archaeology Museum. These re-opened in 1983.

12 Founders Park* was created by the city during the 1970s. It is now one of several parks designed to provide public access to the Potomac River. Watergate developers had planned to construct four high-rise condominiums on the site, but the city arranged a land swap, giving Watergate an abandoned school site for development. An annual Waterfront Festival is held during the first weekend in June at Founders Park.

13 The **Bank of Alexandria*** opened in 1807 at this location. Major renovation of the building was completed in 1980. This is the **oldest bank building** in the state of Virginia, second oldest in the United States. Today the building again serves citizen banking needs as the Bank of Virginia.

14 The exterior of **City Hall*,** along Cameron Street, remains unchanged from the early 1800s. Major interior renovations were completed in 1982 after city courts moved into a new courthouse at 510 King Street. Step inside the Cameron Street entrance to view an exhibit about historic City Hall, the seat of Alexandria's local government.

15 Gadsby's Tavern** was originally a small coffee house, built in 1752. Because it was so popular, a larger addition known as the City Hotel was built in 1792. A jewel of Georgian architecture, Gadsby's Tavern was the site of the preparation of the Fairfax Resolves of George Mason, predecessor document of the Bill of Rights. The tavern was popular with George Washington throughout his life. It also was important to the entertainment world of colonial America. Traveling troupes of actors came frequently and presented their plays there. Gadsby's Tavern has been restored for use as a working tavern. Opening date was appropriately George Washington's Birthday in the Bicentennial year.

Gadsby's Tavern

16 Tavern Square* takes its name from Gadsby's Tavern. This was the first of the six-block Gadsby's Project. The city purchased the properties in the block, razed all structures except Gadsby's Tavern, relocated the former tenants, and resold the cleared land to a private developer, who arranged private financing. Sit down on one of the benches, rest a moment, and enjoy the sights and sounds. The small fountain next to Gadsby's Tavern is made from one of General Braddock's cannons.

17 Banker's Square*—Phase II of the Gadsby project— included four more blocks along King Street, adjoining those of Phase I. In the 500 block of King Street, the United Virginia Bank provides a new central downtown bank as a private renewal undertaking—one that conforms to the city's renewal plan for the area. For the remainder of the block, the designated redeveloper, Banker's Square Associates, developed a project that houses retail businesses and offices.

18 Courthouse Square** was dedicated in May 1980, marking the completion of the Gadsby Urban Renewal Project. This complex includes both public and private enterprise and utilizes a bay of solar-heating panels atop the rear roof.

19 Christ Church** was completed by John Carlyle in 1773, and served as a place of worship for George Washington and Robert E. Lee. It is an English country-style church with panels inscribed by James Wren with the Lord's Prayer and the Ten Commandments. In the old churchyard are many graves of Confederate soldiers who died in city hospitals. Nearly every President of the United States has attended Christ Church, including Ronald Reagan.

20 The Friendship Engine House* was originally manned by the Friendship Fire Company, a volunteer corps of citizens, organized in 1774, which included George Washington as an early member. Today the firehouse serves as a museum. Note signs of current public and private improvements to the area.

21 The Dip*. So called because of its topographic situation, this 13-block area, bounded by Duke, Washington, Henry, and Franklin streets, was originally brought to public attention by the local neighborhood and by the Alfred Street Baptist Church. It was characterized by dilapidated houses, incompatible land uses, and undeveloped land. In 1970 the city council approved the Dip Urban Renewal Project for this area. Groundbreaking occurred in September 1975 in this basically low-income area. The intention was to build new housing that the current residents could afford. The project doubled the amount of housing available in the Dip area to more than 400 units, providing additional housing opportunities for people living in other low-income areas. Unfortunately, inflated building costs drove prices up, drastically changing the nature of the Dip project by the time it was completed in 1980 from that of homeowner to renter-occupied. Real estate agents renamed the area Olde Towne West. Now enjoy your walk back toward the Lyceum.

22 The **Virginia Bicentennial Center***,** also called the **Lyceum** (about 1842), offers information and films about Virginia. For several years the Lyceum remained a boarded-up, dilapidated eyesore. It was restored in 1973. A visit here can be an interesting and worthwhile experience.

24/**Historic Annapolis, Maryland*****

(17th-18th-century port—capital city, U.S. Naval Academy)

by Carol D. and Gary L. Barrett with assistance from
Jacquelyn Rouse

Distance: 1½ miles
Time: 2½ hours
Auto: Take New York Avenue, NW, in Washington to Route
50 and continue to the Rosco Row Boulevard
turnoff. Parking is available at the Naval Academy
Stadium. The city of Annapolis has a shuttle bus
that operates weekdays year-round and weekends
during the summer months. For further information,
phone (301) 267-7790. If you drive into town, park
at the City Garage (entrances both on Duke of
Gloucester Street and Main Street). Annapolis is
about 30 miles from Washington—a one-hour drive.

Our walking tour includes only the historic district of Annapolis. You might wish also to include the U.S. Naval Academy as a side trip. If so, go to Gate 1 of the Academy, located at the intersection of King George Street and Randall Street (no. 29 on your map). Ask directions to the visitor information center at Ricketts Hall (open 9:00 a.m. to 4:00 p.m., seven days a week except Thanksgiving, Christmas, and New Year's Day). Regularly scheduled walking tours are available from early March through Thanksgiving. Private or self-guided tours are available year round. Phone (301) 263-6933.

One attraction at the Academy is the noon meal formation of the Brigade of Midshipmen. Weather permitting, spring, summer and fall formation is held weekdays at 12:05 p.m., Saturdays at 12:10 p.m., and Sundays and holidays at 12:30 p.m.

Professionally guided walking tours are also conducted in Annapolis by:

Historic Annapolis Tours, Old Treasury Building, State Circle (map location no. 6). Phone (301) 267-8149.

Three Centuries Tours, 48 Maryland Avenue (off State Circle). Phone (301) 263-5357.

The narrow, rambling streets of Annapolis make for a delightful walking tour, but the old brick sidewalks necessitate comfortable shoes. Please remember that unlike some colonial cities, Annapolis is a living city and most of the homes are still in use; respect for the owners' privacy will be appreciated.

Annapolis's colonial heritage, and 16 miles of waterfront, make it a unique American city. The town is justifiably proud of its numerous 18th-century colonial homes, considered to be among the finest architectural elements of our history, nestled among a tangle of quaint, narrow streets. In 1965 the National Park Service designated the downtown area a National Historic District.

First settled in 1649 and known as Providence and then Anne Arundel Town, the city took on its final name of Annapolis in honor of Princess Anne, later Queen of England, and became the provincial capital of Maryland.

Annapolis prospered in the 18th century, maintaining a flourishing trade with Europe and the West Indies and exporting tobacco. During the second half of the century, the city was the commercial, political, and social center of Maryland. Many of the great homes built during the era still stand. Among the fine homes were those of the four Maryland signers of the Declaration of Independence; William Paca, Charles Carroll, Samuel Chase, and Thomas Stone. As you walk through the town, note the markers placed on buildings of state and national importance by Historic Annapolis.

1/2 Church Circle**—St. Anne's Church**. First constructed in 1700, the church was supported by an annual tax of 40 pounds of tobacco levied on every taxpayer. The first church fell into disrepair and was torn down before the Revolution. The last colonial governor of Maryland is buried in the churchyard. A silver communion service presented by King William III is still used.

3 Reynolds' Tavern, built about 1747, was operated by William Reynolds as a tavern and hat-making business. The header pattern of burnt-blue bricks is characteristic of 18th-century Annapolis homes. The building was used as the Annapolis library for many years.

4 The **Maryland Inn** is located on the former site of the Drummer's lot, where the Town Crier, in earlier times, called the populace together with a roll of drums to hear official proclamations. The inn was built during Revolutionary times, and the King of France Tavern was presumably named in recognition of France's support during the war.

5 Continue around Church Circle to School Street, where **Government House** is located. This mansion has been the home of Maryland's governors since 1869. It was built in a Victorian design in 1860 and was remodeled in 1935 to match the Georgian structures surrounding it.

6 Continue down School Street to State Circle and walk into the **State House***,** **started in 1669. It burned in 1709 and was replaced with a similar structure, which was used until 1722, when the present building replaced it. Since 1775, only one session of the Maryland legislature has met elsewhere. (The 1861 session was held at Frederick, because of the strong Confederate sentiment of people in Southern Maryland.) The State House is the oldest capitol in the nation still in continuous legislative use. It has the largest wooden dome in the United States and was built entirely without nails. The old Senate Chamber served as the capitol of the United States from November 1783 to June 1784. George Washington resigned his commission as commander-in-chief in 1783, and in 1784 the Treaty of Paris, officially ending the American Revolution, was ratified here. Later, Thomas Jefferson was appointed Minister to European Courts. Other interesting artifacts include historic oil paintings by Charles Wilson Peale, one of the foremost artists of his time, portraits of the four Marylanders who signed the Declaration of Independence, a painting called *Burning of the Peggy Stewart* (see nos. 17 and 30, this tour), and a flag carried by Maryland troops during the Revolution. On the grounds is a cannon from ships that brought Maryland's first settlers to these shores.

7 From the grounds can be seen the **Shaw House** with its captain's-walk along the roof. Shaw was an expert furniture maker and built the chairs and desks in the old Senate Chamber. (His desks sell for $10,000 to $15,000 today!)

8 On the capitol grounds is the **Old Treasury Building***

(beginning of the Historic Annapolis tours). Constructed in 1737, this is the oldest public building still standing in Maryland. Inside is displayed an iron money chest, which held the Treasury's money during colonial times.

9 Walk down **Cornhill Street**,** **which has excellent examples of private restoration of old houses. Note the iron insignias of fire companies hanging on the fronts of many of the homes. If a fire started, the company would extinguish the flames only if the home displayed its logo. At the apex of Fleet and Cornhill streets is an old barber shop. It is said that George Washington was a customer here before his appearance at the State House in 1783.

10 The **Market House*** building is the third market in this location. The first was built in 1788, the second in 1856; the present structure was completed in 1972. Inside, there are a variety of stalls featuring different edibles.

11 Across the street from the Market House is a building believed to be the **Custom House** of colonial days. It is now the Sign of the Whale.

12 Going down Main Street to 77–99, we find the **Victualling Warehouse Maritime Museum**.** **This recently restored 18th-century building now exhibits artifacts and graphics showing commerce as it was when Annapolis was the principal seaport of the Chesapeake Bay. Open to the public from 11 a.m. to 4:30 p.m. daily during the late spring and early summer; Thursday-Sunday other months. Phone (301) 267-8149.

13 Just a few steps farther, at Compromise Street, is the **Shaw Blacksmith Shop,** which is now the home of the Annapolis Summer Garden Theater.

14 Crossing the street again you are at the **City Dock,** a busy hub of activity in downtown Annapolis. Visitors, locals, and workers all gather here to relax and observe water activities. Besides affording a view of the harbor and the many pleasure boats that move in and out in a few hours' time, the dock is the place where you can watch the oyster and clam boats that make up the last commercial sailing fleet still operating in America.

15 Leaving the dock area, we see the **Middleton Tavern*,** which is actually two colonial structures beneath the brick exterior. The original Middleton Tavern was built as a seafarers' inn in 1750 and was the point of departure for ferry trips to the Eastern Shore.

16 Proceed to Pinkney Street, where at no. 4 we find the **Tobacco Prise House*,** originally one of the many warehouses that were clustered around the harbor in the late 18th century. Open by appointment. Phone (301) 267-8144.

17 We continue up Pinkney Street to the **Spicer Shiplap**

House*, built about 1723 as an ordinary for sailors. This building was the Harp and Crown Tavern during the Revolution and later, in the 19th century, home of Frank Mayer, painter of the *Burning of the Peggy Stewart*. The name Shiplap is taken from the wooden siding on the facade. The front yard is planted as a kitchen and medicinal herb garden of the 18th century.

18 At 43 Pinkney Street we see **The Barracks,** which is typical of the primitive small-frame buildings that were the homes of 18th-century artisans.

19 At the East Street intersection we turn right to the **Brice House*,** built in 1776. This is one of the largest Georgian homes in America. The home was partly designed by William Buckland, who came to this country as an indentured servant and later designed many of the best homes in Annapolis. The house once had gardens that stretched to the water, and George Washington and the Marquis de Lafayette were frequently entertained here. A number of legends are attached to the house and residents claim to have seen ghosts and heard knockings in the library where the son of the builder was killed. When a brick wall was removed during the installation of electricity, a secret stairway from the library to an upstairs room, was exposed. Revealed within the stairwell was a woman's skeleton. Legend has it that an insane female relative was hidden away in the house, and when she died, was bricked in the secret stairwell. (The house is closed to visitors.)

20 Retracing our steps a bit we now go up Prince George Street to the **William Paca House and Gardens***,** built in 1763 for William Paca, one of the signers of the Declaration of Independence and a governor of Maryland. The five-part mansion, one of the plainest of the homes designed by Buckland, is being completely restored. The gardens in the rear were covered by asphalt and buildings, but have now been restored to their original condition. Open to the public Tuesday-Saturday, 10 a.m. to 4 p.m., and Sunday, 12 noon to 4 p.m. Phone (301) 267-8149.

21 The **Little Brice House,** 195 Prince George Street, was purchased from Amos Garrett, who was the first mayor of Annapolis in 1708. This house is only part of the original structure—the wings were torn down a number of years ago.

22 The **Dorsey House,** 211 Prince George Street, was the site of meetings of the Maryland Provincial Government before the State House was erected. The house was later used as a residence for Maryland's governors.

23 Walk up Prince George Street to **St. John's College**,** begun as King William's School in 1696 and one of the first public schools in America.

24 The building in the center of the campus, called

McDowell Hall, was originally known to townspeople as Bladen's Folly. Bladen, who was provincial governor, was intent on building a governor's palace more magnificent than the one at Williamsburg, Virginia. In 1746, after four years of work, building funds were cut off by the general assembly, which was aghast at the exorbitant costs of the structures. It was not completed until almost 50 years later, in 1789.

25 To the right is the famous **Liberty Tree*,** a 600-year-old tulip popular. It is said that under this tree the treaty of peace with the Susquehannock Indians was signed in 1652. Later, colonists gathered under the tree to protest British taxation and became known as "Sons of Liberty." General Lafayette and George Washington were honored at picnics beneath this tree.

26 Walk down to the **Charles Carroll—Barrister House,** built on Main Street in 1722. It was saved from destruction by a move to its present site in the 1950s and is now used by St. John's as the admission's office.

27 Proceed down King George Street to the **Ogle House,** built in 1739 for Gov. Samuel Ogle, who was known for his love of horse racing. George Washington often visited here when he attended the races.

28 Walk down the brick sidewalk to 235 King George Street, thought to have been the summer kitchen of the **Chase-Lloyd House.** Around the corner is the front of the home that was begun in 1769 by Samuel Chase, one of the signers of the Declaration of Independence. Chase was originally one of the Sons of Liberty, then a speculator in avail-

Chase-Lloyd House

able flour during the war, and finally a Justice of the Supreme Court who narrowly avoided impeachment. Chase ran out of money in 1771 and sold the unfinished structure to Edward Lloyd. Lloyd, who later became governor of Maryland, wanted the grandest home in Annapolis, so he hired William Buckland to complete the house. The grounds contained extensive stables of race horses, coachhouses, and servants' quarters. Francis Scott Key was married in this house in 1802.

29 Across the street is the **Hammond–Harwood House***,** built in 1769–74, and the last home designed by Buckland. The first owner was Matthias Hammond, one of the Sons of Liberty. Legend notes that he built the house for his fiancee, but she grew impatient with the long involvement with the construction and eloped with another man. The home, which is open to the public, contains a large number of the original pieces of furniture.

30 Continuing down Maryland Avenue, we turn right on Hanover Street to 207, the **Peggy Stewart House,** which was built about 1740. Anthony Stewart, the owner, was a gentlemen of Tory sympathies. In October 1774, Stewart received a shipment of tea aboard his brig, the *Peggy Stewart,* named after his daughter. Annapolitans were so enraged about Stewart's tea and his payment of the tax that they threatened to tar, feather, and hang him from his doorway unless he burned both the brig and its cargo of tea. At first Stewart was defiant, but later he agreed to do as the crowd demanded. He arranged to have the cargo (except the tea) removed under strict supervision and then he sailed the ship out (to an area now covered by the Naval Academy playing field) and set fire to the ship while his wife and daughter watched from the house. This Annapolis Tea Party took place long before the occurrence in Boston. This scene is portrayed in the painting in the capitol painted by Frank Mayer, who lived in the Shiplap House. The home was later sold to Thomas Stone, a signer of the Declaration of Independence.

You may now enter the Naval Academy here or walk down King George Street to Gate 1 (no. **31** on the map). In either case, ask the guard to direct you to the visitor center, where you may pick up a free copy of the walking tour of the Naval Academy. For those who have additional time, a number of other important homes you may wish to see have been added to the map (nos. 32-37).

32 Charles Carroll of **Carrollton House,** St. Mary's Church Grounds. Built by Charles Carroll, father of Charles Carroll of Carrollton.

33 Ridout House, Duke of Gloucester Street.

34 Jonas Green House, Charles Street.

35 Upton Scott House, Shipwright Street.

36 Sands House, Prince George Street.

37 Bordlay—Randall House, Randall Court.

About the Authors and Contributors

Carol P. Barrett is the former Director of Planning for the city of Annapolis and a past president of the NCAC-APA.

Gary L. Barrett is president and cofounder of Touch Technology, a hardware and software computer company.

Floy Brown is a specialist in education programs at the National Endowment for the Humanities.

Robert Cambell, a graduate of Howard University, is currently an ANC commissioner and a planning consultant.

Pierre Childs is a registered architect working with the firm of Harry Weese and Associates. He is also chairman of the Urban Design Committee of the NCAC-APA.

Kathryn Cousins, AICP, is Regional Manager, North Atlantic States Office of Ocean and Coastal Management, Department of Commerce.

Robert Cousins is a staff member of the National Capital Planning Commission.

Charity Vanderbilt Davidson is an urban historian with the Preservation Office of the State of Maryland.

Zachery Domicke is a graduate of George Washington University with a major in Historic Preservation.

Perry Fisher is Executive Director and Librarian of the Columbia Historical Society, a scholarly organization devoted to the history of the District of Columbia. He was one of *Washingtonian* magazine's outstanding Washingtonians in 1982.

John Fondersmith is Chief of Downtown Planning in the District of Columbia's Office of Planning.

Peter Fuchs is an executive with the Saving Associations Financing Enterprises, Inc.

Suzanne Ganschinetz is with the District of Columbia's Historic Preservation Office.

Robert Gray is Director of Development for the Greater Washington Board of Trade.

Fred Greenberg was the original graphic designer for *Washington on Foot*. He has a degree in community planning and was an urban designer with planning agencies in the Washington, D.C., area.

Anthony Hacsi is a writer/editor with the U.S. Public Buildings Service and has lived in Adams-Morgan since 1974.

Susan Harlem is a librarian and a resident of Adams-Morgan.

Alan A. Hodges was the original editor of *Washington on Foot*. He currently resides and practices planning in Boston, and is a board member of the APA.

Carol Hodges participated in the editing of the original version of *Washington on Foot*. She is currently a free-lance consultant in Boston.

Donald Jackson is an urban designer with the National Capital Planning Commission.

Marilyn (Micky) Klein is a free-lance writer on planning and design issues, a member of the Executive Committee of the NCAC-APA for D.C. Affairs, and a Senior Policy Analyst with the U.S. Department of Transportation.

Antoinette J. Lee is an architectural historian and a preservation consultant.

Alvin R. McNeal is currently Chief of Long Range Planning for the D.C. Office of Planning. He has resided in the city for over 15 years and is an active member of the NCAC-APA.

Clifford Moy is an environmental and energy planner with a special interest in relationships between man and the built environment. He is presently the Special Assistant for Regional Affairs at the National Capital Planning Commission.

Sam Parker is a businessman in the Adams-Morgan area.

Audrey Parkinson is an urban and regional planning consultant with international experience.

Julia Pastor is an Area Planner with the D.C. Office of Planning. She holds a master's degree in Urban and Regional Planning from George Washington University.

Ruth Polan is a Senior Librarian with the Library of Congress and has been a resident of the Dupont Circle area since 1980. She resides in one of the oldest COOP apartment houses in the city.

Frederic Protopappas holds a Ph.D. in the Chinese language, is a longtime resident of the Dupont Circle area, and has been a guest speaker at Planning Studio courses in the Washington area.

Jacquelyn Rouse is a member of the city of Annapolis planning staff.

Leo Schmittel was the original production-design editor of *Washington on Foot*. He has studied art at the D'Ambrosio Ecclesiastical Art Studio, N.Y.C., New York, and the Corcoran Museum, Washington, D.C.

Lisa Schwartz recently relocated to the Washington area from Hartford, Connecticut, where she worked in the city's Office of Transportation and was active in local preservation and neighborhood groups.

Barry Steeves is a practicing planner. He received both bachelor's and master's degrees in planning and urban design from the University of Kansas.

Cam Stiver is a member of the Anacostia Community Development Committee.

Charles Szoradi, AIA, is a registered architect and a member of ANC-3C from 1977 to 1982. He is also an active member of the Urban Design Committee of the NCAC-APA.

Sally Kress Tompkins holds a master's degree in Urban Planning. Her thesis was on the Federal Triangle.

Joan Towles is a private consultant in urban planning and development and a veteran resident of the city.

Thurlew Tibbs, Jr., is a seventh-generation Washingtonian native of the Shaw area. He has worked as an urban planner and is currently a facilities' planner with the federal government.

Wilcomb Washburn is Director of the Office of American Studies, Smithsonian Institution, Washington, D.C.

David T. Whitaker is a graduate of the University of Maryland in Urban Geography and a planning assistant in the District of Columbia's Office of Planning. He has conducted historical studies of various Washington neighborhoods.

Deborah White is a graduate of Howard University, with a degree in urban planning. She is currently a practicing planner.

Lindsley Williams is president of the Woodley Park Community Association, a member of ANC-3C from 1977 to 1982, and was appointed by the mayor of Washington to sit on the Zoning Commission in 1981.

James Wilson is a planner with the Alexandria Department of Planning and Community Development. He produces a weekly radio program, "Alexandria Perspectives."

Kathleen Sinclair Wood is an architectural historian who has conducted lectures and walking tours of the Cleveland Park neighborhood for the Smithsonian Resident Associate program. She is currently employed by Lewis and Clark College in Portland, Oregon, to teach a survey on American Art and Architecture during an annual semester in Washington, D.C.